The Year After Childbirth

Sheila Kitzinger has an international reputation as a leading authority on pregnancy, birth, and motherhood. Her passionate commitment to improving our understanding of these experiences has strongly influenced the way in which mothers and babies are treated both during and after childbirth.

Her research on childbirth and midwifery spans cultures as varied as the Caribbean, North America, Europe, South Africa, New Zealand, and Japan. She lectures and conducts seminars and workshops for midwives at universities and treaching hospitals all over the world, and in 1982 was awarded the MBE for her work as a birth educator. She is President of the Oxfordshire Branch of the Royal College of Midwives, a Member of the Royal Society of Medicine, and an Honorary Professor at Thames Valley University. Her many books include *The Experience of Childbirth*, *The New Pregnancy and Childbirth*, *Birth Over Thirty-Five*, *Woman's Experience of Sex*, *Breastfeeding Your Baby*, *Talking with Children about Things that Matter* (with Celia Kitzinger), *The Crying Baby*, *Pregnancy Day by Day*, *Homebirth and Other Alternatives to Hospital*, and *Ourselves as Mothers*.

Sheila Kitzinger's husband, Uwe, has recently retired as President of Templeton College, Oxford. They have five daughters, including twins. Her most recent writing project is *The Grandmother Experience*.

P

The Year

After Childbirth

SURVIVING THE FIRST YEAR OF MOTHERHOOD

SHEILA KITZINGER

Oxford   Melbourne

OXFORD UNIVERSITY PRESS

1994

Photography: Marcia May
Illustrations: Beverley Lees
Schematic drawings: Fran Sewell and Margaret Jones

Oxford University Press, Walton Street, Oxford OX2 6DP
Oxford New York Toronto
Delhi Bombay Calcutta Madras Karachi
Kuala Lumpur Singapore Hong Kong Tokyo
Nairobi Dar es Salaam Cape Town
Melbourne Auckland Madrid

and associated companies in
Berlin Ibadan

Oxford is a trade mark of Oxford University Press

Text © Sheila Kitzinger 1994
Photography © Marcia May 1994
Illustrations © Oxford University Press 1994

First published 1994 as an Oxford University Press paperback
and simultaneously in a hardback edition

British Library Cataloguing in Publication Data
Data available

10 9 8 7 6 5 4 3 2 1

Typeset in Adobe Garamond
Printed in Hong Kong

ACKNOWLEDGEMENTS

In these pages I have drawn on the knowledge and experiences of many women who have added to my understanding of the challenges of the post-partum year. I am grateful to them for everything that they have taught me. I have met these women in countries all over the world. They come from many different backgrounds and have a wide variety of experiences, both positive and negative. I hope that I have enabled their voices to come through vividly and clearly.

Individuals whom I want to thank especially for their help include Vreni Booth, Sissel Fowler, Clare Phillips, Chloe Fisher, Hiromi Takahashi, Janette Brandt in Sweden, Carol Fallows in Australia, Penny Simkin in the United States and Louise Shimitzu in Japan.

The illustrations are based on photographs, often taken in my home, of women and their babies who very generously came together to enable us to have pictures based on real life situations.

Murray Enkin MD FRCS, an obstetrician who is a dear friend, has helped especially with information about episiotomy and the pelvic floor and Bruce Flamm MD, FACOG with information about US practice.

Rosemary Beers is a reliable and enthusiastic secretary, and works on the word-processor at amazing speed, while my daughter Tess has kept the technology running smoothly, another daughter, Nell, has baked delicious bread to keep us fed, and I can always rely on Celia's stimulating comments over the phone to keep me self-critical and intellectually alert.

My husband, Uwe, has been warmly supportive of all my work, is a very good listener, and keeps me highly motivated. My own increasingly happy experiences of the years after the births of our own five children owe a great deal to him.

CONTENTS

1

2

3

The Roller-Coaster Year

How your Body Changes

Enjoying your Body

A new concept of time; love, hate, and anxiety; feeling guilty; stresses on a relationship; physical changes; postnatal euphoria; being unhappy; dealing with advice; the future

Bleeding after the birth; tender tissues; your abdomen; the postnatal check-up; finding a doctor who is right for you; talking to your doctor; after a hard or forced labour; when birth has been violent; after an epidural; after a Caesarean; how to support your abdomen

The flow of energy; how to avoid backache; bending, lifting, and carrying; movements for body awareness; toning your muscles — especially abdomen, back, and bottom; healing backache; massage; exercise for pleasure

4   *5*   *6*

7

8

9

10

Feelings about Your Baby

Bonding; falling in and out of love with your baby; gender stereotypes; feeding behaviour; the second baby; a baby with a disability; the HIV-positive mother; when a baby dies

11

Becoming a Father

Fathers in other cultures; making the transition to fatherhood; powerful new emotions; feeling trapped; becoming engrossed in the baby; building a special relationship

12

Changing Relationships

Turning into 'Mum'; you and your partner — settling down or breaking away, where did yesterday go?, a fresh focus, moving to a new home, topics of dispute; you and your mother; friends; the displaced baby — how the older child feels; the mother alone

13 *14*

Sex

Coming Up for Air

The Year After Childbirth

THE ROLLER-COASTER YEAR

Before your baby was born you probably read books, went to classes, found out what you could about birth. You looked at choices between alternatives, discussed your concerns with a doctor or midwife, and may have worked out a birth plan. Like many other women, you paid special attention to your diet, toned muscles, and helped your body be more flexible with exercises to open your pelvis. If you smoked before you became pregnant, you probably decided to stop, and even to avoid alcohol during pregnancy. Your partner or a friend may have learnt massage techniques, how to hold you upright in supported positions for labour, and what to do when you needed encouragement. All this for the experience of birth.

Now the baby is here! Whatever the birth was like—and it may have been the most exciting event in your life, a dreadful ordeal, or just an anti-climax—with the arrival of your first baby you face a challenge which is different from any you have met before: taking total responsibility for feeding, protecting, understanding, and loving a new human being.

A woman who cares for herself in pregnancy automatically cares for her baby, too, who grows and develops while she is thinking about totally different things, and even when she forgets she is pregnant. If she wakes in the night, it is because of indigestion or because the baby is rolling around like a jumping bean, or she needs to empty her bladder—not because her total attention and all her intelligence is demanded without a moment's delay. When she has a broken night, the chances are she can catch up a little on sleep the next day, or at least at the weekend.

A new concept of time

Once the baby is born everything is different.

Time is no longer your own. New mothers often feel as if it has been snatched from them. They are anxious that they will never catch up, be able to organize themselves, plan ahead with confidence, or take charge of their lives again.

The ordinary divisions of time—into morning, afternoon, evening, and night, and before and after meals—have lost meaning. In their place there seems to be a long, uncoiling, endless ribbon—feeding, changing, cleaning up, soothing and rocking and patting, starting the laundry, tidying up a bit, feeding again, bouncing the baby up and down, managing to wash yourself and pull on some clothes if you are lucky, feeding again, carrying the baby around, drying the baby things, grabbing something to eat, picking the baby up, feeding, dashing to the shops, and then feeding again because the baby is still fretful. There is never any point at which you can say that you have finished.

After some weeks perhaps you return to work outside the home or to work commitments based at home. Time gets split into two qualitatively different sections. This may bring a terrific sense of relief, or the split may be very stressful for you. The part with the baby is still fluid and rather unformed. That at work, especially if it is in a large institution, is rigidly divided into the conventional divisions. You cannot split yourself in the same way, but may struggle to be a different kind of person in each section of your life.

It may be impossible to switch off entirely from the baby when you are at work, and you worry and feel guilty about leaving her. When you are at home work may seem an unreal world and you resent its intrusion via phone calls and other demands on time with the baby, or you may yearn for it because you feel more confident in that section of your life than when playing the part of a mother.

As the year goes on you learn to juggle time, to slot short segments of useful time into almost invisible spaces round the clock, to sandwich 'work' and 'baby' tasks together. Working mothers usually manage time in ways radically different from, say, working fathers. By the end of the year you have become a time-management expert.

Love, hate, and anxiety

Some new mothers say that they did not know what tiredness was until they experienced the exhaustion that comes from straining every nerve, concentrating with set purpose on doing everything right with a new baby, while at the same time feeling powerful emotions of love and hate, hope and fear, joy and depression. For the tiredness is not just a question of needing more sleep, or of trying to fit everything into a twenty-four-hour day that seems suddenly to have shrunk. The emotional intensity of becoming a mother and caring for a new baby is in itself demanding. Nothing is more tiring than being rushed along on that switchback of emotions.

'The birth was great! But looking after a baby twenty-four hours a day seven days a week is hard labour!'

After having a baby a woman confronts enormous emotional challenges while simultaneously facing physical work that may be harder than any she has tackled before. The emotions sweeping through her are partly about the baby, partly about herself—about who she really is and what kind of mother she expects to be, about changes in relationships with those closest to her, perhaps about her work and her future, relationships with bosses and work colleagues, and often, too, about money, housing, and—for women in many different countries—about violence, ethnic conflict, and war.

With the birth of a baby both parents may become more aware of the dangers of the environment and threats to our future. This occurs partly at a personal level—a new father says that he now drives much more carefully; another has stopped smoking so as not to pollute the air the baby breathes—but often also sharpens social and political consciousness. For a new mother, environmental disasters shown on TV—toxic fumes belching from an explosion, poisons seeping into water supplies and the air that we are forced to breathe—may have a significance they never had before. This is not only because they can harm her own child. She may feel very emotional about other children's suffering, too.

Films of children starving in Africa, burnt, maimed, and killed in the Middle East or ex-Yugoslavia, staring from the dark doorways of shacks perched on mountains of rubbish in South America, and of children in the wealthy countries of the West who have been abandoned or are cold, hungry or sexually abused, are all deeply disturbing. Some women say they can no longer risk turning on the TV news because they are bound to be in floods of tears before it has finished.

Taking personal responsibility for a child's life makes you more sensitive to the suffering of children everywhere, and there is an acute awareness of human vulnerability and pain. It may feel as if all your nerve endings have been exposed. The result is that the whole range of your emotional states becomes more intense.

If at times you feel completely unqualified for motherhood because you lose emotional control and—faced with another day of hard slog

3

and jobs that can never be finished—wonder why you ever had this baby, you are not alone. Mothers usually love their children, but also get anxious and angry, and sometimes want to escape from them. Maternal emotions are urgent, raw—and often deeply disturbing.

Feeling guilty

Research into women's lives and personal accounts of the experience of motherhood shows that mothers in Western cultures often feel guilty.[1] It is very different in traditional cultures, where they are not so self-conscious and simply do what mothers have always done—get on with nurturing the baby, usually with practical help from other women in the family.[2] In Western countries professional experts, who often have no personal experience of caring for children twenty-four hours a day, as well as books and magazines, tell mothers what they ought to do, and even how they should feel. There always seem to be other mothers who are coping much better than we are, too. They are better organized, more contented, always consistent, calm, and understanding. Their babies sleep four hours at a stretch from the very beginning, wake, feed, play, and then sleep again. They have regular routines. We are in a state of chaos. They have clean, tidy homes. Ours is a squalid mess. They cook delicious meals, dish them up on time, and enjoy entertaining. We snatch fast food and eat it on the run, because there is no time to do anything else.

Stresses on a relationship

With the birth of a baby the relationship with a partner comes under new stresses, too. A couple may decide to have a baby in the hope of solving difficulties between them. In fact, it often introduces fresh problems. It can shatter an already damaged partnership. Psychological studies show that the time after the birth of a child is stressful for both the woman and the man. What often happens is that a woman who is going through a difficult emotional patch looks for support to her partner. She thinks he is strong and reliable, even when he is not, because that is an essential element in the gender stereotype of masculinity. He may feel helpless, and get angry or retreat from the scene, because he feels under attack. She feels rejected. The birth of a baby, far from being a fulfilment and deepening their understanding of each other, can be the beginning of the end of a relationship.

In childbirth education classes discussion sometimes turns to life after the baby comes. The over-riding questions that men often ask —and many women too—are, 'When shall we be back to normal?', 'When will the baby get into a routine and sleep through the night?', and 'When shall we be able to make love just as we did before?' Men—even men who are loving fathers—sometimes cannot help feeling that the baby is an intruder, and there may be times when they are jealous and demanding. Then the woman feels as if she has two babies to care for.

Physical changes

Any woman who has just had a baby may be anxious about physical changes that result from pregnancy and birth. The shape of her vagina is different. She may not feel the degree of sexual arousal that she did before. It may be hard to lose weight gained in pregnancy, and she may be self-conscious about varicose veins and still-visible stretch marks. These worries are understandable. When a woman has given birth her body alters before her eyes. Her abdomen is at first wrinkled and soft, and feels empty—even cold—in contrast to the firm, rounded, melon shape with the baby kicking inside. With lactation her breasts turn into full, aching globes, with nipples larger and browner than usual. Milk may leak when she thinks about the baby, when there is any pressure on her breasts, if she is sexually aroused, and often for no discernible reason. Her vagina is moist and plump, and feels heavy, since the muscles inside have opened up for the baby to come through, and often remain relaxed for weeks after the birth. The ring of muscle around the urethra, which controls the flow of urine, tends to be softer and looser too. So it may spill urine when she coughs or laughs.

The area between her vagina and anus—the perineum—is often sore, bruised, and tender. Many women endure a knob of aching, prickly scar tissue below the vagina because they have had an episiotomy which had to be sewn up afterwards. This is uncomfortable when sitting, throbs when standing, rubs against the seam if they wear jeans, and may make sexual intercourse so painful that penetration is impossible for several months. It results, at the very least, in self-consciousness and strain in a couple's relationship. Although many women say, 'My husband is so understanding,' it can lead to sexual problems and conflict in a relationship, and almost invariably women believe that it is somehow their 'fault'.

Another problem may be backache. This is common after childbirth, either because the pregnancy has put stress on the body's muscular–skeletal framework, or as a result of straining and unco-ordinated and prolonged pushing in the second stage of labour, or because the mother's legs were lifted and moved carelessly while her lower body was numbed from anaesthesia. This backache tends to be centred in the small of the back where the pelvis joins the spine. Sometimes it is just at the point where an anaesthetic needle was inserted. Occasionally it is lower down over the tail-bone.

With all this happening, it can feel at times as if, in having a baby, an elaborate hoax has been played on you. This sense of being cheated is accentuated because becoming a mother is seen as a great achievement. Congratulation cards flow in, and people say, 'How lovely! A baby!', and smile as if you had done something out of the ordinary and the baby was a special kind of gift.

In fact, for the first weeks after the birth, and in spite of tiredness and physical discomfort, a woman may feel like this herself. She can hardly believe that she has really had a baby. She feels special, and the baby is special.

Postnatal euphoria

Birth is often followed by postnatal euphoria, especially when it has been a peak experience. This euphoria is a state of excitement and alertness, one effect of which is to make the mother acutely aware of everything about her baby, and the signals that alert her to the baby's needs, so that she can get to know and be in tune with him. Through thousands of years of human life this elevated emotional state has had survival value, because it ensures that the newborn baby is nurtured.

Fathers feel it too, but for them it is less physical. After a baby's birth a mother's intense emotions are linked with the rush of milk to her breasts, with nipple erection which make the breasts ready for feeding, and with powerful contractions from her uterus as it actively moulds itself into its pre-pregnancy size, shape, and position in her pelvis, like a firm, plump fig cupped in a hand. Far from being sugar-spun concoctions, maternal emotions are gut feelings. And they stimulate physical reactions that help a woman's rehabilitation after childbirth and that are closely involved with the way she nurtures her baby.

In spite of a difficult labour, or a complicated delivery, a woman often feels an upsurge of energy after birth too, if she and the baby can stay together and get to know each other in their own way and their own time. This is one reason why it is important for a woman to have her baby with her, beside or in her own bed, and to be free to hold, cuddle, and feed the baby whenever she wants. The separation of mothers and their newborn babies in many hospitals denies the woman the closeness with her baby that is the reward of all her striving during birthgiving, denies the baby the security and warmth of his mother, and may interfere with the early development of the intense psycho-physiological process of bonding. Even though a woman may have thought that she needed a rest, and wanted someone else to look after her baby, she may find it very difficult to sleep. She often feels in limbo. She lies longing for the baby, not really understanding what she wants or why. She feels disorientated and odd, lonely and cold inside, and in this state of isolation it is not surprising that she weeps uncontrollably.

I remember gradually waking one morning shortly after having a baby knowing that something wonderful had happened, but for a fleeting moment not being able to remember exactly what. Then I heard a rustle or a little mew from my baby, or I turned and glimpsed her. There was a rush of excitement until my skin prickled and my breasts became warm, and I reached to pick her up.

The almost magnetic pull she feels towards her baby, the keen attention as she gazes at her, that enables a mother to get to know her newborn intimately may be especially important today in societies where members of the extended family are no longer available to help, and where a woman usually has to care for her baby unaided, and—if it is her first child—with no previous practical knowledge of mothering.

Nothing compares with the astonishing reality of a new baby. For many women, feelings about the baby are every bit as strong as those stimulated by sexual passion. The words 'bonding', 'attachment', and 'engrossment', used to describe this new relationship, come nowhere near suggesting the longing to touch and to hold, the outpouring of tenderness, the whirl of joy in flashes of sudden emotion.

'As I lay awake the night he was born, watching his eyes wide open, exploring his new world, I had a strong feeling of "now I know I can do anything".'

Yet even while in this state of euphoria a woman is often emotionally volatile, so that joy quickly changes to tears, and one who was feeling over the moon is unhappy an hour later for what can seem to an outsider as no reason. The result is that she may be accused of being unreasonable, failing to see things 'in perspective'. Those close to her may believe that she should be acting 'normally', and do not realize that for several months after birth it is normal to be in a heightened emotional state.

The paediatrician–psychotherapist Donald Winnicott called this 'primary maternal preoccupation' and pointed out that anyone else who behaved in this way might be considered mentally unbalanced.[3] It is the typical, and normal, state of the mother of a young baby.

Postnatal elation may last for several weeks. But there is bound to come a time when a woman slips down out of this intense emotional state and life is mundane again. No one lives in a state of ecstasy forever. So the 'high' is followed by a 'low', often sometime between five and eight weeks after the birth.[4] There is no way from a mountain top except down!

Being unhappy

Depression after childbirth is often talked about as if it were a cloud that drifts in from nowhere, a kind of mental miasma produced by hormonal disturbance. This ignores the momentous changes that occur in a woman's life, especially with the birth of a first baby. Many women feel they have lost their identity as they struggle to come to terms with the challenges of motherhood. But there is more to it than that. Depression is also often the direct result of treating a woman as a patient, incapable of knowing how to care for her baby, at a time when she is taking on responsibility for a new life and needs to assess information, weigh up alternatives, and come to important decisions. Postnatal unhappiness is frequently the consequence of having been disempowered in childbirth, and for many women this started way back in pregnancy.

Those close to a woman often find it difficult to understand what she is going through and feel frustrated and impatient. They may tell her she is worrying unnecessarily about the baby's health or development, criticize her for letting the baby rule her life, accuse her of being over-emotional, of talking about a distressing birth when she ought to 'forget' it, or of being obsessional about wanting to breastfeed. They try to say the right things and to be sympathetic, but may not know how. So they give advice instead.

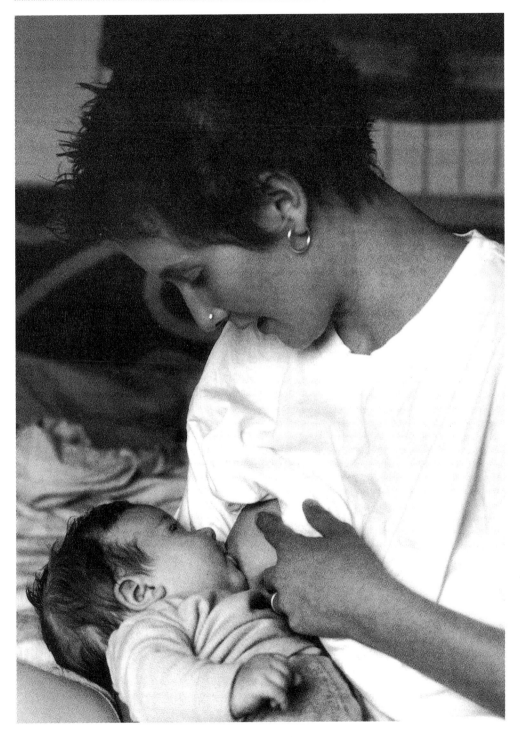

Advice

A new mother is a target for advice—much of it conflicting. Some of it will turn out to be misinformation or completely impractical, even when it appears to come from authoritative sources. One person tells you, for instance, to leave your baby to cry because otherwise he will learn to 'twist you round his little finger', and, anyway, 'it's good for his lungs'. Another says you should keep your baby in close skin contact under your T-shirt and never put her down, because that is how some South American native tribe does it. Someone else says that babies must have water in hot weather or they get dehydrated, and you should test-weigh before and after feeds, while yet another tells you to switch to the bottle and thicken feeds with cereal. Much of this advice runs against your own deep feelings.

Women who are in a 'high-risk' obstetric category—perhaps because they are over 40, are not in a relationship with a man, or have a disability that means they are in a wheelchair or can walk only with crutches or sticks—have been barraged with advice from early pregnancy on. It often felt like a personal attack on their worthiness to have a baby. In one research project on pregnancy and disability it was found that half the women interviewed who had problems with mobility were automatically offered terminations, because their GPs assumed they could not handle a baby.[5] It is vital that doctors, counsellors, and helpers in the social services acknowledge a woman's right to as much autonomy as possible, whatever her disabilities. The important thing is that they should enable the women they are serving to make their own informed decisions.

The advice you get about breastfeeding is likely to be conflicting, and often very dogmatic. Many doctors know little about breastfeeding, but want to help, and are concerned that the baby is crying or not gaining sufficient weight, and so give wrong advice. Good research about breastfeeding has been published since the 1980s, but not all doctors, nurses, and health visitors know of this, so still offer guidance based on outdated textbooks or on their own hunches. A male doctor often gives advice that is derived from his own wife's experience. It may be worth enquiring if she breastfed. If you can find out for how long, so much the better. A caregiver who has had children is most help when she breastfed successfully after overcoming problems, and feels positive about breastfeeding. If she wanted to breastfeed her own baby but was unable to do so, the advice she offers tends to be coloured by her own negative experience and feelings of failure.

Most new mothers need a strategy for dealing with advice. Here are some suggestions that women have made which they found worked for them:

Find two people—not more—whom you feel you can trust, and be open to their suggestions. They may not be the obvious advisers. Often you have to seek them out. You may find these helpers from one of the organizations listed at the end of the book.

Smile when you are given advice, and say thank you. You do not have to act on it.

Remember that the most important thing is to learn from your baby. Even newborn babies give clear signals about what they do like and do not like. Any advice that does not suit your baby is the wrong advice for you, though it may be fine for someone else.

The future

If you are reading these pages before you have given birth, this will probably seem a grim picture. But it is a distorted image, because reading about motherhood can give no idea of the intensity of positive emotions and the shock of joy that a baby brings. This shines through even the darkest days, when everything seems to go wrong. Yes, there are times when you lose all self-confidence and feel that you are a terrible mother and a failure as a woman. But there are other times when you feel a luxurious contentment, like a cat who has been at the cream.

The first year after birth is invariably challenging. Challenges are always uncomfortable, but they stimulate constructive change. That first year can be, above all, a time of personal growth in which you learn a lot about yourself, develop new skills, and discover that you are strong!

How your Body Changes

Amazing changes start to take place in your body the moment your baby is born.

One of the first things to happen is that, with the delivery of the placenta, production of the hormones progesterone and oestrogen is reduced, and a woman's breasts start to change and secrete colostrum (milk in its earliest form). Blood flow in the veins slows down, so that they are clearly etched, purple or blue like branching rivers in the full, swollen globes of a new mother's breasts. In only twenty-four hours they become very sensitive to touch and are easily bruised. By the third or fourth day milk is usually flowing freely.

Other changes, taking place deep inside her body, are not so obvious, but are no less dramatic. The uterus contracts strongly so that in a matter of days it is reduced from the size and shape of a harvest-festival marrow or Thanksgiving pumpkin to that of a ripe fig nestled low in her pelvis. Medical students learn that it takes six weeks for a woman's body to return more or less to its pre-pregnancy state. This period is called the puerperium. In fact, for some healthy women the process is shorter, though for women who have had a traumatic birth it can take longer.

Yet the body of a woman who has had a child is different from that of one who has never given birth. Her uterus is slightly larger than before, and the opening from her vagina into her cervix, the external

13

os, has widened. The soft, velvety lining of her vagina is more relaxed. There is increased softness and fullness, and pelvic muscles and ligaments are looser, or—more positively—have greater suppleness. A woman who is not in top condition because she is not having the right food, enough exercise, or the rest and relaxation she needs, will not have well-toned muscles. Her body sags and bulges in all sorts of places, inside and outside, so that she may really dislike how it looks, and she has aches and pains which make her tired and irritable. This affects her self-confidence, her relationships with others, and her pleasure in the baby.

So the first weeks after childbirth are vital in caring for and toning your body. You can do this in different ways. They include:

deep relaxation—mental and physical—in the brief times when this is possible with a new baby;

physical activity which is fun and increases your sense of well-being: vigorous walking in unpolluted air, swimming, having a rough and tumble with your older children, or a game of catch;

good nutrition which provides the protein, vitamins, and minerals in abundance that a new mother needs.

This does not mean that you must follow strict exercise drills or eat things you hate. It does mean that you owe it to yourself to care for your body and not to be so focused on the baby that you disregard your own needs. Of course, when you have a satisfying relationship with your baby, you cannot separate out what your baby wants from your own wishes. If your baby is contented and happy, you are contented and happy too. You are in partnership, and, for each of you, well-being is to a large extent dependent on the other person.

Though it may seem almost impossible because you are so busy, it is worth while looking for time in your day when you can pamper yourself, and do something you want which is not directly associated with being a mother or with your responsibilities to other people, including a partner, members of your family, or colleagues at work. You need to make space for yourself. Many women find that it helps if they can organize this in advance and fit it into their daily routines. Walking the dog, relaxing in a bath with aromatherapy oils, listening to music on a tape-recorder, doing some gardening, dancing to music on radio or TV—with or without the baby—are all ways which women have of enjoying this space in their lives when they do something for themselves, not for other people.

Bleeding after the birth

Once the baby has slipped out, your uterus continues to contract in order to expel the placenta and membranes—the afterbirth. Though you may not feel these contractions at first, the uterus is squeezing in on itself. The placenta—the blood vessels of which burrowed like the interlacing roots of a tree into the rich lining of your uterus, the endometrium—remains the same size. In a matter of ten to twenty minutes the uterus gets smaller. As a result the placenta is peeled from the lining, and drops into your vagina. With a little pushing from you, just like the pushing that gave birth to the baby, or with controlled cord traction from your midwife or doctor, the afterbirth plops out.

Placenta

'The placenta was amazing! I wasn't sure I wanted to see it, but the midwife explained everything. It's a miraculous organ!'

When it happens naturally it brings an oddly satisfying feeling. Afterwards you feel much lighter.

The placenta looks like a large piece of raw liver, with the membranes lying around it. But if you look more closely you can see branching blood vessels, rather like a bunch of grapes, which nourished your baby inside your uterus. These conveyed food and oxygen from your blood through a fine filter into the baby's bloodstream, and transported its waste products back into your blood for you to excrete.

Immediately after the placenta is delivered your uterus weighs 1 kilo—over 2 pounds. In six weeks' time it will be 95 per cent lighter. It continues to squeeze itself into a more compact shape with contractions which are sometimes called 'afterpains'. The larger your uterus was—if you had twins, for example—the harder it must contract to return to its former shape. Contractions may be so strong in the first two or three days that you gasp or hold your breath. You may be embarrassed at having to break off a conversation. Anticipate these contractions as you put your baby to the breast, and start rhythmic breathing, or they may take you by surprise so that you startle the baby. If you learnt slow, relaxed breathing for labour, use this now for handling these afterbirth contractions. Drop your shoulders and breathe your way through them.

Contractions often continue to be felt for a week or so and touching your nipples excites stronger ones. It is not only when your baby comes to the breast, but if your partner stimulates them in love-making, that you are especially aware of them.

Contractions like these, while unpleasant, help your body to adapt to not being pregnant in a natural way. They squeeze out any remaining blood in 'pockets' of the endometrium that were filled by the placental 'roots'. Mixed with the blood are muscle fragments from the uterus. The huge uterus of pregnancy has the amazing quality of autolysis. It can self-digest excess muscle and the no-longer-needed support system that nourished and provided oxygen for your baby inside you and served as an organ of excretion for the baby's waste products. The flow of lochia that results from this process of regeneration is the bleeding of repair, not of injury.

The bleeding is at first like a period, and may be heavy for a few days. If your uterus is very efficient, this may not last longer than four or five days. The blood gradually changes from being bright red to rusty brown, and after that the lochia gets pale and pink or yellowish. Some women bleed on and off for six weeks, or even longer. Though this is a nuisance, there is not necessarily anything wrong. That is just how their bodies work.

The quicker your uterus tightens up, the sooner the lochia stops. This active process in which the uterus becomes small and firm again is called involution.

It is difficult to estimate accurately the amount of blood lost immediately after the baby is born, but if it is thought to amount to more than 500 millilitres it is recorded as post-partum haemorrhage (PPH). Between two and seven women in every 100 have a PPH. It is more likely when the woman has had pain-relieving drugs in labour or a forceps delivery, or when her uterus has been very large with a great deal of amniotic fluid, or because she has had twins. But the most common reason is probably that there has been what one professor of obstetrics calls 'meddlesome interference with the third stage.'[1]

The definition of abnormal blood loss was worked out in the days when women were less well fed and generally not as healthy. A woman with a good haemoglobin level in pregnancy can cope with losing 1,000 millilitres of blood without any problem.[2] This is because there has been an increase in circulating blood volume during pregnancy by as much as 40 to 50 per cent.[3]

A gush of very heavy bleeding later than the first twenty-four hours after birth is secondary post-partum haemorrhage. Around one woman in every 200 experiences this. If you soak more than three sanitary pads an hour, or see a sudden gush of bright red blood, let your midwife or doctor know.

When you have been lying down for a rest, and when you wake in the morning, some blood will have collected and clotted. Sometimes a woman is alarmed by sudden blood loss after she has been resting in bed, but this is nothing to worry about. These clots can be anything from the size of a small coin to big blobs the size of tomatoes. In the early days, they may come out when you breastfeed, too.

Do not use tampons while the flow is still red, even if you feel comfortable with them; in fact many women do not in the first few months after childbirth. To let the blood flow as freely as possibly, you will need to use old-style sanitary protection, and change your pad frequently. You can buy especially thick sanitary pads for this postnatal period. You need to include them in your budget for the first month or so after birth. If money is tight, you may find that this proves expensive. It is one of the early invisible costs of having a baby.

At first you will probably need two sanitary pads on at night and a spare by the bed to slip on in the morning before you can make it to the bathroom. It is a good idea to have a plastic draw-sheet underneath the bottom sheet to protect the bed, though this can make you feel hot and uncomfortable. Another idea is to buy incontinence pads and slip one under your bottom last thing at night. Old cotton pants will help keep your sanitary pad in place. This heavy bleeding will probably not last longer than a week. Later, when the flow is reduced and is almost colourless, you can switch to tampons if you like. But make sure that you change them frequently, and do not run any risk of toxic shock.

If bits of placenta have been left inside—which occasionally happens when someone has pulled on the cord before the placenta has separated completely (this is what the professor of obstetrics meant by 'meddlesome interference') or because parts of the placenta were adherent and failed to unstick—bright red bleeding continues for several weeks instead of gradually turning paler. There is an unpleasant smell because it is causing infection, and you run a temperature. If you have bleeding like this, take your temperature and get in touch with your doctor or midwife to tell them what is happening. Sometimes a woman needs to go into hospital to have the remaining bits of placenta removed under anaesthetic. This operation is a 'D and C' (dilatation and curettage). Ultrasound can show whether bleeding is being caused by 'retention of products', by which doctors mean bits of the placenta still being stuck inside. Occasionally continued bleeding together with infection results from a doctor accidentally leaving a swab inside after an operative delivery.

Losing a lot of blood for weeks on end reduces your haemoglobin level. Haemoglobin is the pigment that makes blood cells red. It contains iron and enables blood cells to transport oxygen all round your body. When your haemoglobin is low it is likely to make you feel tired and weepy.

If this happens, your doctor can prescribe supplementary iron. Women tend to get constipated with some forms of iron tablets. Let your caregiver know, so that you can switch to another brand, as there are some forms which are much less likely to cause constipation. Make sure that you eat plenty of green vegetables, the darker the green the better. Nuts, beans, peas and lentils, wholemeal bread, egg yolk, prunes, and apricots are also rich in iron. Vitamin C helps absorption of iron, so eat citrus fruits, too.

Tender tissues

You may feel swollen and bruised for a week or two after birth because the pressure of the baby's head, as it came down between your vaginal muscles, pushed against your anus, and spread open the tissues of your vulva, caused small abrasions. Even if you did not have an episiotomy or tear, there are often bruises and grazes which heal naturally. As they heal, the tissues swell to protect them. Some women find that homeopathic treatment is helpful in dealing with sore, tender tissues

and use arnica, as an ointment or tincture. A witchhazel-soaked sanitary pad feels cool and prevents pubic hair sticking to blood.

If the baby was born very quickly because your uterus was contracting powerfully, or if it took a lot of forceful pushing over a long time to get the baby out, you may feel especially sore and tender.

When you empty your bladder urine passing over these sore tissues stings and burns. It is more comfortable to do it in the bath, or to use a shower or bidet to run water between your legs. As you sit on the lavatory, you may be able to tilt your bottom at an angle, so that urine misses the most tender spots. You will want the softest lavatory paper you can find. It may help to keep a jug of cool water in the bathroom and pour water between your legs as you pass urine, and after you have finished, too, so that none is left on your skin.

You may find that essential oils are comforting, in your bath or on a cold, wet compress (a cotton nappy or hand towel), or you can sit in a plastic washing-up bowl or the baby's bath. Chamomile and lavender feel good, and women often say that these help to reduce inflammation. Cyprus is slightly astringent, but may also encourage healing. It should never be used undiluted.[4] A package of frozen peas wrapped in a cloth makes a pain-relieving ice compress.

Your abdomen

Your abdomen is much flatter and you feel slimmer immediately after the placenta has slipped out. Most women start to lose a little weight even before the baby is born because as you approach labour there is increased loss of fluid. With the birth of the baby and the delivery of its baggage you have probably lost another 5 to 6 kilos. But when you look at your abdomen more closely you see that it looks like a soufflé that has sunk. There is a ripple effect, and folds of tissue as if the tide has just gone out from the beach. It is as if you have shrunk, but your skin has not.

At first so much is happening around you with the excitement of the birth, and you are so strongly focused on the baby, that this may not bother you. But when you stand naked in front of a mirror you may be uncomfortably aware of your size compared with how you were before you became pregnant. One reason many women enjoy pregnancy is that they are allowed to look fat. For those who have tried one diet after another, have made good resolutions that they never kept, and have struggled to discipline their bodies, this is threatening. There are times in most women's lives when they are conscious that their figures do not match those of the models in photographs in women's magazines. After being able to eat all they wanted during pregnancy, they now feel under pressure to watch the calories and get

their figures back. This is one of the extra stresses on a new mother in Western culture which can lead to unhappiness.

Any kind of exercise done regularly—running up and down stairs, cleaning the bath, and certainly vigorous sexual intercourse—will tone your abdominal muscles. A muscle is toned when it is energized. This is rather different from the idea of 'strengthening' the muscle, though a side-effect of energy being expressed through using the muscle is that it may be strengthened. You may like doing postnatal exercises, but if you are in good shape after a straightforward birth you do not need special exercises unless you enjoy doing them. Postnatal exercises were first devised when women lay around in bed after having a baby, and so ran a risk of thrombosis—a blood clot forming in a blood vessel.

The stretching of tissues beneath your skin by the huge melon-shaped uterus may have produced a dark line down the centre of your

Separated

Normal

Recti muscles

abdomen, the linea nigra. It is usually more obvious in naturally dark-haired women, but it disappears gradually after the birth.

You may see a puckered section like a ruched ribbon down the middle of your abdomen too, from your navel to the cushion over your pelvic arch, which used to be called, rather charmingly, 'the mound of Venus'. But it tends to leave you feeling less than goddess-like! Sometimes the muscle there has been over-stretched. When you touch it, it feels soft and pulpy. This is where the recti muscles running down the middle of the abdomen have separated into two halves. In advanced pregnancy, especially with a big baby or if you are having twins, these are put under stress, and may peel apart from each other like a zip opening, so that organs inside your abdomen even bulge through.

So co-ordinated, fluid movement is good, whereas straining muscles can damage them. Get someone else to do any heavy lifting that needs to be done if you possibly can. If you have to lift, bend your knees and use your leg muscles rather than abdominal and lower back muscles. Double leg-lifting while you lie on your back is out! That exercise, sometimes advocated in magazines, makes it worse. Even single leg-lifting is bad unless you first press the small of your back down to the floor. You will find special gentle movements to help you tone the recti muscles in Chapter 3. Dancing is very good, too—any kind that you enjoy. Switch on the music, kick off your shoes, pick the baby up, hold her close—and get going!

Your postnatal check-up

'I always felt terribly guilty asking a woman to come for a six-week check-up when I knew it wasn't going to do her any good.'

[An obstetrician]

The postnatal check-up usually takes place six weeks after the birth. It is difficult to understand why it occurs then, not earlier or later. Indeed, it is questionable why it needs to be done routinely, except that some women might be so busy with the baby that they put off seeking medical help though they really need it. In traditional cultures the forty days after birth and after death are often treated as spiritually dangerous and ritually marginal periods. During this time a new mother is considered polluted and it is believed that the baby may be reclaimed by the spirits from whom the child came. In modern technological cultures the medical system controls the gateway to motherhood and has devised its own rituals, so that a woman may not feel safe if she does not attend for her postnatal check-up, though she is completely fit.

You will know yourself whether your body has adjusted smoothly after childbirth, and if you are feeling well the six-week check-up may be rather a waste of time. If you have any worries about your health, however, it provides an opportunity to investigate and discuss problems you are facing. Some women put off seeing a doctor until

this time because they believe they are not justified in seeking help until the statutory check-up. The best time to ask for help is when *you* need it, not when a medical system ordains that you should have it.

A routine check-up may not turn out to be very useful, anyway. Many doctors have no idea how to make the postnatal visit at all helpful for a woman. For some it is another boring chore. Then a woman gets only a cursory glance, is asked if she is feeling 'all right', and has a quick pelvic examination. She finds she is out of the room without having had any chance to ask questions or voice worries.

Before attending your postnatal check-up it is a good idea to think ahead to what you want to get out of it, to list any concerns you have —either physical or emotional—and to work out the most important questions to which you require answers. You can say, 'I've jotted down a few notes because there are some things I'd like to talk about and questions I want to ask. Do you have the time for this now, or would you like me to make another appointment?'

At this visit your caregiver should ask you how you feel, listen to your answers, and discuss any problems. In a study of 11,701 post-partum women, nearly half had health problems within three months after the birth which continued for more than six weeks, and which they had never experienced before. The symptoms of ill-health which they confronted sometimes lasted for months or years afterwards, and many of them never told their doctors about them.[5] This is a serious failure in the care that health services make available for women. The authors of this study write: 'When the women were asked why they had not consulted their doctor, 68% said that they did not consider this symptom to be a serious problem; 25% said the symptoms were too infrequent to warrant treatment, while 20% felt it was just a usual female problem. The extent and nature of long term morbidity following childbirth has not been recognised by the medical profession at large. It is scarcely reported at all in the medical literature, and inadequately mentioned in the textbooks.'[6]

If you are breastfeeding, the postnatal check-up could be an opportunity to talk together with your doctor or midwife about how it is going, unless you have other advisers whom you trust more, or are feeling so confident that you do not want any further advice.

At this visit you will be asked if you still have any lochia. If you are having sexual intercourse, you may be asked whether that is comfortable, and whether your muscles are well toned so that you are not wetting your pants accidentally.

Your caregiver checks your blood pressure, which—even if it rose at the end of pregnancy—should be down again now, and may do a urine

*'He stuck his
fingers inside,
said, "cough"
grunted, then
"right, pop your
clothes on
again", and
wrote up his
notes.'*

and possibly a blood test. He or she feels your abdomen, palpating the uterus to discover if it is firm and small and tucked neatly into your pelvis, examines the place where you had an episiotomy or tear to see if this healed well, and with fingers inside your vagina, feels the strength of the muscles inside, probably asking you to cough or to press down when doing this pelvic examination. Many doctors take the opportunity to do a cervical smear to test for the presence of pre-cancerous cells. It is not the best time to do this, because changes in your cervix after the birth and the presence of lochia may interfere with the results. But it is one occasion when a doctor can be sure that you are up on the examination couch. Tell your doctor if there is any tenderness inside your vagina or outside between the vagina and anus, and, if you wish discuss birth-control.

You will have had a blood test early in pregnancy to find out if you are likely to catch rubella (German measles). If there were no antibodies in your blood, you may have been vaccinated in the couple of days after the birth, so that you were not at risk of contracting the disease in a subsequent pregnancy. This is a good time to have rubella vaccination so that you do not run the risk of rubella in another pregnancy, which could damage the baby. Be careful not to get pregnant for the next three months if you are vaccinated, as the vaccine can do as much harm as the disease.

**Talking to your
doctor**

A postnatal check-up should not be merely a ceremony to demonstrate that a woman is under medical control. Nor should it simply provide a ticket of approval that you are in good physical health, as if it were a matter of being able to wipe your hands of the birth and say, 'Well, that's all over!' You are going through a major life transition, so it should also involve you as a person, and the chance to discuss any challenges you are confronting in your life at the moment which could affect your health. Your doctor should be interested in you as a human being, and want to learn from your experience how to help other women, too.

Over fifty years ago an article in the *Lancet* stated that doctors required from their patients 'an account of their symptoms, as concise as possible and chronological'.[7] That was all that was necessary in the doctor–patient relationship, and if patients played their part in providing this information doctors could give the right treatment.

This is the complete opposite to what patients today say they seek —a doctor who listens. A medical sociologist comments: 'The cornerstone of professional practice has always been that, though patients know what they wanted, doctors (through their specialised knowledge) knew what they needed.' But it is being acknowledged now that 'patients' wants are not capricious whims but needs in themselves'.[8]

It is very difficult talking about such subjects when you are lying flat on your back with your knickers off. Your doctor should sit down with you and talk person-to-person. You can be critical of any doctor who spends much of the time answering the phone, perusing your notes, or talking to someone else in the room as if you were not there, who fails to give you adequate information, or who offers merely a large dose of 'reassurance', as if anything more would be too much for you to digest.

This may sound a rather jaundiced view of doctors, but it comes from having talked with thousands of women in the course of my research and counselling who have had experiences like these. If you have a doctor who gives time to listen and obviously respects you as a person, let her or him know that you value this. As well as being critical of doctors who are not giving good care, it is important to give positive feedback to good doctors. If you find this difficult to say face-to-face, you can always write a letter afterwards.

It is often difficult to take time to talk with doctors if they seem rushed and busy and there are other women waiting to see them. You feel that you may be having an unfair advantage in seizing those extra few minutes. They may appear very overworked, and the whole atmosphere suggests that you should be in and out as fast as you can. But a vital part of health care is acknowledging you as a person, not just a set of organs that are healthy or diseased. No doctor who treats you as an ambulant pelvis, a malfunctioning endocrine system, or a pair of lactating mammary glands, can give adequate care.

When a doctor asks how you are, the temptation may be to reply, 'Very well, thank you,' even though you are feeling miserable or run-down. If a doctor smiles at you, it may be difficult not to smile back and radiate cheerfulness. You may feel so low that you have not sorted out in your mind what you need to discuss, so you give no clues about the help you need. If it feels that your inside is falling out, or it is too painful to have intercourse, or you are exhausted all the time, or cannot bear to face the day when you wake up in the morning, say so. Ask for help. If you are certain that it is a physical problem and your doctor offers tranquillizers, which some doctors prescribe when they cannot think how else to help, you can decline them. You can also ask to be referred to a specialist. If you have made contact previously with other women and learnt about their experiences with medical care, you probably have some idea of the specialist whom you want to consult, so you can ask to see this individual.

An obstetrician is not a psychotherapist. Most GPs aren't either.

But they should have good working relationships with other professionals who can help with emotional difficulties and problems in relationships. So you can ask to talk to a counsellor or to be put in touch with a self-help group in your community.

Finding a doctor who is right for you

If you are dissatisfied with the care you are getting, it is often possible to change to another doctor. In rural areas this can be difficult because there may be only one practice that services everyone in the neighbourhood. Trying to change your doctor can seem like a slap in the face for the doctor you are leaving. It probably makes it easier if you want to change from a male to a female doctor and explain that this is the reason. But you may want to state very clearly in writing why you want to change because you would like it to go on record. In Britain it is also a good idea if you have had very unsatisfactory care to contact the local Community Health Council to tell them what has happened and get their advice. You will find the number in the phone book. They may suggest that a letter to the Family Practitioner Committee for the area is appropriate, and, if you wish, can guide you on how to word it. In Australia it is worth getting in touch with the Consumers' Health Forum of Australia and, if relevant, the Australian College of General Practitioners. Keep copies of any letters you write.

The best way to find out about other doctors, especially if you are new to the area, is to ask women you meet at the health centre, the family-planning clinic, the infant welfare centre, a toddler group —even at the school gate—how they get along with their own GPs, and what they like best about them. Childbirth education organizations and postnatal groups are a good source of suggestions, and addresses of these and other organizations that can help you are at the back of the book.

After a hard labour

Our mothers and grandmothers often accepted a good deal of ill-health as normal following childbirth. Even today there are people who ask a new mother—one who is healthy and has had a normal birth—if she is feeling 'better'. Some doctors, too, take the attitude that aches and pains and muscular weakness must be expected after having a baby, and when a woman asks for help, she is told that it is still early and to return in a few months.

Birth, however, is a normal, though strenuous, physical act. Just as our bodies are constructed to perform smoothly and with rhythmic muscular co-ordination other challenging tasks, such as climbing a mountain, swimming ten lengths or running round the park, if the body of a healthy, well-nourished woman is used correctly during childbirth there is no reason why she should expect to suffer injury or to be in pain afterwards. But childbirth may be complicated by an unavoidable obstetric condition. The baby may not be lying in the right position or does not descend through the cervix. Sometimes a woman's bony structure is too small for the baby's passage. Then prolonged labour or obstetric intervention may result in damage to muscles and ligaments. Unnecessary obstetric intervention may occur too, such as making the uterus contract before it is ready to do so, or contract too strongly, and pain-relieving drugs may have long-term side-effects.

Your well-being in this first year is likely to be linked with the kind of birth you had. This is not just a matter of whether it was an operative delivery, but of how the labour was conducted, whether it was speeded up, for example, and drugs were given, whether or not you were allowed food and drink when you wished, and whether you felt among friends, or in an alien, frightening environment. Some of the effects of a mishandled birth experience are immediate and short term. Others are more lasting.

A woman who has a positive birth experience usually feels marvellous afterwards. She is excited, happy, and has a great energy spurt which is an invaluable start to motherhood. A woman who has a bad birth experience often feels limp and exhausted. She recovers from birth as from an illness. Her muscles ache as if she has flu. She may have pushed so long and hard that she has bulging haemorrhoids and her throat is sore. Blood vessels may have burst in her face and eyes. She may feel as if she has been in a prize fight. She may be unable to pass urine because a catheter has caused bruises. She may suffer sacro-iliac or sacro-lumbar pain, and be unable to sit or walk easily because of perineal stitching to repair an episiotomy or laceration. Instead of an energy spurt, she only feels relief that it is all over.

Perhaps she is in hospital for five days or so, then is expected to snap to, forget about herself, and care for her baby. This may be particularly difficult for a woman who has had a Caesarean birth under general anaesthesia, who may not yet feel that the baby really belongs to her. Though a woman who has had a difficult birth is urged to put her traumatic experience 'behind' her, she may be left with physical damage and pain which is a direct consequence of the birth, such as a 'weak bladder', stretched cervical ligaments, or a too tightly-stitched perineum.

In later chapters we shall look at some of these problems and see what can be done about them. But it is important to say here that, if your body has had this kind of hammering, you need time to recover from it, and you need to be kind to yourself and have other people cherish you. If you try too hard to 'get back to normal', you can cause further harm. Muscles subjected to further stress may bulge and sag. You may get a virus infection. You will probably become exhausted. A new mother needs to be nurtured—especially one who has been through a difficult birth.

After forced labour

When labour has been started off with an induction, especially if the woman was not ready to go into labour, her body may feel battered afterwards. The same may happen after her uterus has been stimulated with hormones during labour because it was considered not to be working efficiently. It is difficult to assess accurately the amount of hormone the uterus needs in order to work efficiently, and it is sometimes speeded up too fast, and made to produce massive contractions which are extremely painful at the time, and leave a woman feeling weak and exhausted afterwards. Another way in which the pace of labour is forced is when a woman is subjected to commands to push more often and harder in the second stage, and when physiological rhythms are ignored. This turns expulsion of the baby into a battle she is forced to fight against her own body. As with the slap-happy use of artificial hormones that stimulate the uterus, physical injury can result, with torn muscles and ligaments, damaged nerve fibres, bruising and bleeding.

Many women's bodies recover quickly from this violence. But in the important days when they are first getting to know their babies they are still aching all over, cannot sit comfortably, and are hardly able to walk. After commanded pushing and prolonged breath-holding as the baby was being pushed out, a woman often has a blotchy face with broken blood vessels, pink eyes, a sore throat, aching shoulders, and sometimes haemorrhoids as well. She probably feels all this is well worth it to get the baby out, but wonders how any woman can enjoy childbirth, and think those who do must be out of their minds.

When birth has been violent

There are things you can do to help yourself after a birth in which there has been a great deal of obstetric intervention, and which leaves you feeling as if you have been assaulted. Here are some suggestions:

Do rhythmic, slow, full breathing, and relaxing completely on a long breath out. After an experience like this you may feel panic, and this breathing will calm you.

Start to move, even if you cannot get out of bed; wiggle your toes a lot, make pelvic floor kisses, and slide your feet up to your bottom and down again.

Even though it hurts, make sure you empty your bladder regularly. If you are holding back because of fear of pain, try running water into the wash basin at the same time; tell yourself you are going to flow with the water.

Drink plenty of fluids. You may feel thirsty anyway, especially when the milk comes in. Fluids will help to prevent constipation, which hurts sore tissue. If you do get constipated, ask for a softening agent or glycerine suppositories. Do not expect to empty your bowels until the third day after childbirth. Many people find bowel movements difficult when in a strange place, such as a hospital, and are only able to relax when they get home.

Soak in several warm baths a day. You will relax better in a bath than under a shower. A sprinkling of lavender essential oil may help you relax as you breathe in the scent slowly and fully. Good smells stimulate fuller, slower breathing and better uptake of oxygen. This not only gives you more energy, but unbuckles the body armour of muscular tension. There is no evidence that the common practice of adding salt to the bath promotes healing, though this was often recommended in the past.[9]

After a bath, when muscles are warm and skin glowing, make some of the movements described in Chapter 3. Do them gently and rhythmically, and breathe *through* each movement. Avoid holding your breath. After each exercise, lie back and relax completely.

If neck and shoulders ache, sit or lie against firm cushions, with a hot water bottle against the tender muscles.

After an epidural

Although in smaller hospitals there is no epidural service, in most large ones there is the choice of epidural anaesthesia. Many women are very glad that they had the opportunity of an epidural, and have no side-effects afterwards. Nowadays it is possible to have a light epidural so that you retain feeling in your feet. Some women find that they can even walk about. But in most hospitals only full epidurals are available, and sensation is removed from the waist down. It can be disconcerting not to feel anything—not being able to empty your bladder, and having your legs plonked on the bed like two logs—but feeling usually returns within a few hours of the birth. The catheter which was inserted into the bladder so that you could pass urine is no longer necessary, and you can at last stumble out of bed and take your first few tottering steps. From then on, every hour brings progress, and you soon feel yourself again.

Women who have had epidurals are especially at risk of long-term backache. Some 14 or 15 per cent of women experience backache for the first time after having a baby, and it usually lasts for many months. Those who have had an epidural or a spinal are even more likely to suffer backache, whether or not the delivery was complicated.[10] This probably happens because a woman is moved when she has no muscle

'I had no idea this could happen. Women should be told. They have a right to know.'

[A woman with backache after an epidural]

tone because of the anaesthesia, and is placed in a strained position for a long time, often in the second stage of labour.[11] The authors of one study, however, suggest that women suffer backache because the idea has been put in their heads by reading a research report of mine.[12] These doctors believe that women get backache because they *expect* it!

Backache may start shortly after birth or much later. After an epidural there may be lower back pain, pain at the bottom of your spine, or extreme tenderness where the catheter was inserted in your back, especially if the anaesthetist had more than one go to get it into the epidural space.

Some women experience both backache and headache or migraine. Women most likely to have headaches alone are those under 25 years old who have more than one child, whether or not they had an epidural. The stresses of motherhood can trigger headaches, especially if you are trying to cope with more than one baby.[13] But having an epidural increases your chance of getting headache or migraine as well as backache.

Some women experience tingling and numbness after an epidural. This is more common when the anaesthetic has been inserted accidentally into the spinal fluid rather than the epidural space. It may continue for some weeks—occasionally for months. A small proportion of women have neckache, either with or without tingling in the hands or feet.

'The baby is 11 months old. My left foot is partially numb and the top of my left leg tingles and burns.'

It may be that childbirth itself—something about the way that it is conducted in hospitals today—exposes some women to backache, neckache, and tingling sensations. But there is a greatly increased chance that they have these symptoms after an epidural.[14] All these physical problems may last longer than a year.

Since backache is the most likely problem after an epidural, and 30 per cent of women experience backache after childbirth anyway, it is clear that there are triggers in the post-partum environment that increase the chances of back pain. These include lifting loads of washing and groceries from supermarket trolleys, bending to pick up and carry the baby, often together with a car seat or carrycot, and perhaps a toddler as well, the spinal twisting that is entailed when you put a baby on one hip and stretch or bend to do housework with your free arm, the combination of heavy lifting and twisting involved with bending to lug packages and boxes from a trolley and heave them into the car boot, and all the work of house-cleaning that entails pushing, pulling, stooping, and using your spine like a crane. If you have had an epidural, it is especially important to avoid movements which misuse and distort your spine. This is easier said than done, because you are likely to be under pressure to complete work in a short time, and thinking about your back may not be top priority at that moment.

After Caesarean birth

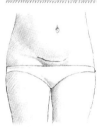

Caesarean scar

'I lay there like an unfinished bride of Frankenstein with fourteen metal clips holding my innards in place.'[16]

Caesarean section is major surgery, and it may take six months to make a complete physical recovery.[15] Changes in the uterus after birth and the flow of lochia are the same as after a vaginal birth. Your abdominal wound is bound to be painful at first, and gas retained in the intestines—common after any abdominal surgery—hurts too. Tightening the abdominal muscles on an outward breath helps get the intestines working again to expel the gas. Pull in your abdominal wall, exhaling at the same time with a huffing sound.

As the wound heals it will burn and itch. Most Caesarean sections performed now are lower section, and as your pubic hair grows back, the scar is almost completely hidden. But as hair grows, the itching is very irritating. Calendula cream may help with this. You can use the kind which is also sold for sore nipples. There is no point in using an antiseptic cream or lotion if you do not have an infection. The scar gradually changes from red to pink, and finally to a thin line, possibly lop-sided, which is silvery, or a little lighter than your skin-colour.

It will hurt to put your baby on your lap to breastfeed. So tuck the baby's legs under one arm, and, with your hand on the opposite side, guide the head to the breast and support it. It may help to put a cushion on your lap to support the baby's head. Some women prefer to lie on their side to breastfeed.

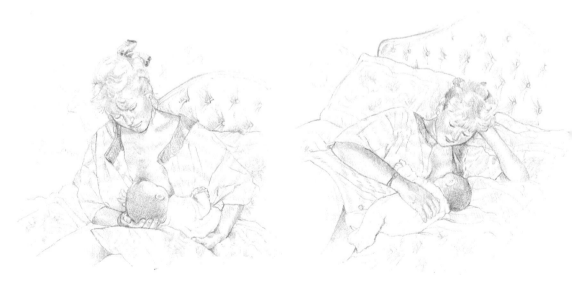

If you have had a failed forceps delivery there will be an episiotomy wound as well as your Caesarean wound, and recovery from this kind of complicated birth takes longest of all. You may find it very difficult to get into any position to breastfeed comfortably. Lying on your side is probably the easiest, and you will need your baby close to you and on the same level so that you can reach her without struggling. It helps if you have someone else who can hand the baby to you in the early days, and be ready to settle the baby down after a feed.

Many women suffer infection in the wound after a Caesarean section. This may occur soon after because bacteria were introduced during surgery, or it can happen weeks after the birth. The wound gets redder, there is swelling and tenderness behind it, it may go damp, pus may ooze from it, and your temperature goes up. Your doctor will prescribe antibiotics. Occasionally the wound unpeels and has to be restitched.

General anaesthetic is still used when it is decided to perform a Caesarean section as an emergency, and when a woman has not been given a previous epidural. Following surgery, secretions collect in the chest, and they need to be cleared by vigorously expelling air from your lungs. It is often suggested that you close your glottis and cough, but since this entails extending the abdominal wall it is painful when your scar is still sore. A far better method is to *suck in* the abdominal wall, in the same way that you use to get your intestines mobilized again, and breathe out forcefully with a 'huff'.

Though you may not be feeling much like it, movement is very important after a Caesarean birth in order to avoid thrombosis, a blood clot. The earlier after the operation you move, the better, and the first movement can be just with your feet. You can draw circles in different directions with your feet and write the letters of the alphabet. This will get the circulation going in your legs, where a clot is most likely to form.

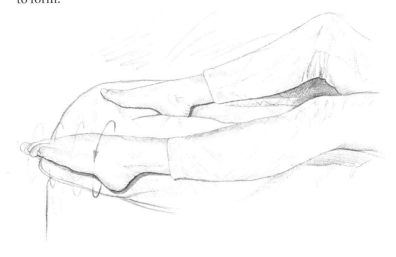

You are helped out of bed within six hours after the birth and take your first difficult steps. From then on it is important to have some gentle exercise each day. When you get home you will be encouraged to rest, and, if you are lucky enough to have people caring for you so that you can stay in bed most of the time, you may need to tell them that exercise is a vital part of care after a Caesarean birth too.

To make the incision the surgeon had to cut through and damage muscles. They will repair naturally in time, but the only way you can tone them is to work them. Good exercises include pelvic tilting, lifting and turning the pelvis, and gentle pelvic rocking. They are described in Chapter 3.

The hara-obi

In the past, and in traditional cultures still almost everywhere, women wore a binder. They say that this makes them much more comfortable, especially when they are out of their homes and have to stand for any length of time, because it encourages good posture. Japanese women still use the hara-obi, a wide sash to give gentle support to their backs and abdominal muscles, from the 'day of the dog' between the sixteenth and nineteenth week of pregnancy until about three weeks after birth. If you have a strip of soft cotton you can devise your own binder. You can use a long crêpe bandage about 15–20 centimetres wide and 4.5 metres long. It needs to go round your body three or four times, so you may not need the whole of it, and can make two or three out of one bandage. Draw the bandage firmly right round your lower abdomen and the small of your back, but not so tightly that you interrupt the circulation. The idea is to lift your uterus up, not press in on it. Continue winding it round until you feel neatly packaged, but not constricted.

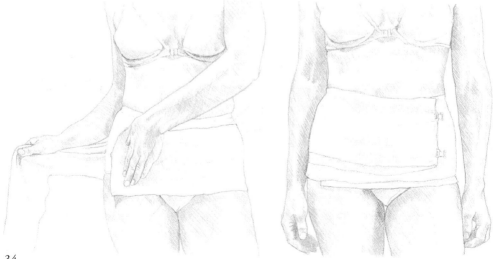

*'The binder I
was given to
wear in the
Japanese
hospital felt
wonderful.'*

Physiotherapists in the West usually advise that exercise is better than any artificial supporting garment, but in Japan it is believed that the combination of a hara-obi and exercise for the abdominal and back muscles prevents and relieves back pain and supports the uterus in its correct position. Because it is quite complicated to put on, some women wear a special light girdle instead, of which there are several different types suitable for wearing through to six months or even one year after birth.

Whatever your experience of birth, in the next chapter you will find suggestions about how to use your spine and muscles in a smooth, co-ordinated way, and so reduce the chances of backache and other muscular–skeletal pain, and ideas for movements to help you feel good about your body after childbirth.

Enjoying your Body

When you have a new baby it almost impossible to plan a regular time to do exercises. Babies vary so much in their sleeping habits, and the same baby changes so completely week by week, that all your plans and good intentions go out of the window. You are glad when you can grab enough time to eat or to have a quick shower.

Telling mothers that they should do regular exercises to be fit and healthy is a sure recipe to make them feel guilty and inadequate. This is why all the movements described in this chapter are ones you can do with the baby beside you, or in your arms, or perched on your lap or legs, or lying across your body. In some the baby is a partner in the movement, whom you bend to kiss or raise up high in your arms.

The way you move, stand, and sit every day, and a sense of positive body awareness, is as important for getting your figure back after childbirth as any movements you do in a half hour set aside for special exercises. Moreover, even when you conscientiously do exercises, habits of bad posture and awkward lifting and bending—tightening muscles in your chest and back, for example—may undo the good done by exercise.

The flow of energy

If you like doing physical exercises, one of the best ways of increasing your sense of well-being after childbirth is to explore movements drawing on ideas from the Feldenkrais method.[1] There is no need to strain or to force your body to perform any actions that do not feel light and easy.

If you are within six or eight weeks of a Caesarean birth you will want to select those movements that you can do comfortably and really enjoy doing. Don't push yourself. It is more important to do simple movements in a flowing way than to demonstrate that you can make exactly the same movements as women who have given birth vaginally. Let your body guide you.

With the Feldenkrais approach to body awareness you learn how to be aware of your body so that it is well balanced, and muscles have minimal work to do and are not tensed unnecessarily or made to work against each other. This is the very opposite of aerobics and the idea that you should push your body beyond the pain barrier. It is also very different from instructions to discipline your body to contract lazy muscles. Instead, the focus is on fluid movement and on experiencing how all parts of your body participate as you move.

Lying on your front

Sometimes it is suggested that in the first days after childbirth a woman ought to lie on her front to help her abdomen get flat. There is no particular reason why squashing your abdomen should reduce its size. But it is often a comfortable position to remove pressure from an episiotomy wound. If your back has been strained because you have had to wait for a doctor with your legs strung in the air, or you have been slung in lithotomy stirrups for a manœuvre, lying on your front allows you to relax your back and abdominal muscles, and can bring relief from pain. So by all means lie like this, but make sure that you are not hollowing your back. This puts strain on ligaments that are already stretched. If you want to sleep, to read, or to watch TV in this position, use a pillow to raise your pelvis and flatten your back. Become aware of stresses in your body, and select only those positions which enable your muscles to be relaxed and your whole body soft and flexible.

Lying on your front puts tender, milk-full breasts under pressure, so you may need to use extra pillows above and below your chest, and make a nest into which your breasts can drop.

Getting up

If you have been lying on your back and want to get up, let your eyes guide you and your body follow where your eyes lead, so that you roll from lying to sitting.

How to avoid backache

The positioning of every other part of your body depends on the alignment of your spine. The flexibility of your spine itself depends on muscles in your chest and shoulders being soft.

In late pregnancy the weight of the uterus and baby tends to pull the lower spine forward. It exaggerates the S curve of the flexible spinal column. This, in turn, pulls on ligaments. It is the reason why many women have backache in the last weeks of pregnancy, when the baby may be putting on as much weight as that of a large potato each week.

Tightening muscles in your chest has an immediate effect on your back. When your chest wall is stiff, your back will be stiff, too. Become aware of the flexibility of your chest. Releasing your chest wall softens your back. Every time you stand up, sit down, or start to walk, release your chest. This tilts your pelvis forward and up. Then your abdomen automatically becomes flatter.

This movement is quite different from deliberately holding your abdomen tight. Isolating and forcing abdominal wall muscles to become rigid results in a general locking of muscles in your back, chest, and many other parts of your body.

The position of your head is important, too. For your head to move freely, neck muscles, shoulders, and chest need to be unlocked. Keep your face and mouth relaxed. Imagine for a moment that your head is like a very heavy crystal bowl perched on top of your spine. Let it drop forward. Feel its weight. Now slowly, slowly, roll it round to one side, and allow it to drop backward with its own weight. Then slowly, slowly, lift it and let it drop to the other side, and roll it round again until it drops back. All the time you are doing this notice what is happening in your spinal vertebrae, the neatly interlocked connecting bones of your spine. Rest one hand on your sternum (the breastbone) and feel how it both supports and moves the head. The position of the head affects the whole length of your spine.

Release your chest wall and breathe slowly and completely, letting the breathing flow down into your pelvis and up again. Listen to the sound of your relaxed breathing, like waves washing on the sea shore. Be aware of what happens to your spine along its whole length as you breathe in and out. Notice what happens to your sternum (the breast bone) and to your abdominal wall.

Standing and sitting

Standing pelvic rock   Imagine a golden wire connecting the middle of your head with the ceiling. Put one hand on your lower back, the other on your chest, and rock gently forwards and backwards between your hands.

Now close your eyes, and make the same rocking movement very

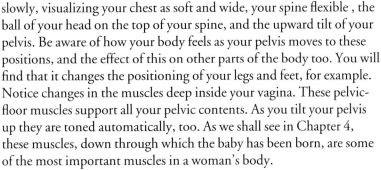

slowly, visualizing your chest as soft and wide, your spine flexible , the ball of your head on the top of your spine, and the upward tilt of your pelvis. Be aware of how your body feels as your pelvis moves to these positions, and the effect of this on other parts of the body too. You will find that it changes the positioning of your legs and feet, for example. Notice changes in the muscles deep inside your vagina. These pelvic-floor muscles support all your pelvic contents. As you tilt your pelvis up they are toned automatically, too. As we shall see in Chapter 4, these muscles, down through which the baby has been born, are some of the most important muscles in a woman's body.

Let your arms drop by your side, loosen your neck, relax your shoulders, and continue this gentle rocking, pausing each time when you get into the position where your chest is relaxed, your bottom is tucked in, and your abdomen firm. This is the posture in which your body can work with ease and freedom without putting strain on muscles and ligaments. It is the position which enables it to shape up naturally after childbirth.

Sitting pelvic rock   Now draw up a chair to a full-length mirror and sit on it so that you have a sideways view. Notice how you sit. Have your knees comfortably apart. Visualize your spinal column and your head and pelvis again. Gently rock your pelvis as you did when you were standing.

41

**Sitting to feed
your baby**

When you sit down to feed your baby make sure that you have good back support and that you are not stiff. If you notice that you tend to round your shoulders, place a cushion on your lap to lift the baby up to your breasts. You may like to raise one thigh by putting your foot on a stool or the rung of a chair.[2]

When you get on the bed to feed your baby, you need enough pillows to support your spine from the bottom to the top. You probably want two or three in the small of your back—but not so many that your chest is forced up—and another behind your shoulders.

But what if you have more than one baby? One answer is to support your arms, and the babies' heads if necessary, with foam cushions at either side. If you have cut-outs in the foam you can scoop up a baby easily without shifting or putting strain on your back.

Working postures

Think about how you sit in a car. If the seat is uncomfortably low, use a cushion so that your knees are level with your pelvis. Consider whether you need extra support for your back, too.

Working postures, at a desk or doing housework, for example, are important. So think about the work you do most often and how this affects tension in your chest, and thus the alignment of your spine, head, and pelvis. When you are at a word processor the chair should be high enough to avoid tightening your chest, shoulders and upper back.

When changing nappies, you may want to do it on the floor, kneeling at the side of the bed, or standing at a changing table which is high enough for you not to have to bend over.

Kitchen units are sometimes uncomfortably low for a tall woman. (American women living in France, for example, usually find that the units are designed for shorter people.) You should be able to stand and rest both hands on the bottom of the sink without having to bend over. If you cannot do this, short of buying a new sink, which may be out of the question, use a bowl placed on another inverted bowl, or insert an upturned rack into the sink and place a bowl on top of that. If you are short, there may be nothing for it but to get someone else to wash the pots and pans!

Bending, lifting, and carrying

Working in the house, doing shopping, lifting children or books and files in the office—the way we use our bodies is important. It is easy to cause strain on ligaments and muscles that leads to pain. Women often suffer backache after having a baby when they never experienced it before, and those who have a tendency to backache anyway find that it gets worse.

If you wear low-heeled shoes you will probably be more comfortable. Be especially careful about good body mechanics and posture when you lift and carry, letting your arms and legs do the work rather than your back. Remember your back is not a crane.

43

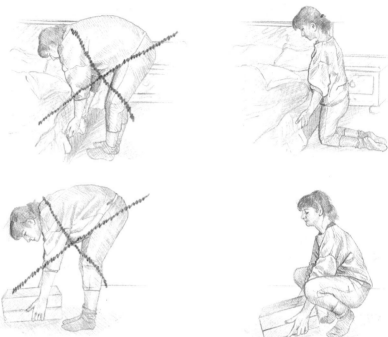

Whenever possible, loosen your knees and go down close to any task below waist level, rather than bending over and straining your back. Making the bed, cleaning the bath, trying to find something on a low shelf or in a drawer, loading or unloading a dishwasher or washing machine, and lifting a toddler, are all much easier when you go down through your thighs and knees to a squatting or kneeling position. If you have rheumatism in your knees so that this kind of movement is difficult, it helps to adapt furniture and apparatus so that you can reach them without bending over, either from a standing position, or from a wheelchair.

When you have to carry a heavy load, you will find that it is more comfortable if you can separate it so that you have two smaller loads, and divide the weight equally each side of your body.

By the time your baby is around six months old, carrying him on your hip for any length of time will distort your spinal column, cause stress to muscles and ligaments, and result in backache. It is much better to have the baby in a carrier on your back.

Movement for body awareness

Setting aside special time to release your body and let energy flow through you is one way to feel good about yourself. Fluid movements will help tone muscles and ligaments that may have been put under stress by pregnancy and birth.

Most of these movements are easily done with the baby snuggled into you in a soft carrier tucked against your breast, or lying against or perched on your body.

'I'm so busy with the baby I thought I couldn't fit in exercises too. But it's important to have a space in the day that's for me.'

45

Or the baby can be in a seat or on a rug where she can watch you do all these interesting things.

In fact, you can often use the weight of your baby, lying, propped up, or supported by your hand or thighs, to make a movement a bit more challenging. When you exercise with your baby, do so on a soft rug in case she rolls off.

Empty your bladder before starting these movements. Avoid any that cause discomfort, or defer them until later, when your muscles are stronger. There is no need to force yourself to do any movements. You can do them at any time of the day, but after a warm bath you will feel relaxed and supple, and this is an especially good time. After each movement take some time to relax completely and breathe slowly and fully.

All movements should be progressive. Start with a simple version and, as you achieve smooth muscular co-ordination, make it a little more difficult. This is particularly important after childbirth. There are no rules about when you can start certain movements, because every woman is different, just as every labour is different. But those that are most suitable for the first two to three weeks after birth are marked with ☆ .

Though these movements focus on certain parts of the body, every one should flow right through your body. When you start to do them, read one paragraph at a time. Then explore the movement, and read the next paragraph only after you have found out what it feels like and what your body can do.

To tone abdominal muscles

Abdominal muscles form a girdle which is constructed of straight and oblique muscle bands in a trellis pattern. You can strengthen this trellis with the following exercises.

☆ *Pelvic rock*   This is one of the first movements for after the birth, and it can be done in bed.[3] It is good to do if your abdomen feels soft and floppy. It will also help you to tone recti muscles if they are separated. If this has happened to you, you can keep your hands pressing in to support each side of the separated recti muscles while you do the movement. Feel what happens to the separated area. At first you may notice that the 'seam' widens as you lift your head. Only when it no longer does so is it the right time to go on to more vigorous movements.

Lie on your back in bed or on the floor without a pillow, knees bent, and the soles of your feet flat. Keeping your knees bent protects your lower back from strain. Cross your hands over your abdomen, and, with one on either side of your waist, breathe out, release your chest wall completely, and push the floor or bed with your feet and allow your pelvis to roll in so that your lower back can flatten. Then 'pull' the floor or bed with your feet so that the rolling of your pelvis enables your lower back to arch. Be aware of what happens all along your spine up to your head whilst pushing and pulling with your feet. You may find that your head begins to roll in response to the rolling of your pelvis so that, as your back flattens, your chin rolls away from your chest, and, as your back arches, your chin rolls towards your chest.

Pelvic rock 2   Another way of doing this movement is to have your baby lying over your abdomen and your arms relaxed and spread out at your sides.

Sideways curl-up   Lie on your back on a rug on the floor, with bent knees again. This time settle your baby where she can watch you. Put your left hand under your head. Breathe in and, as you exhale and soften your chest, lift your head and shoulders and your left knee until your elbow and knee are touching. If you feel comfortable, stay like this for a moment and make sure you are not holding your breath. Return to the starting position gently and gradually, continue the movement on the opposite side, and alternate in this way.

☆ *Unfolding 1*   This is another movement you can do soon after birth. Sit on the floor with your knees bent and close together, holding your baby resting against your thighs. Release your chest and allow your back to drop backwards slowly whilst at the same time beginning

to lengthen your legs. Then fold yourself together again, by moving your nose and knees as close together as you comfortably can, and then separate them again. Lean only as far as it is comfortable. Keep your chest and your mouth soft, and allow vertebra after vertebra to be placed on the floor like a string of pearls slowly lengthening. Hold the position for as long as it feels good, and continue breathing. Be aware of how energy flows from the *centre* of your body.

Unfolding 2   Do this movement without the baby and with your arms folded across your chest. You will find that you gradually increase the distance you can lean back. Think of your body as a book that you open up in the middle.

☆ *Leg slide*   Lie on your back, your baby lying on your chest or abdomen, knees bent and feet flat on the floor. Put one hand in the small of your back. Notice how your back is in contact with it. Release your chest. Push the floor gently with your feet, an action which flattens your back further so that it squeezes your hand against the floor.

Soften your mouth and, keeping the pressure against your hand, slowly, slowly, let both feet slide forward so that your legs lengthen. Notice how far you can go. As your legs withdraw their support, abdominal muscles take over. So press more firmly with your back against your hand. Allow your toes to come up off the floor so that your leg muscles are not tense. Remember to go on breathing. If at any point you feel the small of your back lifting off the floor, do not move your feet any further. Slide one foot back to the starting position, then the other. Repeat this four or five times.

Up, up, and away   Lie on your back, knees bent and feet flat on the floor. Rest your baby on your chest, holding her under the arms. Then slowly and gently lift your baby high in the air above your face, feeling the pressure of your lower back against the floor as you do so. Hold the baby in this position and talk to her. Slowly lower her on to your body again and, with chest soft, rock her gently.[4]

Rocking the baby   Lie on your back, knees bent and raised, with your lower legs parallel to the floor, and put your baby face down on your lower legs, holding her under the arms. Tuck your chin in, slowly raise your head and shoulders, and rock forward. Continue breathing. Then gently rock back, lowering your head and shoulders to the floor.[5]

To tone muscles of back and bottom

☆ *Swinging hammock*   Lie on your back with your knees bent and your feet flat on the floor. Your arms are spread at your sides, palms up. Release your chest, and slowly lift your pelvis off the floor until there is a straight line from your feet to your shoulders; keep your chest relaxed so that you do not hollow your back. Hold the position for a count of five or six. Imagine a hammock swayed by the wind, and let your pelvis rock. Then gently return to the starting position. You can do this while holding your baby too.

Bottom shuffle   Sit on the floor with your legs straight out and your baby resting on your thighs facing you. Hold her back with one hand and her head with the other. With your back straight, allow one leg to lengthen further, and shuffle forward on your bottom, extending first your right leg from your hip bone downwards and then your left. Let your head turn as you move, and keep your ankles soft. Notice how your chest is involved in the movement, too. You will be moving rather like a camel—left leg and left shoulder, then right leg and right shoulder. After this, switch to shuffling backwards.

51

Roll-up 1   Lying on your back, without your baby this time, with your hands behind your head and knees bent, elbows facing forward, allow your knees and elbows to roll together. Then let them roll apart from each other.

Roll-up 2   Lying on your back, without your baby, knees bent, allow your knees and shoulders to roll together and rest your hands loosely on your lower legs. There is no need to pull your legs, since the folding movement happens in your chest and the lengthening movement in your back.

'I'm beginning to feel like a baby again, I'm feeling so soft.'

Complete rock   Lying on your back, with knees bent, lift your feet off the floor and support your legs with your hands under your knees. Rock backwards and forwards, keeping the distance between your nose and knees more or less constant. Rock your spine more and more until eventually you find yourself sitting upright. Don't aim to rock right up. Just let it happen. Keep your back rounded the whole time. This is a great back relaxer.

The twist Sit on the floor upright, legs crossed, with your baby in your lap. Stretch out one arm at shoulder level and turn so that it is extended behind you. Hold your baby with your free hand. Turn your head to look at your outstretched arm. Lower your hand to the floor behind you and continue looking over your shoulder. Go on breathing, and hold the position for a count of ten to fifteen. Go back to the starting position. Breathe slowly and fully and repeat the movement on the other side.

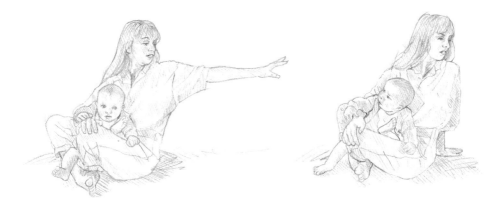

As you finish each movement session, use the wall to help you stand straight and relaxed, so that you maintain good posture. Stand with your back to the wall, your heels about a hand's breadth away from it. Drop your shoulders, relax your chest wall and unlock your knees. Be aware of how the small of your back touches the wall and how the whole length of your spine makes contact with the wall. Stand like this for half a minute or so, breathing slowly and fully in through your nose and out through a soft, relaxed mouth, feeling the breathing movement flow right down into your pelvis and up again.

To heal backache

As abdominal muscles stretch in late pregnancy, muscles in the small of the back tend to shorten. Elizabeth Noble calls this a 'bowstring effect'.[7] Abdominal muscles are stretched like the string of a bow pulling on muscles and ligaments in the lower back, so that they become tense and shortened, and ligaments, already softened by the hormones of pregnancy, are overloaded. By toning the muscles of your lower abdomen and your buttocks—the gluteals—you can protect the pelvic joints.

All the movements to tone abdominal muscles will help your back, too. Here are two extra movements that will help.

Sitting wall stretch   Sit cross-legged with your back against a wall. Release your chest muscles so that you can easily rest the small of your back against the wall. Slowly and gently move both arms out sideways and up so that they are extended above your head. Breathe slowly in and out four or five times. Then bring your arms down again, and relax forward. Let your forehead sink towards the floor in front of you, with your arms spread wide, the palms of your hands face down, and your back long and broad.

Standing wall stretch   With your feet comfortably apart and your knees unlocked and bent, stand with your back to a wall. Release your chest muscles so that you feel the contact of the small of your back with the wall. With arms straight, let them draw a circle against the wall from the level of your knees, out and up over your head. Continue breathing. Be aware of how, when your chest is relaxed and wide, your pelvis is tilted so that your head and shoulders and the small of your back are touching the wall.

Massage

Massage helps you feel good about your body. It can be either stimulating or soothing, depending on what you prefer at the time. It releases muscle tension, helps you sleep deeply—so that you use whatever sleeping time you have to best advantage—and when you are busy caring for the baby, enables you to relax and feel good about yourself. Women often like it before they settle down at night, after the late feed. If you don't have a live-in partner it may be possible to arrange a once-a-week session with a friend. In France and Belgium, as in Third World countries, postnatal massage is often a normal part of care of the new mother.

Massage can help backache (and feels wonderful even if your back is fine), but it must be skilfully done. It is not just a matter of a helper rubbing as hard as possible. This can be very painful. In fact, it usually

helps if whoever is doing it receives massage first, to find out how it feels. It may be best not to massage directly over a painful area, but to concentrate on releasing the muscles of your back and buttocks.

Lie on your front in a warm room with a pillow under your pelvis so that your back is straight. Your helper kneels at one side and starts by massaging with warm, oiled, relaxed hands right up your back at either side of your spine to your neck, and then lightly down again in slow, firm movements. When massaging the back it is important to do so at either side of the spine, not directly on the vertebrae. The hands move up and down your back three or four times.

Whole back massage feels good, too, if your helper makes big finger circles, moving the flesh on the muscles right down your back, repeating this three or four times.

Since the lumbar curve is exaggerated by tension in the chest and shoulders, massage of your *upper* back can help reduce *low* backache. With warm, oiled hands your helper rests fingers on your shoulders and massages slowly with the thumbs in big circles over the muscles at either side of your upper spine, and into the little valleys beside your spine.

Now your helper does the same thing moving down over your buttocks too, massaging the gluteal muscles with deep, firm movements. This is repeated three or four times, too.

Then you can see how it feels if your helper makes long, slow firm strokes with the palms of the hands from your shoulders down to your bottom, alternating the hand movements so that there is a continuous stroking.

Exercise for pleasure

There is nothing like having a break from a baby and then meeting up with each other and falling in love all over again! Any physical activity or sport that you enjoyed before you were pregnant, and for which you can clear space in your busy life, will be invigorating now. It is not the time to take up any new athletic activity, but if you liked jogging, running, swimming, cycling, aerobics or any kind of exercise class, racket games, riding, or dancing before the baby came it will be a refreshing break from baby care and the other work you do if you can manage to make time for this now.

Swimming is one of the best forms of exercise after having a baby. Some childbirth groups arrange for sole use of a pool, and heat it especially warm, for mothers and babies together. There may be a nursery where you can leave the baby in good care while you swim alone, too.

Walking is a superb exercise, but not if it is a stroll round the shopping mall. If you can get into the countryside or a park you can walk vigorously, swinging your arms. In Japan women have specially constructed coats, called 'mamma coats', which contain a pocket into which the baby can be placed, and the coat buttons up round both mother and baby. They are often designed so that they can be suitable for almost any weather, with detachable arms, turning the coat into a cool waistcoat for warmer weather. Women wear these in both town and country, so that they are able to move freely with unencumbered arms. You can move freely if you have a comfortable carrier so that the baby is nestled against your body. Wear trainers or other shoes that support your feet well.

If you prefer to walk with other people, there may be a group that enjoys cross-country walking in your area, or you could form one yourself with other people who have babies. If you want to find out about groups and classes in your area, look on the notice boards in the leisure centre, public library, the health centre, and your Citizens Advice Bureau. A sports equipment shop may be able to let you know about local walking groups. Look in your local newspaper, too, and if you are still in the first six months after birth, ask local childbirth organizations about postnatal exercises, swimming, and Yoga classes. The great advantage of these groups is that all the members have young babies, and, as well as the activity, it is fun to get together to talk.

If you enjoy dancing there may be classes that are suitable. Belly dancing and African dance are ideal, with their exciting rhythms and powerful pelvic movements.

You may feel too tired to think about exercise. But, paradoxically, a woman who cannot make any time for enjoying her body through movement is likely to feel even more tired. If you are exhausted, try three things: deep relaxation—breathing slowly, and listening to the sound of your breaths in and out, like waves flowing on to the beach and back again; activity that gets you moving; and finding a space in the day in which your mind and energy is not entirely focused on your baby.

While you are lactating, your breasts may be too uncomfortably full for any athletic activity in which they are bounced up and down. Jogging can cause painful friction of clothing against your nipples, for instance. Some women say it is easier if they wear two well fitted sports bras, one on top of the other. Exercising just after a feed may be the answer. But even then, it is too uncomfortable for some women. Let your body guide you.

It is also worth noting that, if your breasts become engorged because the baby is switching to a cup and solids, or just does not want to breastfeed so often as before, any activity in which you move your arms energetically helps free the milk ducts and results in leaking. Once you are leaking, it is easy to express by hand or machine till you are comfortable. Do not express more than this, or you will make more milk. So a game of tennis, swimming a few lengths, or more humdrum tasks such as polishing, washing a floor on hands and knees, or gardening—anything that entails vigorous arm movements—can help free breast engorgement.

Both you and your baby benefit when you enjoy and express yourself through your body, and you are charged with fresh energy.

Your Pelvic Floor, Bladder, and Vagina

The pelvic-floor muscles are some of the most important muscles in a woman's body. They are slung like wide, stretchy elastic between the bones that form the base of her pelvis. These are the coccyx at the very bottom of the spine and the pubic symphysis which forms the front of the pelvis. There are three openings through the layers of muscles: the urethra, through which urine is passed from her bladder, the vagina, and the anus. Every time a woman empties her bowels or bladder she uses these muscles. She uses them in love-making and intercourse, too. And when she gives birth, the baby's head is pressed down through the pelvic-floor muscles to be born. Because it has these openings, the pelvic floor needs to be both strong and flexible. It has to hold in and to give, to close firmly and to open freely.

The term 'floor' suggests a rigid surface. In fact, it isn't like that at all. These muscles are supple and multi-layered, like hammocks sloping one on top of the other, and at different angles. They are capable of subtle, flowing movement. They are rich with nerve endings that convey feelings of fullness and pressure which stimulate their opening, and they can also produce pain—and feelings of satisfaction and intense pleasure. When a woman has an orgasm, they contract and release spontaneously in a rapid succession of tight clasps, like kisses inside, and once the orgasm is over they are very soft and relaxed.

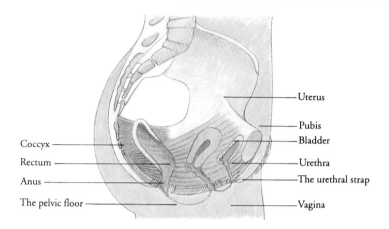

Coccyx ——

Rectum ——

Anus ——

The pelvic floor ——

—— Uterus

—— Pubis

—— Bladder

—— Urethra

—— The urethral strap

—— Vagina

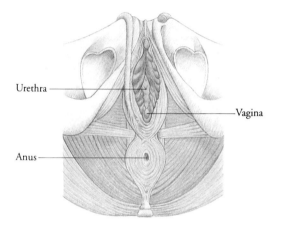

Urethra ——

Anus ——

—— Vagina

The pelvic floor

Pelvic-floor muscles are important right through a woman's life, not only when she is pregnant and after childbirth. They may get slack if she is constipated and strains to empty her bowels, or if she has to do very heavy lifting that puts her pelvic floor under stress. When the muscles are weak she cannot stop her bladder leaking as she sneezes, coughs, or laughs, if she exercises vigorously, or when the weather is cold and windy. It is estimated that one in every three women suffers from incontinence like this.

It is often taken for granted that incontinence is an inevitable consequence of ageing, especially for a woman who has had babies. A doctor writes, 'Childbearing inevitably stretches the muscles of the pelvic floor... Repeating the procedure four or five times almost always causes irreparable loss of tone in both muscles and ligaments even though the births appear uncomplicated.'[1] When oestrogen levels are reduced with the menopause, a process of 'degeneration' begins, with what this doctor describes as 'tissue wasting, hormone deficiency, and the onset of other disorders that may raise the intra-abdominal pressure'.

This very common medical view of women's bodies as inherently flawed, of birth as a pathological process, and the menopause as a disaster, can be challenged by many healthy older women who have cared for their bodies and have firm pelvic-floor muscles. The assumption that nothing can be done to improve the condition of weak muscles is ridiculous, too. Any muscles that are under voluntary control can be toned by movement.

Nevertheless, it is true that urinary incontinence is common in women who have had babies, especially in the first year after birth, and sometimes for much longer. It sometimes occurs because a forceps delivery has pulled on muscles that support the openings in the pelvic floor and probably also dragged down the soft lining of the vagina, so

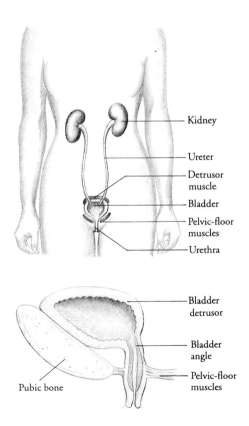

Kidney

Ureter

Detrusor muscle

Bladder

Pelvic-floor muscles

Urethra

Bladder detrusor

Bladder angle

Pelvic-floor muscles

Pubic bone

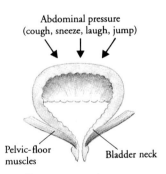

Abdominal pressure (cough, sneeze, laugh, jump)

Pelvic-floor muscles

Bladder neck

Poor support – urine escapes

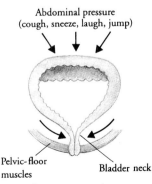

Abdominal pressure (cough, sneeze, laugh, jump)

Pelvic-floor muscles

Bladder neck

Good support – no urine escapes

that it hangs like clothes on a slack washing line. Muscles may also have been weakened by commanded pushing in the second stage of labour before the woman has a spontaneous urgent desire to push the baby out, by a violent delivery in which the baby was pulled out forcibly, and by other interventions, including manipulations to get the baby into a better position for delivery, and possibly the artificial stimulation of uterine activity with synthetic oxytocin introduced into the woman's bloodstream.

Perhaps we should ask what there is about what women do in pregnancy, or about the conduct of childbirth, or what is done or not done in the days after birth, which damages women physically, and often leaves them coping with long-term bladder problems.

In Asian and African countries mothers often teach their adolescent daughters how to control their pelvic muscles because it is considered an important part of being a woman, and necessary for sex and childbirth. In Western culture, however, it is a neglected subject, and girls grow up not knowing that they have pelvic-floor muscles.

'I'd never **heard** *of pelvic-floor muscles until I went to childbirth classes!'*

In traditional cultures, too, women often carry loads on their heads. They stand tall and walk with a swinging movement from the pelvis. This may stimulate contraction of pelvic-floor muscles, so that they are well toned. You can try this with a book on your head—an exercise which was considered an essential element in 'deportment lessons' for young ladies in Victorian England. Maybe they knew more about women's bodies than we realize!

Any muscle of the body that is not used atrophies. For this reason, after operations physiotherapists help to mobilize muscles that have been weakened by giving patients special exercises. But this is not enough to keep the pelvic floor active. It needs to be used regularly, and right through a woman's life, if it is to be supple and strong. We should be able to mobilize pelvic-floor muscles like the muscles around our mouths. Just as expressions on our face change and we use facial muscles as we talk, so our pelvic-floor muscles can be active, too, rather than simply left to hang there.

To locate your pelvic-floor muscles, press a finger of one hand on to the smallest bone at the bottom of your spine—the coccyx—and a finger of the other hand on the bony ridge at the front of your pelvis—the pubic symphysis. Now tighten up inside as if you could pull your fingers towards each other. Your pelvic-floor muscles are working.

You can, in fact, 'smile' with your pelvic floor. This is a good exercise to greet each day. Wake up every morning with a pelvic-floor smile. As you pull in the muscles and tighten them, and hold the smile as if for a photograph, they become well toned. If these muscles start to tremble because they are not yet strong enough to hold the smile, release them and smile again. Women who are anxious about getting them into shape sometimes drive themselves to discipline them even though they are trembling with the effort. This over-strains the muscles, and may cause damage, especially in the first six months after birth. It may be the reason why research suggests that some women who exercise enthusiastically have pelvic-floor muscles which are weaker than those of other women who are physically active but who do not do regular pelvic-floor exercises.

Pelvic-floor muscles—like any other muscles in the body—can be affected by strong emotions. When a woman is depressed, it is not only the muscles of her face that sag, but also those of the pelvic floor. So it is important to make pelvic-floor 'smiles' at any time when you are feeling low or tired out.

Some years ago a survey was undertaken to examine the relation between pre- and post-natal exercises and prolapse. The results were not definitive, but they discovered in the course of research that of the 728 women who answered the questionnaire 269 (37 per cent) suffered from stress incontinence, and most of them dated the onset of this from pregnancy or childbirth. One woman, for example, could only go to the beach if there was a public lavatory nearby. She had to wear a pad all the time, so she could not wear a swimsuit. Many of these women felt ashamed about it and dirty, and some had been too embarrassed to seek help from their doctors.[2]

When pelvic-floor muscles are weak a woman may have some of these symptoms:

a dragging feeling low in the abdomen
a feeling of something falling out inside
low backache
difficulty keeping tampons in place
reduced sensation during intercourse
urinary incontinence (wetting pants with sudden movements, with exercise, or on a cold day)
frequency of urination (having to empty the bladder a lot, though there is hardly any urine there)
vaginal flatus (passing gas)
haemorrhoids (piles)
pain on emptying the bowels
bowel incontinence

You can test the strength of your pelvic-floor muscles in two different ways. You can interrupt a stream of urine when you are emptying your bladder. If you can do this, your muscles are well-toned. You can also slip a finger deep inside your vagina and squeeze it with your pelvic-floor muscles. If you can feel this squeeze as if you were pursing up your mouth inside, they are well-toned.

Both these methods of checking to find out if pelvic-floor muscles are strong are also ways of toning them. Do not interrupt urine more than about once a week in case you get into a habit of not completely emptying your bladder. Never interrupt the flow if you have a bladder infection, or you may make it worse.

Eileen Montgomery, a physiotherapist who specializes in bladder problems, suggests that a good test of pelvic-floor tone is to jump up and down, with a full bladder, alternating your feet between together and apart. After three or four cups of tea or coffee, this demands almost bionic strength![3] An alternative recommended by some physiotherapists is to get a child's skipping rope and skip with feet apart. The chances are that you will get tangled in the rope and go crashing to the floor, so it may do more harm than good!

There is an exercise, however, which can be done any time, any place—because it is invisible. It is the Pelvic Lift.

The Pelvic Lift

Imagine that you have a lift inside your body which can go up as far as your waist. It is composed of your pelvic-floor muscles and you can make them ascend, floor by floor, from the ground floor, up to the fourth floor, stopping at each level on the way. Hold the contraction only so long as it is comfortable. If muscles tremble it shows that they are over-strained. At the end of the exercise let your pelvic-floor muscles relax a little, but not drop right down to the ground floor again. Hold them curved into a pelvic-floor smile. As you do this, go on breathing, and don't pull upwards with your shoulders. This is an internal movement only. You won't need to tighten your buttock muscles either. If you do so, you may feel you are pulling up inside strongly when you are only getting a flicker of movement. So focus on getting the feeling of the lift going up without tensing any other muscles in your body.

When you first start doing this you may look as if you are concentrating very hard, and even have to explain what you are doing. But once you get into the habit of it, you will be able to do it easily as you talk on the phone, wait for the lights to turn green when you are driving, change the baby's nappy, and stand at the supermarket check-out. This is not a once a day exercise, but one for repeating again and again whenever you have a moment to do it. If you tackle the strengthening of your pelvic-floor muscles in this way, you can incorporate pelvic-floor movements into your everyday life and mobilize the muscles just as much as those in your face, hands, and feet.

Even if you do not have a problem with weakness in these muscles in the year after childbirth, as you get older you may find that they do not work so well for you and there are difficulties with bladder control, especially in old age. If you activate the muscles, there is every chance that you will go through life with a well-toned pelvic floor and the sense of vitality that this brings.

Prolapse

In countries where there is extreme poverty and long-term malnutrition women may suffer genital prolapse because they have never had enough protein in their diet to make muscles and ligaments strong. In the West, anorexia may contribute to some women's muscular weakness. But most women are well fed and muscles should be able to function well.

'I felt a bulge inside my vagina and thought it must be a prolapse. But it turned out to be a cervical polyp and was nothing to worry about.'

There are four different kinds of prolapse. The most common after childbirth is cystocele. This occurs when the front surface of the bladder sags into the vagina. With rectocele, the rectum sags into the anus. It is difficult to empty your bowels completely. Enterocele is the sagging of the intestine into the deepest part of the vagina. When there is uterine prolapse, the uterus sags into the vagina. A prolapse is caused not only by weak pelvic-floor muscles but by the stretching of ligaments that usually support the bladder and uterus.

If you have some degree of prolapse you may be unable to move your pelvic floor at all when you are standing, because the weight of your abdominal and pelvic organs is pressing down on the muscles, and they cannot work against it. So do the Pelvic Lift lying down. Since it is easier to isolate these muscles when your knees are bent, too, the answer is to lie down on the floor with your feet up on a coffee table or the bed, and do the exercise in this position.

If you can feel something like a cherry protruding in your vagina, or it is as if something like a tampon is stuck halfway in,[4] gently replace this small bulge with your finger first of all. Then make pelvic-floor kisses. Exercising in this way four or five times a day gradually strengthens the muscles so a slight prolapse is repaired.

Surgery is rarely necessary for these conditions unless the prolapse is causing low back or abdominal pain, or pain with intercourse. You may not be able to cure a prolapse simply by muscle action, but pelvic-floor exercises strengthen the 'safety net' so that prolapse does not become worse.[5]

Perineal pain

Some women find it impossible to mobilize the pelvic floor after having a baby because of perineal trauma. Sometimes this is short lived. It is usually because they had an episiotomy, a cut through skin and muscles to speed delivery. Sometimes it is because they had a bad tear. Either way, the perineum has been sutured afterwards. In the first year after birth pain from a perineal wound often deters women from moving these muscles.

You cannot mobilize pelvic-floor muscles if you have perineal pain. More important, however, you should not be exercising if it hurts. It is fine to contract them to the point of pain, but not beyond this, and never hold on to a contraction until the muscles quiver.

A woman's perineum and the muscles deep inside often feel numb for the first few days after birth. It is almost as if this is no longer part of her body. Then, as sensation returns, she feels bruised and sore. But by ten days after—and often earlier—a woman with an intact perineum, or one who has had a small graze or simple tear, is easily able to contract and release these muscles again and to restore their tone.

After a forceps delivery it may take much longer. It need not be a complicated forceps delivery, either. Nowadays lift-out forceps are often employed when a woman has had epidural anaesthesia, and obstetricians tend to treat this as a minor intervention. But a study of women's experiences of forceps delivery revealed that many women experienced 'unbearable discomfort' on the third or fourth day after the birth, and that when forceps deliveries were compared with vacuum extractor deliveries three times as many women were in severe pain in the forceps group. As the authors comment, 'Operative deliveries are commonplace for the obstetrician but not for the woman.'[6]

In Scandinavia forceps deliveries are rarely performed. They have been almost entirely replaced by vacuum extraction. In Britain the majority of obstetricians still rely on their skill with forceps. This may be fine for them, but the consequence is unnecessary pain for women. In North America obstetricians perform Caesarean sections in place of either forceps or vacuum extraction, and women suffer the trauma of a major surgical operation.

Physiotherapists are skilled in treating pelvic-floor dysfunction. If you need extra help, ask your GP to refer you to an obstetric physiotherapist. She will assess the strength of your pelvic-floor muscles, perhaps using a perineometer, which tests how hard you can squeeze them. This may be off-putting to look at, as it usually resembles a large artificial penis with a dial attached. Sometimes a woman can take it home to practise, or a DIY one is put together with a condom and a measuring device so that she can experiment at leisure. Sometimes the physiotherapist may advise faradism, using low electrical currents, or that you wear vaginal cones to stimulate reflex activity in the muscles. Cones are a kind of weight-training for the vagina. They come in sets which the woman takes home. They are the same shape and size, but one is very lightweight and the others heavier. When a cone is placed in the vagina it stimulates the muscles to contract so that it does not fall out.[7] Electrical stimulation can be used at home, too. A vaginal electrode stimulates muscles to contract, and the current can be adjusted until it feels right. It is used for twenty minutes a day for one month.[8] Some obstetric physiotherapists say that cones and electrodes are just gimmicky and a waste of money. Certainly for most women with poor muscle tone, pelvic-floor exercises are more effective. And the great advantage is that you do not need an operation or any special equipment.

You can visualize your pelvic floor as an internal trampoline of muscle which forms the springy base for everything in your pelvis and abdomen. Or you may prefer to visualize it as a strong, flexible stem with wide-sweeping branches that support these organs in your lower body. Your pelvic-floor muscles are beautifully and intricately constructed to perform this function well. All it needs of you is that you keep them alive through movement.

Episiotomy

In Western culture it is accepted as normal for a woman to have stitches after childbirth. Doctors sometimes say that we should be grateful that episiotomies can be performed and suturing done afterwards, because otherwise many of us would suffer from rectovaginal fistula—a tear from the vagina into the rectum—and, as in some South African tribes, would become outcasts because we were incontinent. But there are many traditional societies from which evidence is now coming that midwives have known how to help women give birth to babies without injuring themselves, and without needing to be cut. The most important element in this may simply be that the second stage of labour—the expulsive phase—is not rushed, and that there is no time limit on it. Where a woman can give birth at her own pace, injury to the perineum, and to the muscles, ligaments, and nerve endings deep inside it, is much less likely.

Episiotomy—the incision of a woman's genitals to enlarge the birth outlet—is by far the most commonly performed obstetric operation. In some countries hardly any woman escapes without one, and those who do are likely to have had Caesarean sections. In Spain and Italy, for example, the rate is over 90 per cent. In Australia there is no formal requirement for obstetricians to report the number of episiotomies performed. But in some areas it is estimated by midwives and researchers to vary between 80 and 95 per cent. British hospitals did not start to report episiotomy rates until the practice came under critical scrutiny in the early 1980s. It was then that my two surveys of women's experiences of care in maternity units were published, the National Childbirth Trust produced my two studies on episiotomy, and women started asking searching questions about it.[9]

There is a very wide range of obstetric practice between countries, and often also within a country. The Netherlands, for example, has a rate of episiotomy which is under 10 per cent. In Britain it has now dropped to about 30 per cent for midwife-attended births (the vast majority), but with obstetrician-conducted deliveries it is probably around 90 per cent, even when births are otherwise straightforward. More women have episiotomies who opt for private care than those who have NHS care, just as they can expect more interventions of every kind, including more operative deliveries.

It makes sense to keep the option of episiotomy open when a delivery is complicated because the baby is in the wrong position or needs to be born quickly because there are concerns about its oxygen supply. But episiotomy does not make sense as a routine procedure. It is our Western way of female genital mutilation.

After having a baby, many women are shocked and distressed by the episiotomy and its after-effects. As one woman put it, 'It is as though I have been attacked with scissors during a private sexual act. If someone cut you deliberately with scissors while you were making love because you weren't the right size it would be in all the newspapers, wouldn't it?... I now have an 8-month-old baby and an 8-month-old episiotomy scar and they feature equally large in my life.' Women are horrified that this ritual mutilation of women can take place without public protest. They often feel violated. Certainly, if men were forced to have their

'I had been pushing so long and so hard and was so exhausted that I was really grateful for the episiotomy.'

'I did not know my own body. I felt damaged—mutilated.'

testicles surgically incised and sewn up afterwards before they could become fathers it would be discussed widely, and there would be concerted efforts to do away with the practice.

Research reveals that routine episiotomy is not only unnecessary, but harmful. Episiotomy does not maintain the strength of pelvic-floor musculature, as obstetricians have often claimed. It is exercise that does this. In fact, episiotomy may have the opposite effect and cause problems with the pelvic-floor muscles for many months.[10] It cannot prevent prolapse. It does not prevent urinary incontinence.[11] Even though, when repairing episiotomies, US obstetricians often insert an extra, unnecessary suture to tighten a woman's vagina—which they call 'the husband's stitch'—episiotomy and tight suturing do not preserve the size and shape of the vagina, either to enhance a man's pleasure in intercourse, or to increase the frequency of female orgasm. On the contrary, suturing often results in prolonged dyspareunia —pain when intercourse is attempted.[12] And episiotomy does not prevent fourth-degree perineal lacerations—tears into the rectum —when a baby is born so quickly that its head shoots out like a cork out of a champagne bottle.

You may have been given no choice about whether to have an episiotomy, or were advised that you ought to have one for the sake of the baby. Or perhaps you did not know the possible effects of an episiotomy before you went into labour, and though in retrospect you would have said that you did not want one unless absolutely necessary, you are now landed with the pain and the sense of outrage that many women experience.

'I don't know what all the fuss is about! My episiotomy healed in a week and caused no trouble.'

Not all women feel like this. You may have been lucky and been cut skilfully and sutured quickly afterwards, with only minor perineal trauma. Like any operation, episiotomy can be done with good reason or unnecessarily, and it can be performed skilfully or in a slap-dash way. If you are happy about having had an episiotomy, and comfortable physically now, you may want to skip the rest of this section.

A small tear—first degree, which affects skin only—which is stitched within half an hour rarely causes any problem, and heals completely in twenty-four hours. Even a second-degree tear—that goes through muscle as well as skin—which is stitched within half an hour rarely causes difficulty if it is sutured correctly. The perineum is well supplied with blood vessels, so there is no shortage of nutrients for rapid healing.

An episiotomy is usually the equivalent of a second-degree tear. The cut is either medio-lateral or mid-line. When tears occur they are usually in the mid-line, though some women have small labial tears. These labial tears hurt for three or four days, and sting terribly as urine passes over them, but usually heal spontaneously. Some episiotomies are larger and deeper than a second-degree tear. Occasionally a woman has a bilateral episiotomy—one on each side—prior to a forceps delivery because the baby is in an awkward position—a breech, for example.

In the early days, when you empty your bowels, it may be frightening because you feel that you are going to split in two. But you can overcome this fear if you support the front part of your perineum with a sanitary pad or wad of tissues, and press this firmly with your hand, while at the same time relaxing your pelvic-floor muscles.

Cross-infection is to be expected in hospitals where newly delivered women use the same often inadequately cleaned lavatories and baths. When a wound becomes infected sometimes an abscess forms, which delays healing further and damages tissue. The wound may break open and have to be resutured. Scrupulous cleanliness is vital. The best way to wash is with a bidet or by pouring a jug of water over the tender area. Avoid using any substance which might irritate the sore tissue, such as scented soap.

Pain after a straightforward episiotomy which heals well should have almost completely disappeared by two weeks post-partum, though many women cannot face love-making that involves any kind of penetration and recoil from the idea of intercourse until three or four months later. For some it is as long as six months. If this is how you feel, you are not unusual.

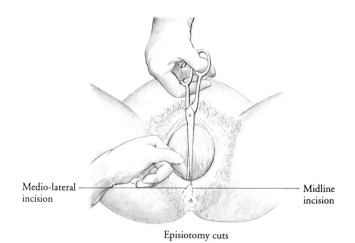

Medio-lateral incision   Midline incision

Episiotomy cuts

**Episiotomies
that go wrong**

An episiotomy may be done badly. The most frequent cause of perineal trauma is that an episiotomy has been medio-lateral rather than median—in the mid-line.[13] In Britain most obstetricians perform medio-lateral episiotomies, and midwives are taught to do them, too. They believe that this avoids tears into the rectum, fourth-degree tears. Many Australian obstetricians have had at least part of their training in British hospitals, so they tend to medio-lateral episiotomies, too. Although the rate of fourth-degree lacerations is slightly lower with medio-lateral than with median episiotomy, when a severe tear does occur it can be horrendous.

In North America the medio-lateral incision is considered archaic. One Canadian professor of obstetrics claims that 'medio-lateral episiotomy is tantamount to malpractice. Nowhere else in any form of surgery would a surgeon cut across the belly of a muscle.'[14] A randomized controlled trial comparing the two types of incision revealed that there was far less trauma after a mid-line incision.[15] The dip between the two sides of the pubo-coccygeous muscle has few blood vessels, so that a cut there is almost bloodless. It is relatively pain-free, because nerves do not cross the mid-line between the muscle. It is easier and quicker to repair, because the two sections can be aligned more easily, and the cosmetic result is better.

An episiotomy often goes wrong because the operator is nervous, and pecks away with the scissors in a series of small incisions, rather than making one clear cut. Sometimes the scissors are not sharp enough, and tissues are crushed rather than cut, which can produce massive bruising. Episiotomy is the only operation performed with scissors rather than a scalpel. The explanation is that doctors and midwives are anxious that, when the baby's head is low on the perineum, they may nick it accidentally if they use a knife. In practice, a finger should always be introduced underneath the tissues when making the cut, so that if anything is going to be damaged, it will be the operator's finger, not the baby's head.

Women tend to suffer most pain, and it lasts longest, if they have had a medio-lateral episiotomy which has extended into a tear when either the baby's head or shoulders came through.[16] A fourth-degree laceration is the most severe kind of tear. It passes into the rectum, and it is vital that it is repaired expertly. Otherwise a woman may suffer bowel incontinence and pass faeces through her vagina. It is more likely to occur when an episiotomy has been performed than when a woman has been helped to give birth spontaneously.[17] The repair of a mid-line fourth-degree laceration is relatively simple because it is easy to align the muscle and other tissues. The repair of a fourth-degree laceration extending from a medio-lateral episiotomy may be extremely complicated.

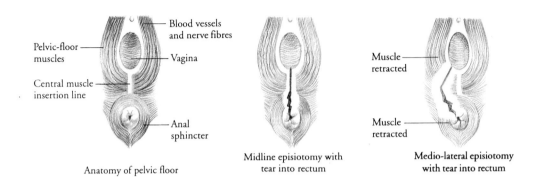

Pelvic-floor muscles — Blood vessels and nerve fibres

Vagina

Central muscle insertion line

Anal sphincter

Anatomy of pelvic floor

Midline episiotomy with tear into rectum

Muscle retracted

Muscle retracted

Medio-lateral episiotomy with tear into rectum

There used to be a theory that episiotomy should be performed before the baby's head was on the perineum, and this is still done in some hospitals. The idea is that doing it early on protects ligaments and muscles. But this is not so. The baby's head has already exerted pressure on ligaments and on the pubo-coccygeous muscles on its journey out, and the only muscle which an episiotomy can protect is the transverse perineal muscle. This runs across the centre of the figure 8 of pelvic-floor muscles, and it is relatively unimportant. Performing an episiotomy before the baby's head is pressing against the perineum and blanching the tissues there results in excessive bleeding and is often extremely painful.

An episiotomy cuts across not only soft tissues and muscles, but also nerves. Some women develop a neuroma where cut nerve fibres have tangled, and this is very painful. A doctor may examine you and say that you are perfectly all right and that the suturing has been done beautifully, because there is nothing to see. But you know yourself that you are in terrible pain.

Nerves do heal eventually, and in the meantime there may be no alternative but to use an anaesethetic gel. Even so, intercourse may be impossible, and there may be times of the month when, because of hormonal changes and engorgement of tissues, you feel that thorns are stuck into the most tender part of your body. If you are in this kind of pain, it is real. It is not your imagination, and you have not invented the condition because you are rejecting your sexual partner, or because you hate your body. With episiotomy pain, as in many other aspects of women's lives, the victim is often blamed.

'While examining my perineum the consultant said the problem must be "up there" (pointing at my head) rather than "down here". I couldn't explain my feelings and stayed silent.'

Suturing that goes wrong	The worst mistake that anyone can make when repairing an episiotomy or tear is to suture the skin, but not the underlying tissues. The danger is that there is a fistula—an opening between the vagina and the rectum—which goes unrecognized. Then the sutures disintegrate as the underlying tissues break down.

Women often say that they have been too tightly stitched. This happens when no room is left for the swelling of tissues that always follows injury. Perineal tissues swell a lot. If you have ever had a wasp sting near your eye, you will have had a similar swelling. When swelling pulls on stitches and causes pain it is usually possible to remove some of them, so in the early days after childbirth tell your midwife or doctor if it feels as if you are sitting on glass splinters. When her vagina is made artificially small, a woman is bound to have problems with penetration. The result for some women is that muscles go into spasm, a reflex response to touch or the fear of touch.

Sometimes the underlying muscles have been distorted during suturing, so that the perineum, lining of the vagina, and labia are incorrectly aligned to each other. One woman who took a photograph of her badly sutured episiotomy commented: 'I am competent at sewing, and it does not require a great deal of sewing expertise to realize that the relative tension of two edges to be joined must be equal. If this was something I had sewn I would have put it in the dustbin.'

When repairing an episiotomy, it is the deep structures that matter most. Skin heals in around twenty-four hours, anyway. It is not surprising that there is often poor alignment of muscles and superficial tissues if you bear in mind that a junior doctor may be unsupervised when performing a perineal repair. Doctors learning how to do suturing should *always* be supervised. Some have only ever had the opportunity before this to stitch a cut hand in casualty, and some have only seen women's labia and vaginas in medical textbooks.

Stitches may get infected and break down. This is most likely to occur when there is a haematoma—a swelling filled with blood. A pool of blood is a very efficient culture medium for infection. Then the wound gapes open, and after having antibiotics a woman has to be resutured.

Surgery	For some women with prolapse or with a botched episiotomy surgery is the only answer. If you decide that this is the route you want to follow, ask the surgeon exactly what is to be done and which bit is to be sewn where. Ask about side-effects of the operation, too. Prolapse operations are successful in about 80 per cent of cases, but in about 20 per cent the prolapse recurs.

75

You can take the baby with you into hospital and continue to breastfeed. By the time you are alert enough to breastfeed after the operation the amount of anaesthetic in your milk will be negligible.[18]

Express milk in the days prior to the operation and store it in the fridge. Get your baby accustomed to taking milk from a spoon or bottle, so that you can relax and know that the baby will be fed during the short time that you cannot breastfeed.

When the anal sphincter has been torn, the nerve supply to this muscle is likely to have been damaged, so repair of the sphincter may not be enough and you have pelvic-floor surgery—deeper inside—as well.[19]

'I'm off to be restitched, tucked up. I'm taking the baby with me as I'll be in hospital a week to ten days.'

Immediate complications of surgery may be haemorrhage, infection, or trauma to the ureter, bladder, or rectum. Of course, any operation on the perineum leads to pain in the days afterwards. Sometimes this proves to be long-lasting, and it may make sexual intercourse distressing. If you are thinking of having surgery because intercourse is difficult already, and you feel too tight—if, for example, there is a painful knob of tissue which makes penetration difficult, or you have pain high up inside your vagina—it is important to discuss with the gynaecologist the risks and benefits of the operation, and to find out whether it is going to be right for you.

Colporrhaphy is the name of the operation to repair damage to the vagina. If it involves tissues at the front for the repair of a cystocele, it is an anterior colporrhaphy. If it is done at the back of the vagina for repair of the rectocele, it is a posterior colporrhaphy.

Fothergill's operation, or the Manchester repair, is a very old surgical technique which entails repair of a cystocele, amputation of part of the cervix, and repair of the perineum. The most dramatic way of curing prolapse is hysterectomy. This is removal of the uterus, and of course you cannot bear a child after this has been done. Vaginal hysterectomy is removal of the uterus through the vagina. Subtotal hysterectomy removes the uterus, but leaves the cervix, whereas total hysterectomy excises the uterus and the cervix together.

These operations can be performed under either epidural or general anaesthesia. You usually need to be in hospital for about a week afterwards. If you want, arrange to take your baby with you into hospital, knowing that nurses on the ward will be delighted to help and will take great pleasure in having a baby there.

Most women do not need an operation, however. Muscles that are damaged have an amazing capacity to heal. A woman came to me for help who was about to have a prolapse repaired surgically. There was a waiting list and she could not have it done for six weeks, so I suggested that she used the time to tone her pelvic-floor muscles through movement. At first she could not mobilize the muscles at all, because the cystocele prevented her from locating and squeezing them. So I asked her to lie down with her legs raised, so that her own weight was not pressing on the pelvic floor, and gently to replace the prolapsed tissues with a fingertip in her vagina. Once she had done this she found that she could use her muscles and do the Pelvic Lift. She continued to activate these muscles until the time she was admitted for the repair operation. On examining her, the gynaecologist remarked that she must have been placed on the list by mistake, and that she did not need surgery.

If you are concerned that your pelvic-floor muscles are not strong enough and that you need to learn how to tone them, you may want to speak to your GP, who can refer you to a physiotherapist. It is also worth contacting one of the organizations listed at the end of the book. These will have leaflets and other useful information that can help you help yourself.

Breastfeeding

You probably decided long before you had the baby whether you wanted to breastfeed. Most women make up their minds before the sixth month. Even if you decided on formula, there is a strong case to be made for breastfeeding in the first few weeks, so that the baby gets the immunological benefits of colostrum, the first form of milk, and the gut is lined with a protective layer of milk.

In this chapter I want to help you breastfeed if you need some extra support to do so. If you are already happily settled with bottle-feeding, you will obviously want to continue with formula, and these pages are unlikely to contain any useful information for you, at least until the next time round. If you are thinking of switching from breast to bottle, however, because breastfeeding is proving difficult, this chapter may help. And if you are happily breastfeeding, it will probably confirm what you already know from experience.

The uniqueness of breastmilk

Human milk has evolved over many thousands of years to be perfectly adapted to the needs of babies. It is one of the world's greatest natural economic resources. Everywhere women breastfeed, in war, famine, and extreme poverty. Breastmilk enables their babies to survive, and to flourish, in circumstances where bottle-fed babies die, and where those who do not die often succumb to gastroenteritis, convulsions, respiratory illnesses, and intestinal diseases.

Formula manufacturers have never succeeded in copying breastmilk. It is impossible that they will, because human milk is a living organism. Though cow's milk is modified to seem like breastmilk, and nowadays formula does not have the high sodium content that used to interfere with a baby's electrolyte balance and sometimes cause fits, it is quite different from human milk. Breastmilk adapts itself, in quantity, its constituents, and the ratio of milk solids to fluid, to the needs of a particular baby at different stages of growth. It varies according to whether one or two babies are being suckled. It is a nutritionally ideal food through the first nine months, and, with the addition of other foods, well into the second year.

When breastfeeding is a pleasure for mother and baby, both can enjoy this time together long after it is needed as food. In many cultures children are breastfed often during the day and unrestrictedly at night up to 3 and 4 years old. Through the first months the mother sleeps with her baby at her breast, who suckles more or less continuously. Having the breast close gives older babies valuable additional protein and the comfort of their mothers' presence. It also has an important contraceptive effect in countries where another mouth to feed might be disastrous. The contraceptive effect, however, works only when breastfeeding is unrestricted. It is not a reliable form

of birth-control for a woman who is offering other fluids or foods, who times breastfeeds, or who is trying to achieve some sort of schedule.

Breastmilk is produced according to supply and demand. Demand stimulates milk production. If there is no demand, milk dries up. If demand is restricted because a woman is feeding only every four hours, for example, the supply is reduced. If she has twins and they are fully breastfed, with no formula or other fluids, she automatically produces more milk. A lactating breast is never completely empty. Milk rushes in to take the place of milk which is suckled, so that it is impossible to drain the breasts completely.

Breastfeeding is more than a way of getting milk into a baby. It is more, even, than giving the comfort and closeness of the breast. It is a way of communicating. If the mother is stressed and anxious, it communicates her tension. If she is relaxed and positive, her confidence and pleasure are communicated.

This physical communication draws a woman to become deeply involved in a small human being's experience, open to all the emotions that a baby may express while at the breast, and to share an intimate, secret dance with her baby. A blind mother discovered with delight exactly how a smile feels when her baby paused and smiled with lips still touching the curves of her breast.[1]

'I don't think I've ever felt so relaxed and contented in my life before.'

One problem in Western culture is that most women, especially first-time mothers, have never seen babies breastfed. In traditional communities girls grow up with babies being casually breastfed around them. They know how they are held and handled. They absorb information about breastfeeding without needing to learn it consciously. When a woman picks up her baby for the first time and puts her to the breast, it may seem that this is a purely instinctive act. Though powerful instincts are involved, it is learned behaviour. In industrial countries that learning is often painfully acquired: mothers get sore nipples, their babies do not put on weight, or do not settle after feeds. Yet when a woman persists in breastfeeding in spite of initial difficulties, she is usually successful. It is a question of surmounting those first problems.

Opting for formula

A woman may have good reasons for not breastfeeding, and these should be respected. Many women start out determined to make a success of it, but find it so difficult and painful that they give up, either reluctantly or with relief. Almost invariably they have not received the right kind of help in the first days after childbirth, and have often been given incorrect and conflicting advice. Many give up because their babies are unhappy and are not putting on weight. They do not know how to increase their milk supply, and cannot get the practical help and emotional support they need. Many give up because of sore and cracked nipples which make breastfeeding torture.

Women also have to confront an anti-breastfeeding culture. Not only have many children never seen a baby breastfed, but little girls are given dolls with feeding bottles. Breasts are perceived exclusively as sexual objects. Women are segregated behind four walls to feed their babies, and directed to public lavatories to breastfeed when they are outside their homes. Feeding a baby with milk from one's body is treated either as obscene or polluting, and often as an act of aggressive sexual display. When women breastfeed in public, however discreet they try to be, they take on a society which is hostile to breastfeeding mothers. Understandably, there are many who feel that they cannot face this ordeal.

'I heard two women whispering, "Look at her! She's breastfeeding. How disgusting!" But I just went on and did it.'

International baby food manufacturers, no longer permitted to advertise direct to the public because of the major health risks of artificial feeding, soft-sell formula by sponsoring medical conferences and research trips, advertise in midwifery and nursing journals, offer free samples in bounty bags for new mothers, and give refrigerators and other equipment to hospitals and clinics.

Emotional elements play an important part in the choice to feed a baby artificially, too. The best reason for a woman to bottle-feed is that she chooses to do so. She may feel it is going to be too much of a struggle because she has a partner who is emotionally unsupportive and who is embarrassed about breastfeeding, or one who thinks that her breasts belong to him, not the baby. To breastfeed is to offer part of your body to another human being. A woman who has been sexually abused in childhood, or who has experienced rape, should not to have to justify her choice of bottle-feeding.

For some women there are health reasons why they decide not to breastfeed. The most important of these is active TB. If a mother has active TB the baby should not breastfeed until he has been given BCG—a vaccine against tuberculosis. She can express during this time—probably not longer than two weeks—and then put the baby to the breast when antibodies are present in his bloodstream. A woman who is receiving cytotoxic drugs for cancer or radioactive iodine should not breastfeed. But apart from this, there are very few conditions which mean that a woman should probably be advised not to breastfeed if formula is available and can be given under hygienic conditions.

For others, the practical arrangements of a job outside the home, and travelling to and from work, make breastfeeding difficult for longer than a few weeks of maternity leave. Every woman should have the accurate information she needs to weigh up the advantages of different kinds of feeding. The conclusion to which she comes is not just a matter of the scientific data available, but has to do with her life experience, her emotions, and her relationships. Only a woman herself can decide what is best for her.

A good latch

Many women start breastfeeding hoping that it will work, but give up because they encounter insuperable difficulties. Sore nipples and an inadequate milk supply are the reasons usually given for switching from breast to bottle. Both stem from one cause—*not getting the baby well latched on to the breast.*[2]

'It was incredibly painful. Every feed was an ordeal until Chloe showed me how to latch her on. Then it didn't hurt at all.'

If a baby does not have a mouthful of breast, with the lower jaw well down over the areola (the darker circle of skin around the nipple), every suck causes friction on the nipple, and it quickly becomes sore.

When the baby comes to the breast the nipple needs to be drawn deeply into his mouth, so that a teat is formed out of both nipple and breast tissue. As the baby suckles, the combined action of the jaws, tongue, and palate presses on the milk sinuses so that milk squirts into the baby's throat. It is the jaws, not the baby's lips, which press down on to the bunched milk sacs deep inside the breast.

When you are breastfeeding you cannot see exactly where the baby's lower jaw is, of course. So you have to judge by *feeling* whether the baby is latched on well. One thing that helps is to notice where the chin is. It should be resting firmly against your breast, rather than being tilted away from it. Changes in breast shape during pregnancy and after childbirth as lactation begins, with the resulting heavier curve of the lower breast, make it easier to position the baby correctly than if you had a neat, tight teenage breast.[3]

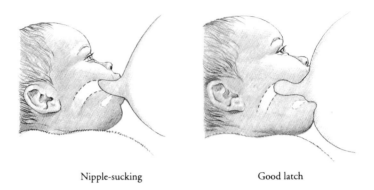

Nipple-sucking   Good latch

You make it more difficult to get your baby latched on if you try to do it with her head in the crook of your arm, because it is awkward to have to swing your elbow forward and back towards your body in one smooth movement. You can fix her more easily if you have her head cupped in one hand to place her on the breast, and support it from behind with your forearm as she suckles.

You will notice that, when the baby is well positioned, her lips are rolled back, rather than pouting. The action of suckling is very different from that of sucking through a straw. It entails movement in the muscles over the baby's ears. When a baby is suckling strongly, it often looks as if her ears are wiggling.

'It's a thrill to hear those long, slow, satisfied sucks, and to see her completely content.'

'It's a thrill to hear those long, slow, satisfied sucks, and to see her completely content.'

You can also hear whether your baby is well latched by listening to the pattern of suckling. It begins with quick, short sucks. Then there is a point at which the sucks change to become long, deep, and slow. This shows that milk is flowing into the baby's throat.

The baby should always come to the breast, not the breast to the baby. Sit comfortably. Drop your shoulders, breathe out, and relax. If you lean back, your nipples will be tipped upwards making it difficult for the baby to latch on. If you lean over your baby, the nipples are tilted downwards, which also makes it difficult. Sitting up straight makes it much easier for the baby.

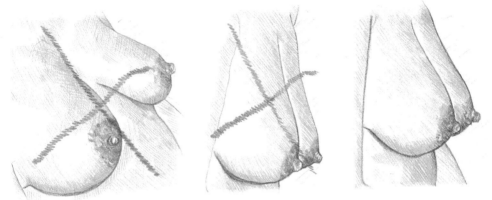

You may want to cup your breast with one hand under it, but avoid grasping it and using your hand like scissors pressing on the breast. This may pull forward the skin and surface tissues, lifting them away from the milk sacs, so that the baby's jaw cannot press in on them to extract the milk.

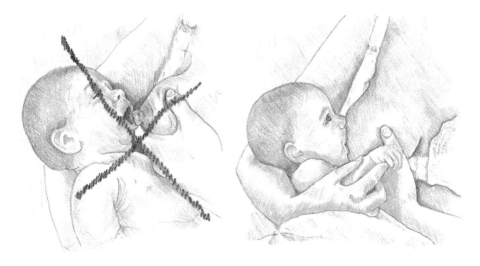

Have your baby facing you, his back straight and his body turned towards you. He should not have to twist his neck to reach the breast. His mouth should be at the same level as your nipple, and his chin slightly raised. If he does not seem interested, tease his lips with the nipple until he opens his mouth wide. Plant him on the breast with a single firm movement, rather as if you were pressing a circular biscuit cutter on to dough. Most women need some practice with this before getting it right.

There is no need to restrict yourself to one position. It is restful to feed lying on your side, for example. Have a firm pillow under your upper body, and both arms free if you can. Bring your baby's head toward you cradled in your hand. Do not lift the breast and put it in the baby's mouth.

When you are sitting to breastfeed, it sometimes helps to have a pillow on your lap to raise a small baby to the level of your nipple, or you can raise one knee with your foot on a low stool, and support your baby against your thigh.

If your baby is big, it may be easier to position him correctly by parting your legs so that he sits between them.

Sometimes a baby seems to prefer one breast to the other. Often a mother herself finds it easier to feed one side rather than the other, too. If this is the case with you, try tucking the baby's legs under your arm on the more difficult side, and use the same hand as you would for the other breast.

If your baby is crying desperately, you will both be too fussed to get a good latch. So move him away from the breast, give him time to calm down by putting him over your shoulder or in someone else's arms for a moment, where he cannot smell your breast, and soothe and pat him before bringing him to the breast again.

How breasts make milk

During pregnancy levels of the hormone prolactin rise in a woman's bloodstream. After the placenta is delivered, production of the placental hormones, progesterone and oestrogen, is reduced. As levels of these two hormones drop, prolactin starts to stimulate the production of milk.

87

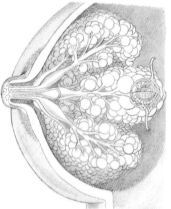

The milk is made in small cells that line the breast glands. It is stored in grape-like clusters, the alveoli. A network of muscles surrounds each of these sacs. When stimulated, the muscle walls squeeze the milk sacs and eject milk. So lactation starts off as a hormonal process. But once this has happened, more milk is not produced unless the milk that is already there is removed.

Lactating breast

The milk-ejection reflex

As your baby suckles, you may feel a warm tingling and buzzing in your breast. This often occurs as the baby begins to suckle, but sometimes not until a minute or so later. It is the milk ejection or 'let-down' reflex. Some women are not aware of it, but it happens nevertheless. You may enjoy the feeling, dislike it, or even find it painful. During a feed it occurs again and again, but you probably do not notice it unless the baby comes off the breast for a while to play, and then goes on again after an interval.

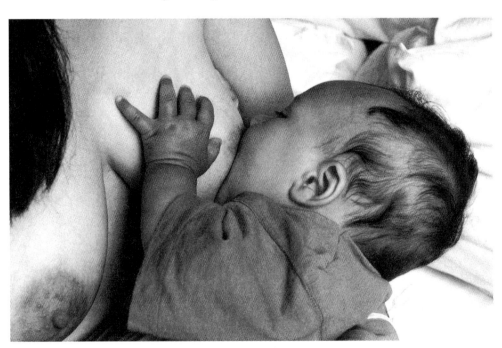

When the milk-ejection reflex occurs, the combined action of the hormones oxytocin and prolactin is causing contractions in the muscle walls of the milk sacs. These squeeze milk into the ducts, from where it flows down to the nipples.

After the first few days of breastfeeding, just thinking about or seeing your baby may stimulate the ejection reflex. If you know it is time the baby is likely to want to be fed, it may occur spontaneously. Sometimes glancing at something you associate in your mind with making milk can stimulate it. Even seeing a hungry, crying baby on TV may spark off the milk-ejection reflex. On the other hand, once breastfeeding is established, if you are anxious or embarrassed, or feel that you have to put on a breastfeeding performance in front of someone who is sceptical, the reflex may be slow in coming. It may not happen at all until you find a private place in which to breastfeed in a relaxed way.

Your milk alters during the course of a feed. At the beginning of each feed there is a gush of low-calorie milk. As the baby goes on suckling, this changes to a smaller amount of high-calorie milk. The 'hindmilk' at the end of the feed is the richest of all.[4]

Breasts and nipples

Women with breasts and nipples of all different sizes and shapes can breastfeed.[5] There is no ideal model. The baby moulds the nipple and breast tissue that is drawn into her mouth to form a teat which is right for her.

If your breast is heavy, it may help to support it underneath with one hand, or to rest the palm of your hand against your ribs. Or you could tuck your baby with legs under your arms and cradle her head in your hand, so that you can easily 'plant' her on the breast.

If your breasts are small, it often helps to lie the baby on a pillow on your lap.

Retracted nipple

'*A nurse told me I'd never be able to breastfeed. But the midwife who helped me get him on was superb and I had no problems.*'

A woman with large nipples should take special care to see that the baby's mouth is gaping wide before bringing his head to the breast, because only then can he draw the nipple and surrounding tissue deeply into his mouth.

Some women have nipples that are flat or retracted. These are ones which are dimpled instead of projecting. Your baby will mould this kind of nipple to a good shape if you ensure that she gets a good mouthful of breast. If she cannot get a good mouthful, you will get sore, the milk cannot flow freely, she becomes distressed, and you may develop a breast infection. It takes five or six days while you initiate lactation for your breasts to change and become more elastic. If you cannot get the baby latched on during this time, keep the milk flowing by expressing it and feeding it to your baby. But go on with the rehearsals to get the baby on the breast. Make sure that the baby's mouth is as wide open as it can be. This may not be easy with a tiny newborn, and needs great patience. But dimpled nipples often prove less of a problem than very large nipples, provided that you get the baby in a good position.

Nipples respond quickly to the stimulus of touch. If you stroke your areola or the nipple itself, a dimpled nipple will develop a firmer shape. Using a hand-held breast pump just before a feed draws nipples out, too, or spraying them with cold water from a small plant spray. Seeing that a dimpled nipple changes shape rapidly can help give you the confidence to breastfeed.

Caring for your breasts

In the past women were told to wash before and after feeds, and a form of nipple hygiene was insisted on that often dried the skin and made injury more likely. In some Eastern European countries women on postnatal wards still have gentian violet painted around their nipples routinely before they are allowed to put their babies to the breast.

Many creams and sprays that are available do no good at all, and some do harm because they contain alcohol which dries the skin. These substances, especially if they contain antiseptics, also interfere with the normal bacterial flora which keep skin healthy, and change the flora inside the baby's mouth.

It is sensible not to use soap on your nipples for the same reason. Simply splash your breasts with water to keep them clean.

Baby-led feeding

Baby-led feeding is feeding a baby when she wants for as long as she wants. Ignore any advice you may be given about keeping the baby on the breast for ten or twenty minutes, or any other length of time. Your baby is the best judge of how much milk she needs, and how often she should feed. Babies who are fed this way tend to put on weight more rapidly than those fed by the clock and, because breastfeeding is a more satisfying experience for the mother, they are breastfed longer.

Your baby knows how long a feed is needed. The clock can tell you nothing. The milk that one baby gets in four minutes takes another twenty-four minutes to obtain. Timing feeds is a major obstacle to successful breastfeeding. Always let the baby suckle as long as she wants on one side. Then switch to the other to finish the feed. Sometimes the time at the second breast is brief. Sometimes one side is enough. If your baby has had a period of good, active feeding, and then looks as if she has had enough, trust your own judgement. The important thing is to recognize good feeding behaviour, rather than making rules about how long the baby should take. With the next feed you will want to start with the breast that feels most full.[6]

Night feeds

Most babies need to be fed at night, at least for the first few months. Their stomachs are only about the size of a fig, and breastmilk is readily absorbed. Moreover, your breasts need a regular suckling stimulus if you are to make enough milk. Levels of prolactin are highest at night. So if you want to keep up or increase milk production, you get a valuable prolactin boost from night feeds.[7]

'Nightfeeds are the best of all. There are no interruptions. They're so peaceful.'

It is easy to feed your baby while lying on your side, something which would be very difficult to do if you were bottle-feeding. In fact, once you have the knack of helping the baby get well latched on, the baby can suckle while you sleep.

You may be urged to introduce solids to get your baby to sleep through the night. This does not work. Babies who are given a milk feed thickened with cereal in the evening are just as likely to wake at night as a baby who has milk only. Some wake more often, because they have difficulty in digesting solid foods and pass large bowel movements at night. Sleeping through the night is a developmental stage that occurs independently of the introduction of solids and may be delayed by stuffing a baby with solid food.

No extra fluids

A breastfed baby does not need anything else to drink. Even in hot weather, drinks of water are unnecessary.[8] Giving fluids other than breastmilk means that the baby suckles less at the breast. This automatically reduces your milk supply.[9] Until babies are about six months old they do not benefit from other food or drink unless there are clear medical reasons for this. Sips of water or juice can be given for fun, but the breast satisfies thirst as well as hunger.

Growth spurts

Babies have growth spurts when they need more milk. They spontaneously feed more often and may need longer at the breast, too. This does not mean that you do not have enough milk, only that this is a time when the supply must be built up to satisfy increased demand. It usually takes no longer than twenty-four hours for this to happen.

Babies often seem to go on these feeding 'binges' at 3–4 weeks, 6–7 weeks, and at 12–13 weeks. If you feel self-conscious about feeding so often because people comment and suggest that the baby needs topping up with formula, if may help if you go into another room to breastfeed in private. If it helps you relax, take a book or magazine or listen to music. But above all, avoid timing these feeds or recording them like a taxi meter ticking up. Sometimes babies who are contented during the day want to feed all evening, just when you are most tired. If it is possible for you to get a rest in the afternoon, and for someone else to prepare the evening meal, it will be easier to cope with this feeding marathon.

When there are problems

Sore nipples

Nipples are made sore when they are drawn in and out over the baby's tongue and gums, causing friction and damaging tissues. The important thing is to get the baby in a better position and to ensure that part of the curved area of breast below the nipple, as well as the nipple itself, goes into the baby's mouth.

Sometimes it is difficult to do this because you are engorged and the breast feels so tight that it is inflexible. It is as if the baby is trying to latch on to a huge balloon. Sponging your breast with warm water before the feed and then gently expressing, using your hands to massage, is comforting and helps soften them. It may be easiest when you are under a warm shower or in a bath. Or you can stand over a wash basin filled with warm water and let your breasts hang down in the water before expressing by hand. Once milk is flowing, simple pressure is often enough to make the breasts more comfortable and flexible.

Then ensure that the baby is in a good position at the breast and is well latched on. *Breastfeeding should not hurt*. If it does, there is something wrong and you need to correct it.

A satisfied baby often drops off the breast at the end of a feed. But some babies stay latched on because it is their favourite place to be. Don't pull the baby off whatever you do. Break the suction by inserting a finger into the baby's mouth.

If a nipple is cracked, a thin latex nipple shield sometimes helps for a while, but because the baby gets less milk you need to feed for longer. The thick old rubber nipple shields reduced transfer of milk by around

56 per cent. The newer, thinner latex ones still reduce it by 22 per cent.[10] Some women find that the nipple shield itself produces friction, too. So if you decide to use one, do so for not more than a day at a time.

Do not stuff cotton wool, toilet paper, or tissues against your nipples to protect your clothing. This way bits of paper or cotton wool stick to your nipples. Use either breastpads which you change frequently or one-way nappy liners with soft toilet paper tucked inside.

Another cause of sore nipples, independent of how you position the baby for a feed, is thrush in the baby's mouth. This is a yeast infection, candida albicans, that flourishes in warm, moist conditions. It is usually associated with taking antibiotics, which change the natural flora of your vagina. You then pass the infection on your fingers to the baby. Nipples get shiny and red, like raspberries, and cracks appear in them. You may have shooting pains in your breasts as well. The infection can spread to the milk ducts if untreated.

In the baby's mouth thrush looks like white milk curds, but you can see they are not when you gently try to wipe them with a finger, and they stay put.

Treatment of both the nipples and the baby's mouth is usually with nystatin or clotrimazone. If your nipples are itching a great deal, a teaspoon of bicarbonate of soda in a cup of cold boiled water can be swabbed on to them after feeds. It eases the itching, but does not stop the infection.

A tender, red patch

A tender red patch on your breast is a sign that you have a blocked milk-secreting duct. It is not mastitis.

Sometimes in the early days of breastfeeding a woman produces so much milk that the baby hardly has to suckle at all. He can just wait there with his mouth open, and it pours in. If the baby is not positioned well and latched on to the breast, problems develop because he is not actually working for milk. Milk is stored in the alveoli, but if the baby is not really suckling the muscle networks around each sac do not squeeze the milk out to empty the sacs. So milk builds up, the alveoli become distended, and milk-secreting cells are stretched to the point of rupture.[11] The milk is blocked and a sore patch appears on the breast. If the condition is not treated, infection may result, with fever, and even perhaps an abscess. Certainly there will be a very hungry baby.

The cure is to get the milk flowing. Warming the breast, by placing a hot flannel over the red patch, and gently stroking from above the tender area down towards the nipple, will start this process. But the real solution is to get the baby well latched on, and to feed as often and as long as the baby will.

If you do not get milk flowing, substances in the milk are pressed through the cell walls into small blood vessels and connective tissue, and the blockage gets larger and harder. You can feel a definite lump there. You react to the leakage of substances in your milk through the cell wall as you would to a mis-matched blood transfusion. It is a foreign protein, and your body fights it. Then your temperature rises, your pulse rate goes up, and you may wonder if you have flu. These are symptoms of mastitis. But at this stage it is not necessarily infected, so there is no advantage in taking antibiotics. Perhaps it is better to call it 'non-infectious inflammation of the breast'. The fever is a reaction of your immune system to the foreign substances in your bloodstream. Inflammation like this is always the result of poor breastfeeding technique, which results in one or more segments of the breast being inadequately milked.

The best treatment then, too, is still to keep milk flowing as much as possible. The worst thing is to 'rest' the breast. You need to get the baby latched on, and to continue feeding as frequently and for as long as possible.

When a simple blockage has not been freed, it may lead to bacterial infection. This is infective mastitis, and antibiotics are needed.[12]

Continue breastfeeding. If at this stage you wean your baby, you are much more likely to develop a breast abscess. This is a pocket of pus in the breast. The treatment is to make an incision and drain it. Depending on where the abscess is, you may need to stop breastfeeding on that side for a few days because it is too painful. But you should put the baby to the breast as soon as possible afterwards. Women who do not get the baby back on to that breast are more likely to develop a second abscess.

Not enough milk

Your baby is crying again, and your doctor or health visitor has warned you that she has not gained weight since your last visit and are advising you to supplement with formula. Anxiously you try and squeeze out milk between feeds and are unable to do so. You notice that your breasts are no longer as full as they were in the six weeks after birth. When any of these things happen, alarm signals ring, 'I can't have enough milk!' It is difficult to think calmly because, unlike feeding a baby with artificial milk, you do not *see* it going in. The modern woman might feel more confident if she had plastic, see-through breasts, but they certainly would not be as comforting or as flexible as human breasts, which are ideally suited to babies' needs.

'The antibiotics gave her a rather sore bottom, but apart from that she was fine, and it was a great relief that I didn't have to give up breastfeeding.'

It is important to realize that breastmilk is more easily and quickly digested than modified cow's milk. So a baby is usually ready to suckle again in two to two and a half hours. The idea that a baby should be able to last three or four hours between feeds was a twentieth-century invention of doctors who believed that feeding a baby on formula was more scientific, and it enabled them to have more control over infant nutrition.

When your breastmilk first comes in, three or four stained nappies a day are not uncommon. It may continue like this. But later breastmilk may be so completely digested that you only get a dirty nappy every second day. There is very wide variation between babies. But you need not worry about constipation. A fully breastfed baby cannot be constipated. As lactation settles down, your breasts will no longer seem so full, except in the early mornings, and when the baby skips a feed. It does not mean that you have lost your milk.

You may also have had milk dripping from your nipples in the early weeks, but as your breasts adapt to established lactation that, too, stops. So some signs of milk production have disappeared. You cannot conclude from this that you have lost your milk. A reasonable conclusion is that your breasts have adapted to feeding an older baby.

Ease of milk expression varies, too, both between women, and depending on how you feel at the time. Some women who are lactating well never get the knack of hand expression. Some breast pumps are more efficient than others. But no pump really imitates a baby's suckling. It does not stimulate nerve endings in the areola, so you do not get the prolactin surge that results from this. Nor do you have the positive feelings you have when your baby is at the breast, so milk flow may be inhibited. Any check on your lactation performance is stressful. Do not come to the conclusion that you have insufficient milk on the grounds that a few sessions with a breast pump produced very little.

If your baby is not gaining weight, you are bound to be anxious. You feel that no one *trusts* you to provide enough milk. You may wonder whether you are being self-indulgent in wanting to breastfeed, and feel very guilty about depriving your baby of nourishment.

You may be advised to drink more fluids, especially milk. There is no point in drinking more than you want. You may well feel thirstier when you are breastfeeding, and many women settle down to breastfeed with a glass of water or juice beside them to sip. You need not drink milk at all, unless you like it. It has nothing to do with making milk. After all, cows do not drink milk.

Unless a woman is very severely malnourished, changing her diet will not increase the quantity of milk that she makes. In the Gambia women's milk volume varies only slightly between seasons of the year when they are hungry and others in which they are fairly well fed, and the quality of the milk is no different.[13] There is no benefit in forcing yourself to eat anything you do not enjoy, nor in stuffing yourself with food, either. Women can make good milk even when they are not well nourished themselves. During famine in Ethiopia, for example, women who were hungry and desperately thin had thriving breastfed babies.

Weight-gain charts were devised with bottle-fed babies in mind. The pattern of weight gain for breastfed babies is different. They tend to put on more weight than formula-fed babies in the first eight to twelve weeks. Then it slows down. After six months, breastfed babies put on less weight than formula-fed babies, who often get very fat at this stage.

Breastfed babies often gain weight in hops, skips, and jumps, too —two ounces one week, eight ounces the next, then perhaps five ounces, ten ounces, nothing. The important thing is that the overall picture is one of weight gain.

If your baby is slow to gain weight, the first thing to do is to check that she has a good latch on your breast. A baby who was well latched on when she was smaller may have grown so much that you need to find a slightly different position for feeding, because her mouth is no longer level with the nipple.

If you are sure your baby is well latched, but she is still not gaining weight, you need to stimulate production. You might like to put into action the Peak Production Plan.

The twenty-four-hour Peak Production Plan

The basic idea is that you are alert to respond to every signal from your baby that she is willing to suckle. So cut out everything else that you do not have to do. If someone else will take on household jobs and look after an older child, you are free to make milk. The best place to be is in bed. Make it a sanctuary where you and the baby can cuddle together. There is no need to drink any more than you want. Let your thirst guide you. If a friend or partner can bring you meals on a tray, this can be a special time of luxurious relaxation.[14]

When it is impossible to clear a full twenty-four hours, you may be able to arrange a couple of mornings or afternoons off to go to bed with your baby and make milk. If necessary, pick a special stash of playthings, picture books, and tapes, and have your toddler with you, too. It is amazing what a good feed the baby can have while you and your older child are watching Sesame Street.

'I could never have done it without my husband's support. He believed in me.'

No test-weighing

Weighing a baby before and after feeds to try to determine how much milk has been taken used to be the standard routine when there was concern that a baby was not gaining enough weight. But it is difficult to produce accurate results. Sometimes the scales themselves may be inaccurate, but, whether they are or not, it would be necessary to test-weigh a baby for every feed of the twenty-four hours to achieve the correct measurement, because babies get different amounts of milk at different feeds. Just as adults are not equally hungry at every meal, and do not eat the same quantity, the baby's intake varies, too.

Nothing could be calculated to raise more anxiety in a breastfeeding woman than test-weighing her baby. Nothing is better designed to make her feel that her breastfeeding performance is on trial, and thus to reduce the chances of her continuing to breastfeed.

If there is a query about how much milk you are making and test-weighing is proposed, you can decline it, on the grounds that there is scientific evidence that it makes breastfeeding success less likely.

The simplest way to tell whether a baby is getting enough milk is to look at, feel, and hold the baby. A well-fed baby has bright eyes, firm

muscles, plump, rounded arms and legs, and is energetic. Another way to check how much milk the baby is getting is to note how many wet nappies there are. If your baby is having no other fluids, six to eight wet nappies in the twenty-four hours tell you that your baby is getting sufficient milk.

Returning to work

If you are going back to work outside the home you need to choose whether to switch to formula, to continue breastfeeding—expressing and storing your milk for the baby to have while you are away—or to combine bottle and breastfeeding.

You will want to take into account your baby's age. There is a strong case to be made for breastfeeding if possible, in terms of your baby's health and your mutual closeness, until the baby is 4 months old. But for a woman who is in full-time employment, who also has a long journey to and from work, and has no childcare available at or near her place of employment, this may be too complicated. Perhaps you can negotiate a gradual return to work, with a shorter working day, or to start part-time.

Few women are fortunate enough to be able to take their babies to work and to feed them when they want. With this in mind, plan ahead. Teats taste, smell, and feel different from breasts, and some babies take a long time to get used to them. First introduce a bottle for one of the feeds that you will miss when you are at work, and allow at least a week for the baby to get accustomed to it. Then switch to another bottlefeed during what will be your working day, and so on. The whole process may take five or six weeks. A breastfed baby often accepts a bottle more readily from someone other than his mother, from whom he expects the comfort of the breast, so it may be best for your partner or baby-sitter to give the bottle.

If you would like to combine breast and formula-feeding, you can keep up the early morning and late night breastfeeds while you still have breastmilk: after the first three or four months, when the milk supply is well established many women are very successful at this. It is much more difficult to succeed if your baby is still under 4 months. If you have a copious milk supply, combined breast and formula-feeding may result in your breasts filling up uncomfortably, or milk squirting out, while you are at work. If this is the case, you will need to find some private place to express milk, either by hand or with a breast pump.

But you may decide that you would like to continue breastfeeding fully if possible. You then have two options. You can leave your own milk to be given to the baby by bottle or cup while you are away from home. This works well for many women, but it requires careful organization. Alternatively, perhaps you can find childcare near your workplace and make arrangements with your employer to go there to

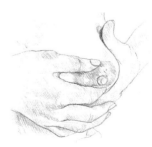

breastfeed during meals and coffee breaks, or at other convenient times.

If your baby is going to be fed with expressed breastmilk, start expressing your milk, manually or with a pump, and freezing it, about four weeks before you return to work. Expression at the end of a breastfeed may be easiest. Or you may prefer to do it some time between feeds. Another alternative is to express first thing in the morning, a time when your breasts feel full and when you are likely to produce most milk. That may be the feed when you and the baby enjoy cuddling together for a breastfeed, so you do not want to cut out that feed, but you can express immediately after it.

Expressing milk is often tricky at first, and babies are often much more efficient at getting milk than breastpumps. Stimulating the milk ejection reflex *before* you pump will help the milk to flow. Have any equipment you are going to use sterilized beforehand, and a glass of water to sip beside you. Rest a warm face cloth against your breast and massage it slowly down from your armpit towards the areola. Nipple stimulation may help, too. Some women need only think of feeding the baby and the milk starts to pour out. You will be able to express more milk if you manage to get it dripping out before you start manual expression or operating the pump.

'I express into a thermos and put it in the canteen fridge till I go home. Then it goes in the fridge for feeds the following day.'

Various types of breast pumps

Once you are back to work it will help if you can find a private place where you can express without hassle, and do this at times when you would be feeding the baby if you were at home.

Although all this may sound incredibly complicated, and colleagues at work may make amused or embarrassing comments, if you can stay relaxed but determined, you can, if you wish, continue this method for many months.

In fact, it is surprising how often women can keep up their milk supply even when they do not express while they are separated from their babies. In Fiji, for example, women often nurse their babies only once or twice a day, without expressing.[15] A study of thirty Anglo-Canadian mothers who were doing much the same thing revealed that lactation was maintained for as long as the baby or the mother wished. In this study, working mothers used what the authors called 'minimal breastfeeding' for a mean of 19.77 weeks. So, if you do not want to express milk, or it is very inconvenient to do so, you can still continue to breastfeed, if this is what you would like to do.

Weaning

Weaning is often treated as if it were taking something *away* from a baby. It is better to think of it as *giving* food in addition to milk to a baby who is ready to explore new tastes. This should be a gradual and unhurried transition.

Most babies enjoy additional foods from around 6 months of age. That is a good time to introduce tastes of foods that can be rolled in the tongue and slurped, and, as soon as teeth are coming through, things like baked rusks that can be chewed and gnawed. Through the first year of life, however, milk should form the main part of their diet.

The first cereal should be rice-based, just in case your baby cannot tolerate wheat at this early age. Fruit and vegetable purées which are rich in iron are a useful addition to the breastfed baby's diet after six months. All these foods should be offered in very small amounts at first. Wait to see how the baby digests each before giving it again.

Weaning is also often used to describe the process of switching from breast to formula. If you want to wean your baby off the breast on to a cup or bottle, this should be done very gradually too, cutting out one breastfeed a week and replacing it with formula. Some babies want to suck more than others and you will need to judge whether your baby of, say, 7 months should be offered a bottle, or whether he will be happy to be weaned straight on to a cup.

As soon as you introduce other foods and fluids, your breastmilk supply is reduced. But even when your baby is missing two breastfeeds a day, it is possible to keep up your supply if you set aside some time in the twenty-four hours when you breastfeed lavishly and without clockwatching. This is very convenient for a woman who is going back to work in a place where there is no day care. She can also stimulate milk production if she is able to express during working hours. She can store this milk for the baby if a fridge is available. Most portable breast pumps have containers for this purpose.

The point about breastfeeding is that, even when it has been a struggle at first, it is an opportunity for a physical and emotional relationship with another human being, small, dependent and completely trusting, which is like no other relationship that exists.

Many women in Western society who try to breastfeed are given no skilled help. They are isolated, they lack emotional support, and they

are subjected to criticism if they persevere. No wonder they switch to formula. There are bound to be breastfeeding organizations and counsellors in your community who can give you skilled help. You will find a list of these organizations at the back of this book.

For some women breastfeeding is very simple and straightforward. For others, it is an art that needs to be learnt. A woman needs around her other women who have breastfed successfully, women who can help her overcome any difficulties, and who support her utterly. Then, whatever challenges she confronts, she can breastfeed.

EATING WELL

When you have a baby there is little time to think about food, still less to shop for, cook and serve it. A woman who enjoyed delicious dinners *à deux* before the baby came, or who gave serious attention to working out nutritionally balanced meals, sits with the baby at the breast while her partner feeds her a cheese sandwich, or wolfs down a bar of chocolate because there is nothing else around to satisfy her hunger, and she has had no chance to get out to buy anything. There are unidentified furry objects at the back of the fridge, since cleaning it is a major operation. Fruit from last week is rotting in the bowl, because it is too complicated to peel one-handed.

All the books tell her that she should be careful about nutrition, especially if she is breastfeeding. She tries to calculate whether she is getting sufficient vitamins and trace minerals. Meanwhile pop-psychology articles in magazines advise her not to neglect her husband, and to put the baby out of sight and hearing, slip into something slinky, and produce the food he likes best, in case he comes to dislike the baby because it has come between them, and their sex life is destroyed. Munching her way through a packet of biscuits with the infant plugged on her breast, as it has been for the last forty-five minutes, she wonders what is wrong with her. Why can't she organize herself?

For many women in the West food is associated with guilt. We feel we should not be eating so much, or that we are eating the wrong things. It is good to relax and enjoy your food, especially when you have a baby and there are new stresses on you. There may be no time to prepare a *cordon-bleu* dish, to add all the trimmings you would like, or to present it so that it looks like the illustrations in magazines and cookery books, but at least you can savour it, and give yourself a chance to digest it.

The fine balancing of menus is not top priority when you have a baby. It will be even less important when the baby grows into a child with strong personal likes and dislikes who spits out anything which does not meet approval, or later still if several children have to be fed, and baked beans, a potato, and a mug of orange juice are devoured like manna from heaven.

So, provided that you do not go in for food stuffed with sugar, excess fat, unnecessary artificial preservatives and colouring, you can afford to be rather laid back about nutrition now you have a baby. This advice is the opposite to other advice you will receive. But if you already know what nourishing food is, now is not the time to raise anxiety levels. Yes, you want to be a good mother, but important elements in this are being relaxed (some of the time), happy (some of the time), and able to enjoy your child (some of the time). All that is made much more difficult if you are worrying about what you eat.

Your diet and breastfeeding

Maternal diet affects the composition of breastmilk, but this is usually important only at the extremes of deprivation and abundance.[1] Even a woman who is undernourished herself can have a well nourished breastfed baby, though it may be at the expense of her own health. This has been acknowledged for a long time. As Trollope remarked, 'How is it that poor men's wives, who have no cold fowl or port wine on which to be coshered up, nurse their children without difficulty, whereas the wives of rich men, who eat and drink everything that is good, cannot do so, we will for the present leave to the doctors and mothers to settle between them.'[2]

Anyone reading this book is unlikely to be missing out on protein, vitamins, minerals, and other food nutrients unless they are very short of money, on a crash slimming diet, or on any other very restricted diet.

Protein

Protein is needed for easy repair of tissues that may have been damaged in childbirth. Animal proteins are 'readymade' and can therefore be eaten in relatively small quantities. But proteins do not have to be only meat, fish, eggs, cheese, and milk. These used to be called 'first-class' proteins and it was thought that they were the only ones that really mattered. Yet when nutritionists looked carefully at the diet of most of the people of the world they discovered that these animal proteins were often a small element in nutrition, and that whole populations flourished on plant proteins in grains, vegetables, nut oils, and berries, with occasional animal protein from fish, meat, and dairy foods. Italian food abounds in recipes for risottos and pastas in which plant foods are combined to form full proteins, often with the addition of a little cheese.

High-protein diets are often recommended for breastfeeding. This raises the question of how thousands upon thousands of women manage to breastfeed so successfully in the developing world even though they are hungry, whereas women in affluent societies often have difficulty in doing so. It is true that you may have a larger appetite while breastfeeding, but you do not need to eat more than you want, nor do you have to stuff yourself with protein in order to make milk.

I have been a lacto-vegetarian since I was a child and breastfed my five babies without any problems and without feeling in any way deprived of energy myself. In fact, vegetarians think rather more carefully about food values than many meat-eaters, especially when

they have children. Sources of proteins for vegetarians include: soya beans, tofu, miso, shoyu, tamari, soya milk and soya flour; pulses of all kinds—e.g. lentils, mung beans, black-eyed peas, aduki beans, flageolets, haricot beans, kidney beans, chick peas, other dried peas; seeds—e.g. pumpkin, sunflower, and sesame seeds; nuts—e.g. pistachios, almonds, cashews, walnuts, brazil nuts, hazelnuts, peanuts; wheatgerm and wholewheat flour, cracked wheat, rye flour, buckwheat flour, buckwheat, barley, brown rice; oats and oatmeal, yeast extract, broad beans; cheeses—e.g. cheddar, parmesan, brie, cottage cheese; yogurt; eggs. You can combine grains with dairy products, grains with dried beans and peas, and dried beans and peas with nuts and seeds.

If you increase the protein content of your diet, you may make more milk, but the ratio of protein to other constituents in your milk is reduced. The production of high-protein milk depends on you having enough *calories*. When the breastmilk of mothers in India is compared with that of women in Sweden or the United States, for example, there is little variation in protein, although no one really knows why. The pattern of fatty acids, however, is based on the kinds of fats you eat.[3]

Vitamins

It is paradoxical that people who have a good diet anyway tend to take more vitamin supplements than those who have nutritional inadequacies.[4] Moreover, the wrong people take the wrong doses of vitamins.[5] Pill-popping is expensive and wasteful, and it can be dangerous, too, because if you do not flush most of it down the lavatory, as with excess vitamin C and iron, it can build up in your body to toxic levels, as does vitamin D.

In affluent societies the only vitamin which is often short in the diets of women who are pregnant or breastfeeding is folic acid. This is essential for normal cell function and the production of red blood cells. It is not incorporated into most multi-vitamin capsules. You can buy it over the counter in 300-microgram doses combined with vitamin B_{12} and iron. You can also get a good supply from dried beans, from green vegetables like spinach and lettuce if they are fresh, especially if you eat them raw in salads, and from wholewheat bread, oranges, and orange juice. Folic acid is absorbed more effectively if you also have foods rich in vitamin B and a generous supply of vitamin C. Liver is packed with folic acid, but, since the toxins an animal has absorbed in its feed are concentrated in the liver, too, you may want to avoid it. Animals that have vitamin A added to their food may have toxic levels of this vitamin in their liver, which can cause foetal deformities in early pregnancy. This is why any woman likely to get pregnant is advised not to eat liver or liver products.[6]

Vitamin-B rich foods help make milk, but diet in early pregnancy may be more important than the amount you are getting now. In Britain older midwives used to recommend Guinness, and it was available free in some NHS hospitals, because brewer's yeast is packed with B vitamins. You will not lack vitamin B if you eat whole grains and animal protein in any form. One of the first signs of vitamin-B deficiency is fatigue, irritability, and emotional instability. Most mothers probably feel like that anyway by the end of the day. If you get sores around your mouth or cracks in the corners of your mouth, you could try adding more riboflavin (vitamin B2) to your diet. This is present in eggs, beans, and milk. You are unlikely to go short of it if you have a poached egg or beans on wholewheat toast.

But what if you eat no dairy foods? Supplementary vitamin B12 is essential for a vegan breastfeeding mother. The milk a woman makes if she has no animal products at all lacks vitamin B12. This vitamin is necessary for the baby's nervous system and mental development, and there is a severe form of anaemia which may result from a diet deficient in vitamin B12. You can buy vitamin B12 over the counter, too.[7]

When you are losing blood, either because you are still bleeding from the birth or because menstruation has returned, food high in iron will help to replace haemoglobin. This can come from meat or plant sources. To aid absorption of iron, have plenty of vitamin-C rich foods—oranges, for example. With every period a woman loses 30 millilitres of blood. That is 0.5 milligrams of iron a day. If you have heavy periods, you lose more. If at the same time you are trying to lose weight and are on a calorie-controlled diet, it is difficult to get enough iron from food alone, and you may need supplementation.[8]

A woman who has not had enough vitamin A in her diet during pregnancy and who does not eat vitamin-A rich foods while she is breastfeeding makes milk which is low in this vitamin. But anyone who eats carrots, other vegetables, butter, or fish and meat has enough vitamin A, unless they suffer from a disease such as coeliac disease, which interferes with absorption. Women who survive on polished rice and little else make milk which is low in thiamine (vitamin B1), and riboflavin also varies depending on the mother's intake of this vitamin. If you eat wholegrain cereals or bread every day, you will have adequate supplies of the B complex vitamins, so there is no need to worry about this, either. The vitamin C content of breastmilk varies as well, but it is possible that a woman's milk-producing mechanism may be able to make up for a diet low in vitamin C by manufacturing this vitamin itself.[9]

**Balanced
nutrition**

After an injury to the pelvic floor a high-fibre diet will help to avoid constipation, so that you empty your bowels without straining. Straining on the lavatory puts stress on pelvic-floor muscles. Eat wholegrain bread of different kinds, muesli and oat cereals, dried beans, brown rice, and vegetables and fruit. If your intestines need further help, buy a box of bran—the outer layer of wheat kernels —and sprinkle some on soup or cereal. Two tablespoonfuls a day are ample. Drink six glasses of water a day, too, especially if you are eating bran.

Any woman who puts on extra weight during pregnancy probably wants to lose it. But this is not the time to go on a slimming diet. It is best to cut down on fatty foods and have plenty of salads, vegetables and fruit, fresh or frozen, with potatoes and bread or other cereals cooked with herbs and spices to fill you up. If you have time to browse round a bookshop, look for recipe books that describe the Mediterranean diet—that of southern Italy, Spain, Greece, Turkey, and the rest of the Middle East. Olive oil is an unsaturated fat, and —used in small quantities if you are trying to lose weight—is healthier than butter.

*'The baby cried
and cried and I
cut out one food
after another
until I was down
to rice and
potatoes. The
baby still cried!
And I was
starving!'*

Breastfeeding women get thirsty. So it helps to have plenty of juices and milk in the fridge, and to stock up with any special teas you like. You do not need to drink more than you want. Let your thirst guide you. Excess fluids actually reduce the milk supply.[10]

All societies seem to have rules about what a breastfeeding mother may or may not eat. In Britain grapes, onion, garlic, and curry spices are believed to contaminate milk, and to cause colic. It is difficult to know how babies in the southern Mediterranean and India could have survived if this is accurate. You would at least expect them to be crying much of the time, whereas in many of these societies it is rare to hear a crying baby. It is possible that unusual foods, things you are not accustomed to eating, may affect a baby. Some babies seem unable to cope with high levels of dairy-food proteins in their mother's diet: when a woman cuts down or omits milk and cheese and has plant proteins instead, the baby may have fewer digestive upsets and bouts of crying. Galactologues—foods believed to enhance production of breastmilk—are often recommended. Most of these have no proven scientific effect, but if you *think* that a food is helping you make copious, nourishing milk, this is likely to help lactation.

Enjoying meals

When you get down to the practicalities of shopping and cooking, motherhood demands new priorities about food. It is not enough for it to be nutritious and tasty. It must be easy to get, from a shop that is close by or has spacious parking, and which, with any luck, you can get out of with speed. Some of it, at least, must entail little or no preparation. It must not cost the earth. Ideally, it should be edible hot, cold, or in between. If you have other children, they have to be willing to eat it, too. You should be able to combine it with other foods to make dishes that taste very different. And it must not produce many left-overs that you feel you will have to do something about.

If you can get someone else to shop and cook for you, at least occasionally, accept the offer with open arms. But if shopping is the only chance for you to get out of the house, or you feel you need to make some other human contact because otherwise you are stuck inside four walls with the baby, do the shopping yourself.

'We lived on take-aways. We only ate a meal when my mother-in-law came and cooked, because she was worried about her son.'

When you make a meal, do not be tempted by elaborate dishes, but go for fast food. Fast food can be quick to prepare either because you can dash into the kitchen and make it on the spot, or you can prepare much of it in advance, or it can be left to cook without your active participation. Buy the best quality ingredients you can afford and choose the simplest way of preparing them. Use recipes that do not demand that you are ready to add an ingredient or do an essential operation at any particular time.

'We decided we could afford one meal out a week, and took the baby with us—me breastfeeding discreetly under a cape.'

Should your partner be skilled at making special dishes, even if they are more complicated, welcome this, *provided* the shopping, clearing away, and washing up is done too.

If there is a chance to eat out occasionally, with or without the baby, this gives you a break and an opportunity to have a meal in a relaxed setting and to choose more elaborate dishes.

Time takes on new dimensions when you have a baby, and the regular three meals a day may become strung out in a series of snacks. Even if you do get round to proper meals, you may get hungry between them, especially if you are breastfeeding or if you have had a broken night which has made you feel washed-out by mid-morning.

Your baby joins in

In the second half of the first year of life your baby enjoys tastes of food you are eating. Start by puréeing an apple, banana, or cooked carrot in a small food processor, and offer just a teaspoonful. Then you can try a little mashed baked potato with some grated cheese, other puréed vegetables, such as avocado, cooked parsnip or spinach, or rice mashed with home-made soup, for example. There is no need to produce special dishes for a baby. If you do, and the child will not eat what you have made so lovingly, the temptation is to coax the baby to eat it up. This is how food battles often begin. It pays to be laid back about what your baby eats. You have food preferences, and your child is bound to be selective, too. Being able to make food choices may be a good basis for making other choices in life.

Towards the end of the first year your baby will delight in finger foods, and can eat them with great delicacy and skill. Offer fingers of bread and butter, peas, peeled apple slices, or segments of clementine which your baby can enjoy sucking, and any fruit or vegetable which goes down sweetly.

Once a child can sit in a high chair to share your meal it is fun to have a real taste experience, instead of being presented with a bowl of sugary stodge which looks like wallpaper paste. Baby gourmets tend to be uninhibited in their behaviour when eating, and in introducing them to nutritious, attractively presented food of different colours and textures, you are inviting them to share in one of the lasting pleasures of life.

Feelings about Yourself

The birth of a child is a passage to adulthood, and it can be so for both parents. There are other ways in which you can mature, of course —taking responsibility for and developing ideas or organizations, and personal commitment to other people's lives or to creative action. Yet even when they have already done these things, women find that motherhood confronts them with new aspects of themselves and digs deep into the most profound and often disturbing emotions. Because most men are less directly and constantly involved with fatherhood, this maturational process passes some of them by, and is for others slower and more long drawn out.

Caring for a baby is often talked about as a series of tasks that you have to execute. You service the infant, and, if you do it right, the baby is clean, dry, warm, contented, and fed.

But a woman cannot separate herself from all these acts. She is caught up in them, body and soul. As she fumbles at first to get into the rhythm of apparently simple manœuvres like changing a nappy, soaking a slippery little body in the bath, drying in all the extraordinary tortoise-necked creases of folds under the arms, and odd dips and recesses in the bottom, behind the ears, and where a soft spot throbs alarmingly, she may feel awkward and inept. Yet even while she learns these new skills, something enormous is happening at the deepest level of her emotions. As she pulls a vest over a protesting

'I don't think I've ever loved like this before. Plenty of relationships—but that was my need to be loved.'

115

baby's head, draws a jacket over a knobbly fist or splayed starfish fingers that get caught in the knitting, as she cleans up, soothes, rocks, and, above all, as she feeds—sustaining life—she looks into the eyes of another human being who is seeing the world, seeing her, for the first time. And through the child's eyes she sees herself anew.

Sometimes this forces her to ask many searching questions of herself. Where am I? How did I get here? Is this what I want? What is going to happen in the future? Sometimes there is no time for questioning, because the reality of the baby and of her own commitment to the child is so overwhelming that she is in no doubt that, whatever her previous priorities, this is what she wants most of all.

A woman who has become a mother for the first time often feels bewildered at the amazing complexity of her life as it is going to be from now on, at the myriad demands made on her as a mother, and often also as a wife, a worker, a manager, a daughter—someone on a stage already peopled by characters, and where she must play different parts in a script that is already written and which treats her motherhood as incidental and trivial. She often feels, too, as if she has previously been centre-stage, in her job, in her relationship with her partner, and as a pregnant woman, but is now relegated to a minor role. Everything revolves around the baby. Only the baby matters. While she dutifully changes, washes, dresses, and feeds her baby, part of her may be inwardly protesting that *she* matters, too.

These things are rarely talked about, and rarely admitted by a woman, even to herself. The cultural idiom of motherhood, and the only one that people find bearable, is that once a woman has produced a child she bonds with it in utter devotion, forgets her own wishes, and sacrifices herself for her baby. When she does not slip easily into this role, she risks the accusation of being a bad mother.

To say that this involves a process of self-assessment is inaccurate. When you are head down in motherhood, there is no time to stand back and analyse. Becoming a mother brings with it excitement, pleasure, a sense of triumph, and often deep content. A woman may be shaken by waves of tenderness as the tide of her love for this child sweeps in and submerges her. Yet there are more disturbing emotions, too. The greatest of these is simply *shock*.

Many women are astonished that no one warned them that the birth of a child would catapult them into facing new challenges, conflicting emotions, and a constant race against time; that looking after a baby would demand all their energy, stamina, and intelligence. Life before the baby looks, in comparison, leisurely and even self-indulgent. Sometimes people tried to make them aware of the chaos

'Your priorities change. Most of the things I worried about before seem insignificant now I have a baby.'

'The way his eyes light up when he sees me, the way he trusts me utterly—it is an incredible joy that I never realized was possible!'

'No one told me it would be like this. What have I got myself into?'

'No one told me it would be like this. What have I got myself into?'

'I know how to control a class of rowdy 11-year-olds, but I have absolutely no control over the baby, or over my own emotions.'

and confusion of new motherhood, but they did not hear. In pregnancy attention is turned towards the birth. If the subject of 'life after baby' is introduced by childbirth educators into discussion groups, women often brush it aside as being unimportant compared with the major task of preparing for birth.

When a woman imagines what it will be like having a baby, she knows it is going to be hard work, but it is impossible to foresee the stresses ahead, and how they will make her feel about herself. Her self-perception often changes dramatically. The woman who saw herself as capable, calm, confident, and well organized, may now feel inadequate, anxious, and completely disorganized.

Women with disabilities—those who have arthritis or cerebral palsy, or who have artificial limbs, for example—sometimes sail through this experience, whereas those who have previously relied on good health, smooth physical co-ordination, and abundant energy, may find the sheer physical stress of early motherhood very difficult. Women who are used to coping with physical challenges have learnt how to handle difficulties and invent solutions in their everyday life. A woman with a disability usually feels great triumph after having a baby. Other people did not think she could do it. She may have had all kinds of advice warning her that she should not have a baby. Doctors may have recommended abortion. She starts out on motherhood victorious over her disability and other people's stereotyped perceptions of it. When mothers with disabilities are in new mothers' groups, they have a great deal to give. Other women tend to feel, 'If she can do that, so can I,' and are spurred to come up with their own imaginative solutions to problems.

One of the biggest challenges is shortage of sleep. This is something that a woman who suffers night-time asthma knows all about anyway. She realizes that she may have to catnap during the day or go to bed really early to get some rest in the evening. A baby who needs to be fed during the night interrupts sleep, and most mothers probably go short of REM sleep—the rapid-eye-movement kind that is important if you are to feel fresh on waking—through most or all of that first year after birth. The result is that they are permanently tired. This means that they are on a short fuse emotionally. Sleep deprivation is a form of torture.

There is also the matter of understanding what is virtually a new language. Babies speak a language that needs to be learnt. And with each baby you need to start discovering this one's special language. It takes time. Meanwhile there is confusion, and irritation that the baby's messages are not clearer, and that your own efforts to understand are

not appreciated. You have read books about childcare, but somehow the baby is not playing by the rules. Remember that, though you are trying your best, your baby has not read the same books.

The weight of the baby is out of all proportion to the burden of responsibility you feel. Here is this scrap of a human being who demands all your capacities of management, inventiveness, analytical problem-solving, loving tenderness, and instant action when she cries. Even women who have cared for other people's babies before, those who have had jobs as nurses or nannies, say that the responsibility is heavier when it comes to their own babies.

An older mother

In medical literature older motherhood is usually treated as a problem. Doctors tend to see child-bearing after 35—even after 28—as risky. There is a higher rate of Down's syndrome and other chromosome abnormalities as a woman gets older, and mothers are sometimes warned by their obstetricians that they must accept high-tech help to get their babies born safely. They may even be told that they should not expect to lactate successfully. It is true that older women giving birth are more likely to have obstetric interventions, including

Caesarean sections, but this seems to be more the result of obstetric anxiety, and insistence on continuous electronic fetal monitoring, than anything else.

A five-year hospital study of pregnancies in women having their first babies aged 35 and over reveals that birth was just as safe for these mothers and babies as it was for younger women. The research report reveals, however, that there was a higher induction rate and a lower rate of spontaneous deliveries. 'Both these differences were largely accounted for by cases where the intervention was prompted solely on grounds of the patient's age.' The authors conclude that 'the automatic classification of an otherwise healthy primigravida aged 35 or over as at high risk should be reconsidered'.[1]

Journalists who address the theme of older motherhood treat it as problematic, too. We read that an older mother tires more quickly, her health is likely to be bad, she needs more sleep than a younger woman, she is inflexible and stuck in her ways, old-fashioned in her ideas about childcare, out of touch with young people's interests, and is friendless because people she knows are work colleagues who either are childless or have children who are much older. As one newspaper heading put it, quoting a consultant obstetrician, 'Don't risk it ... stop having babies after 35—it's a game for younger players'.[2]

More and more women over 35 are having their *first* babies than were doing so thirty years ago. Yet in the first half of the century much larger numbers of women gave birth in their forties. These babies were the last of large families. Going back still further, the Victorian woman in her forties was often a grandmother by the time she had her last baby. So women have always been having babies in their thirties and forties. The difference is that now many more women delay having their *first* baby till this age.

Newspaper and magazine editors are often under the impression that an alarming social phenomenon is sweeping the Western world as thousands of women in their forties are suddenly deciding to get pregnant. The image of the older mother is of a woman who puts off having a baby because she has a brilliant career and cannot find space in her Filofax for a baby. Once she has pushed the infant out of her body she cannot wait to hand it over to a nanny, put on her business suit, and stride out, brief-case in hand, to get on with her life.

This is a crude stereotype. It gives an entirely false impression of what older mothers are like. A psychological study of women having babies after 40 reveals that only 5 per cent of women delay having a baby for career reasons, and these mothers, on the whole, feel very positive about late motherhood. Those who already have children are

'I'd been too self-seeking before. I wasn't grown-up enough to be interested in a child for his or her own sake. I would have wanted to show how I could do it better than anyone else!'

119

much more relaxed than with earlier babies, and those having their first babies at this age say that they have more patience than they could possibly have had when they were younger.[3] So there is no reason to expect that motherhood will be difficult or that you will find it any more tough going than a younger mother.

Dream baby, perfect mother

Women's expectations about babies and themselves as mothers vary widely. In pregnancy some fantasize about a baby who is cuddly and cooing, or fast asleep tucked in a cot, and who is usually at least 3 months old. The baby is pretty, spotlessly clean, and self-comforting, like the illustrations on birth-announcement cards. Often women whose dream babies are like this are very young. Sometimes they have low self-esteem and are lonely. Having a baby holds for them the promise of someone who will love *them*, and something that they will have for their very own. Other women have more realistic expectations. But a strong element in the dream image is their own idealistic expectations of themselves.

A first-time mother may yearn for a relationship with a baby which is one of bonded bliss. She aims to be in perfect unity with her child, her love free-flowing, and to have a baby who does not cry because all needs are satisfied by an understanding, all-giving mother.

'I was going to be the perfect mother. Trouble was—I didn't know anything about babies.'

Another plans ahead so that she can establish a routine, organize herself efficiently, have time for other interests, and foresees that the baby will fit into this programme—provided that she is a good enough manager.

Each of these women is bound to be disappointed. Joan Raphael-Leff, a social psychologist and psychoanalyst, calls the first woman a 'facilitator' and the second a 'regulator'.[4] A facilitator is concerned to adapt to her baby. A regulator expects the baby to adapt to her. The thing the first woman fears is that she may never manage to achieve synchrony with her baby—or that she might even hate him. The second woman is afraid that she may fall helplessly in love with her baby, and be unable to regulate his needs and drives; she might produce a monster whose demands cannot be controlled, and who would take over her life.

Most of us swing between these two styles of caring and ways of seeing ourselves as mothers—because neither of them works. It is impossible to be in complete harmony with a baby all the time. It is equally impossible to slot a baby into your life as if he were merely a puppy that has to be trained.

120

**Feelings when
your baby cries**

A baby who cries inconsolably can seem like an alien from outer space. Communication is impossible. You feel helpless, and a failure as a mother. Relentless crying often seems like an attack on you. The baby appears not only to be rejecting you as a mother, but also to be aggressive and threatening. So it is not surprising that sometimes a mother needs to escape from her baby. This escape may be as much to protect the baby from her violent emotions as to protect her from the baby.

Women are often surprised at the strength of feelings that this small creature can generate. They do not associate hatred and resentment with being 'motherly', and they feel guilty. They blame themselves, and anger at the baby may be turned inwards and become depression, or may be expressed towards the nearest other person, often the partner.

A woman looks down at her baby who has at last cried himself to sleep and wonders how she could feel anything but tenderness for this helpless being. Yet only minutes before he had seemed so menacing. She hates herself for not giving the baby her unconditional love. She thinks that there must be something wrong with her.

A sense of failure

A new mother who has low self-esteem comes to value herself more as she gets into a rhythm with her baby and learns to understand and respond to the child's needs. But self-esteem is eroded further if she feels that they are at loggerheads with each other, in a battle where the baby is winning. It is as if the child is telling her, 'You are not good enough to be a mother.'

Even though the media often claims that we are in a 'post-feminist' era, girls growing up are still conditioned to be apologetic and placatory, and to underrate their achievements. When it comes to childbirth and motherhood, women are expected to look to male experts for guidance, and to distrust their own knowledge and the shared experiences of women. This learned helplessness is like a stretch of quicksand through which they must pick their way as they learn how to be mothers. While they do this they are in danger of being sucked down into guilt and an overwhelming sense of failure.

The romanticizing of motherhood makes this journey even more difficult. Mothers usually want to conform. A novice mother looks around for cues as to what other women are doing. There is no shortage of advice and precept. From magazines, TV, classes, books, health professionals' instructions, and from women's competitive struggles to do the right thing, an ideal of the 'mother' is erected.

The motherhood ideal is impossible to achieve, because it ignores reality. Romanticizing motherhood, denying the strong conflicting emotions that are an integral part of being a mother, can tear you apart.

Acknowledging these feelings— realizing that other women experience them too, and that you are not alone—is an important part of coming to terms with them. So it is a good idea to make

opportunities to talk and share with other women, especially those who have babies of the same age. One of the best ways of doing this is to contact women who were in your antenatal class and arrange regular get-togethers. Pot-luck lunches or suppers with babies, a picnic in the park, a buffet in which you each bring one dish, baby-sitting for each other (with a chance of a chat beforehand), a country walk with babies in carriers front or back, a mother and baby session at your local swimming pool, or meeting for yoga or other postnatal exercise classes—these are all ways of breaking through the isolation, releasing tension, and discovering that other mothers of under-ones encounter many of the same challenges.

If your conflicting emotions are so strong that you are frightened that you may lose control, you can build in safeguards, take preventive action. You will know when to put the baby down in a secure place and leave the room, when it is sensible to go outside, be with other people, or hand the baby to a neighbour, your mother, or a friend and say, 'I need a break. Can you have him just for half an hour?' Sometimes you will want to use that time to catch up on work which desperately needs to be done. Other times you may want to lie back and listen to music, or run round the park, or take a bath.

Grieving

Perhaps the most surprising and unacknowledged feelings that a woman has after giving birth are to do with grieving. She expected to feel happy and triumphant, and she does. But underneath the joy there is often a thread of sadness which she cannot explain. It is not that she is depressed, but rather as if the intensity of delight she feels in having produced the baby, her wonder as she holds and strokes her child, casts a shadow.

For some women it is the loss of the baby inside them—the sense of closeness, the partnership with this emergent life, the body-rolls and somersaults, twists and turns, the roundness of the head bouncing against the trampoline of pelvic-floor muscles, the dancing, thudding feet and the hop, skip, and jump of legs now flexed, now extended. A pregnant woman has never been so close to anyone else before. With the birth of the baby she may feel very alone again. No longer automatically nurtured inside her body, the baby is now 'another' who needs her attention.

When a woman has enjoyed pregnancy, the birth may also make her feel somehow diminished, her body no longer fecund, fruitful. This, too, brings a sense of loss as she tries to come to terms with her no-longer-pregnant body, which is wrinkled and soft as if it were the discarded skin of a mother goddess. Now she is ordinary again.

With the birth, attention turns from the mother who enfolded and encased the fetus to the baby, whom she is expected to serve with no thought for her needs. For this reason she may feel that she has lost her special value as a pregnant woman, as a woman with a future, the meaning of whose life lies in something wonderful that is about to happen. She has had the baby. People know what it is and whether it has Uncle John's nose or Aunt Sarah's chin, and if it looks more like its father or mother around the eyes. A mystery has gone, and with it the excitement. It is as if she has plunged her hand into the lucky dip, pulled out a package, unwrapped it, and the expectation and adventure is over.

The way in which a woman experiences birth, and the memories with which she is left, may cause grief. This often goes unrecognized and she is supposed to be grateful for having a beautiful baby. When a birth was not what was hoped for, a woman needs time to grieve. Often her own behaviour in childbirth was not what she had hoped for and planned. Sometimes her partner did not behave as she had hoped. She sees herself in a new light and may come to see the father of her child in a different way. In Chapter 8 we can explore this in more depth, because it is often a strong element in depression after childbirth. Perhaps it is enough now to say that this grieving is normal, and that it needs to take place if a woman is to be able to go on freely into motherhood without being submerged by her recollections of an unhappy birth.

'She came to my arms, and it was meeting someone I already knew well—the delicious roundness of her limbs, and her kicking feet. I'm sure she knew me, too.'

Even when the birth went well, a woman's encounter with the real baby entails the loss of a dream baby. It often happens that a mother greets her baby with astonished wonder, and, as she reaches out to draw the child to her, the image of the dream baby fades, or becomes incorporated into that of the corporeal baby in her arms. She is no longer aware of any distinction.

But sometimes this mingling does not occur. The baby is the wrong sex, looks entirely different from what she expected, seems to ignore her, fails to appreciate the efforts she is making to understand and nurture, clings to her in a dependent way that she cannot tolerate, or seems to be aggressive, is too large and tough, or too frail and small. She cannot relate the baby in her arms to the baby who was inside her uterus, and mourns the death of her dream baby. It is as if the pregnancy was a confidence trick, promising her something of which she has now been cheated.

There are social pressures to produce a perfect baby, one who is vigorous and healthy, or of a particular sex, and a mother is blamed if she fails to produce the baby that society demands. A woman who gave birth to a girl when her husband's family wanted a boy said, 'Nine months wasted!'

For some women, especially those who became pregnant shortly after the start of a relationship, the birth of a baby also spells the loss of romance. This may be very threatening. Babies bring disorder and mess. A couple who believed that a baby would draw them closer may find that they are wedged apart. Intimacy is invaded. In Chapter 12 we shall explore how a baby can often bring new depth and meaning to a relationship, too. Yet for many women motherhood means losing an aspect of the self—as young, vibrant, and sexually attractive. As a result a woman may feel resentful. She is the victim of the confidence trick of romance, and grieves over the loss of part of herself, part of her life.

'I felt grotty— fat bulging, milk dripping everywhere, hair lank. Then Josh said, "You're beautiful!" and I saw myself through his eyes, and it was all wonderful!'

When you become a mother, you say goodbye to yourself as a child. This cannot be an instantaneous process. In the weeks immediately following birth a woman often feels the need to be nurtured and helped by her mother, or by other women who fill much the same role. Many traditional cultures organize a lying-in time after birth which enables a woman to pass gently over the bridge to motherhood, while being cared for and relieved of duties like housework and cooking, and all the work on the farm and in the fields. At the end of this transitional period a ceremony takes place, and she emerges as a mother able to take full responsibility for her child.

In Britain the midwife visits mother and baby at home for at least ten days. In The Netherlands the maternity home help gives a great deal of practical assistance, and may even live in. In other countries the woman may have to cope alone immediately. In the United States she can visit her paediatrician with queries and problems, but there is rarely anyone one who will come to *her*.

Women are expected to transform themselves into mothers simply by the biological act of birth, by nature of their female hormones. Even if a woman was unable to give birth, and was delivered by Caesarean section, she has to make the instant switch to being a mother just because a baby has arrived. Miraculously, many women achieve this metamorphosis without difficulty. For others it is a long, and perhaps painful, journey.

Something else is happening during this time. A woman may start to have fleeting sensations of what it was to be a baby herself. Memories of your own childhood are reborn, things that you thought you had forgotten, odd impressions and sensory experiences, such as how it felt to stroke your mother's dress or breathe her scent, to be empty and hungry and cold, the feeling of being tucked tightly into your pram, the startling bright light of a room, or a voice singing. These half-formed memories may seem trivial, but they are part of an awareness which enables a woman to feel empathy for her baby. She knows when a coat is too rough and prickly to be comfortable, for example, or when light is too bright; she understands the things that make a baby feel insecure and frightened. For we have been through all this ourselves.

When we have had good experiences in infancy, it is easier for us spontaneously to do the right thing for a baby. But when these experiences have been bad, it may take a great deal of thinking and problem-solving to work out how to soothe and comfort a baby, and to feel relaxed and confident as a mother.

As she handles her baby, a woman may long to be looked after herself in a loving way. She may ache to be the nurtured, not only the nurturer. Yet her partner, if she has one, is back at work or out with his friends, other people are getting on with their lives, and her mother may live far away or have other commitments. During the pregnancy or shortly after the birth, a woman has often moved house and is living among strangers with whom she has no contact at all. There may be nobody who realizes how great her need is.

So it is not surprising that she grieves the loss of her own infancy and childhood. Sometimes memories are bitter. She may remember —perhaps for the first time—that she was neglected or abused, and grieves for the childhood of which she was cheated. She often strives to make up for it to her baby, to give her own child the love which she was denied. But if she has a jumpy baby who startles and cries, and who is

'They told me that, because he was in an incubator, I shouldn't expect to bond quickly. But the moment I looked into his eyes and touched him, I knew he was mine.'

'I watch my mother with the baby and think, "That's how she touched me. She loved me like that, too."'

difficult to console, one who does not relax and curl into the crook of her arm and give her the assurance that she is a good mother, she may come to resent the child. She may compete with her baby for any affection and tenderness that is going.

When a woman has had a job and is now at home with the baby, either because she is on maternity leave, or later on if she is not returning to work, she may feel either cocooned or trapped. Sometimes she snuggles into the cocoon, luxuriating in its protection, and being able to do things in her own—and the baby's—time. Sometimes she beats against the bars of what has become a cage.

A woman who had a baby before she was really ready for it, before she knows who she is and what she wants in life, may experience motherhood as a trap. One in her early twenties, or anyone who has had an accidental pregnancy, whatever age she is, may need some time to grieve for her interrupted life. For in most industrial societies motherhood entails loss of mobility, loss of job opportunities, reduction in human contacts, reduction in income, and reduction in leisure time and time shared with a partner.

'This time at home was like a sanctuary—just me and the baby in a milky timelessness.'

A teenager comes across friends of her own age having fun, experimenting with life, and being part of a crowd of which she is now an outsider. A woman who has just left college has news of contemporaries starting out on high-flying careers. One who was already in a career structure is aware that she has lost a place on the ladder to success, and sees less-able people with the jobs she wanted. The baby probably more than makes up for this loss. Nevertheless, in Western culture there are times in most mothers' lives when they feel marginalized and degraded. They grieve for life unlived, opportunities lost, an inner potential which is not realized. As they become bogged down in childcare through that first year after birth, many feel more and more trapped. They may feel guilty about confessing it, even to themselves.

Competition between mothers

Every woman is under pressure to be a perfect mother—from society, from her own internalized picture of an ideal mother, and, later, from her children. The gap between what we want to be and what we actually feel and do is wide, and the higher our ideals the wider the gap. The result is that much of the time we feel we are failing in one of the most important tasks in life.

Mothers often measure their own performance against other women's. Does her baby go four hours between feeds and sleep through the night? Is she breastfeeding successfully? Is her baby putting on more weight than mine? Is she on to solid foods yet? Is that baby crawling, pulling herself up, walking, ahead of mine? Is her child smiling, saying 'mamma'? How is potty-training going? Mothers try to assess their success in these ways.

Competition between mothers, often criticized in the baby books, but promoted by the same books in the emphasis they put on 'developmental milestones', is a sign of women's low self-esteem. The main element is neither self-centred pride, nor envy, but lack of self-confidence, which impels women to compare babies and to claim marks for being a good mother.

'About 11 o'clock each night I congratulate myself. The baby's thriving. We've both survived. We're doing well!'

Babies, in fact, do not need super-mothers. All they need are 'good-enough' mothers. They thrive even while we are making mistakes. The moment we think we are into an established routine, know what we are doing, and begin to be rather pleased with ourselves, problems often crop up, for motherhood is like an obstacle course, one in which the obstacles are always on the move.

There is no such thing as a perfect mother, only many different ways of being a mother.[5] A mother socializes her developing child. But it is not only the child who changes and adapts. Motherhood itself is shaped by culture, and changes historically. When social change is rapid, as it is in Western countries today, daughters and mothers may be in conflict about the right way to bring up the baby, or the older woman may sit back and try not to interfere because she thinks anything she does to help will be irrelevant. Either way, this can lead to pain in the relationship between a mother and daughter, something we shall explore further in Chapter 12.

A woman may devote a great deal of energy to trying to be as good as her own mother—or to be the opposite of her and to show that her way works best. There are often things we want to emulate, and others we are determined to do differently. Yet we find ourselves slipping into saying and doing exactly the same things as our own mothers, almost as if we have been pre-programmed. When this happens to you, you may feel irritated about it, or it may give you a new understanding of your own mother's experience of being a mother.

'Since my son was born the memories of my childhood have become sharper and more painful. I'm angrier than I ever was before.'

Since caring for a baby often reawakens in both parents memories of their own childhood, each of them may have very strong feelings about how they were treated then. When you hold your baby, it is almost as if you are also the baby who is held. When your baby cries or is in pain, it is as if you, too, are enraged and suffering.

So at the same time that we are learning how to care for and relate to a baby, we also have to come to terms with memories of our own babyhood—not just what was done to us, but the intense emotions that were stimulated. In having a baby and moving forward into the future, we gather up and incorporate our own past experience. Whatever this was like, whether it felt warm and secure or cold and rejecting, these memories, and acceptance of them, can help us learn how to be mothers and fathers.

Unhappiness after Childbirth

To open your body, or to have it opened forcibly by someone else, in order to produce another human being, to be handed a new creature who has slipped from darkness and wetness, from the pulsing rhythm of your blood and the drumming of your heart—birth is such an extraordinary, yet everyday, event that it is not surprising that many women pass through a transitional time afterwards when they feel emotionally chaotic.

Birth is a life crisis. Like any crisis, it may precipitate confusion, anxiety, and unhappiness. When women become distressed after having a baby it is usually called postnatal or 'puerperal' depression.

Yet it is doubtful whether the clinical condition called 'puerperal depression' exists. Researchers find that women are often depressed in the time following birth because that is the only period which they are investigating. Being a mother and having young children is in itself a risk factor for depression. With all its joys—and these can be vivid and exultant—motherhood is intensely stressful. Research might be more productive and realistic if it examined why some mothers are *not* depressed. Mothers, especially mothers of babies and young children, are often unhappy, and are no more likely to be depressed in the six weeks after childbirth than when their babies are 6 months old.[1]

In spite of this many people still think that unhappiness in the weeks following childbirth is a special condition, different from all other kinds of emotional suffering. This means that a woman's distress when her baby is, say, 9 months or a year old is ignored, or she is blamed for not being able to cope and for being self-centred.

In the nineteenth century the word 'hysteria' (from the Greek *hustera*—womb) was invented by doctors to describe madness caused by the womb. There was a still older idea that the womb could slip its moorings, and that this had a terrible effect on the woman's mind. A theory of 'the wandering womb' developed to account for a wide range of female conditions and what men saw as women's irrational behaviour. It was impossible for men to be hysterical, because they did not have wombs. Even today unhappiness after childbirth is often explained as being the result of hormonal disturbance that is peculiar to women. In Sweden, for instance, a woman who is distressed may be told that she has 'breastfeeding madness', and doctors may perform a spinal tap to measure substances in her spinal fluid. Some medical researchers try to find physical differences between women who are distressed and those who are calm. Yet no correlation has been discovered between hormone levels and any individual woman's unhappiness after giving birth.

Hospital 'blues'

On about the third or fourth day after a baby is born women are often shaky and tearful, and feel that they just cannot cope. This is usually described as the 'blues'. Depression at this time is usually explained as being due to hormone imbalance, and considered to be physiological in origin, because immediately after a baby is born the production of oestrogen drops sharply in a woman's body. But just because two things occur at the same time it is wrong to conclude that one is the cause of the other.

The 'blues' are considered quite normal, and the implication is that nothing can be done about them, except to give a new mother a strong shoulder to cry on. As many as eight out of ten women experience this kind of depression. In hospital whole wards of women are often weeping at the same time. But it rarely occurs after a homebirth.[2] It is a hospital-induced emotional state. The remedy is speedy hospital discharge so that a woman can return home and get to know her baby in her own way, in relative peace, and in her own time.

Recognizing that the standard post-partum ward, with rows of dejected women propped in bed while their babies lie in plastic boxes under bright lights in a central nursery, is a quite inappropriate setting for women to get to know their babies and to start breastfeeding, hospitals are changing. If a woman is forcibly separated from her baby, she is bound to be sad. Now in many hospitals mothers can have their

'Now that we have switched to twenty-four hour rooming-in we hardly ever see a woman with the "blues".'
[A midwife]

babies with them right through the twenty-four hours, can pick them up whenever they like, and can cuddle and sleep with them in their own beds. It is beginning to be acknowledged that the baby belongs to the mother— not to the hospital.

Yet even in a hospital where this positive change has taken place women often feel out of control because, although the system has changed, they have no choice about whether or not they want their babies with them. For while there are women who do not wish to be separated from their babies under any circumstances, there are others who prefer hospital staff to look after their babies so that they can get some rest. In any large, hierarchical institution those at the bottom, the new mothers, who are merely in transit, are powerless. The 'blues' are short lived because most women stay in hospital only a brief time after having a baby. If they had to remain in hospital longer, the chances are that this transitory form of depression would continue.

Postnatal depression

In medical and psychology texts post-partum or puerperal depression is defined as a psychiatric illness, the symptoms of which are distress, fatigue, irritability, anxiety, tearfulness, feelings of inadequacy, marital difficulties, and inability to cope with the duties of a housewife and mother.[3] A woman often 'presents' with psychosomatic symptoms, too — described this way: ' The symptoms of postnatal depression include somatic symptoms such as headaches or palpitations, excessive anxiety about the baby, sadness and difficulty to cope with household tasks.'[4] Psychiatrists conclude that as many as two in every ten women experience depression of this kind.[5]

'People look at you and point out that your baby is healthy. For that I am grateful. But it doesn't make me feel any better.'

What comes over clearly in the medical diagnosis of depression is that it is very inconvenient for everyone else, particularly those living in the same house, who expect the woman to clean it, cook meals, and deal with the baby efficiently. It may be their unease that forces a woman to seek medical help as much as anything in her own mental state. This means that some women turn up at the doctor's at an early stage in depression, while others go on trying to cope, often for many months, managing to produce a semblance of normality, and to service their husbands and children, while suffering profound distress.

If a baby is obviously healthy and thriving, it can be difficult for other people — including those closest to her — to 'see' a mother's distress at all. Their attention is drawn to the baby, and they may take it for granted that the woman is happy and well.

A woman who is depressed often cares for her baby like a robot. She may manage to function competently, though she thinks that she is being a very bad mother. She often carries on mechanically with routine housework and cooking, but may get to a state in which she is unable to tackle tasks which have become too demanding. She cannot remember where she put things or what she meant to do, so her life may be totally disorganized. She feels drained of energy, as if the baby has drawn all strength out of her. She wakes up every morning tired, unwilling to face the day. She often feels at her lowest in the mornings, and copes better as the day goes on. She may veer between being withdrawn and feeling irritable, between determination to do something positive and utter despair.

'I had all these alien feelings. I was in turmoil.'

She may blame herself for not being able to cope, feel that it is her fault that she feels so awful, and deny that she is depressed.[6] She does not necessarily weep. Some women cry a lot. Others do not cry at all. She may be depressed yet *unable* to cry. She may lie awake in the night worrying, and, with the baby waking to be fed as well, this means that she gets little sleep. She feels that she is like a fly on the wall, outside herself, watching herself. It is as if she is cut off from contact with other people by an invisible sheet of glass. So friends and family who want to help feel unwanted and rejected. When she does start to share her feelings, she may burst out in an uncontrollable flood of emotion that seems as if it will never stop.

Often, however, she finds it painful to speak about how she feels, and blanks out the worst bits. When she tries to talk, there may be long pauses. She may be terrified that she is going to hurt the baby. Or she is convinced that the baby is harming her, perhaps by sucking her dry and draining all her strength if she is breastfeeding, or by eating her up — consuming her essence. In her worst moments she feels that she would be better dead. She is often terrified of telling anyone about these thoughts, since she is afraid that some authority will take the baby away from her because she is a bad mother or is insane.

'I felt I was about to do something dreadful to her — like drowning her or letting her drop out of a window.'

Depression can occur after any major life crisis, after the death of someone we love, when we lose or retire from a job, following surgery, and even after moving house. These are all situations in which we may be in a state of shock and are not given the emotional support that we desperately need. Depression can overwhelm a woman after adopting a baby, too — further evidence that depression after birth is not hormone-related.

One obstacle to helping women who are suffering from depression in the year after childbirth is that it is considered a 'woman's problem', along with premenstrual tension and depression at the menopause. It is seen either as an almost inevitable consequence of upheaval in her uterus or ovaries, as a result of breastfeeding, or as a figment of the female imagination which need not be taken seriously.

To ignore or trivialize unhappiness of this kind is to fail a woman when she needs love and care from people who can support her in down-to-earth practical ways. This includes unobtrusively helping with housework and cooking, and giving time to listen to whatever she wants to say without being judgemental or offering advice.

Anti-depressives A woman who is depressed after childbirth is often prescribed anti-depressive drugs. These, like tranquillizers, are excreted in breastmilk, though no significant ill-effects on the baby have been observed. But it should be remembered that all drugs have side-effects, and it is important to monitor these carefully and to take the minimum dose needed to treat the condition. Some doctors feel very strongly that prescribing anti-depressives to a new mother is a way of avoiding giving what is really needed—mothering of the new mother.

Tranquillizers Tranquillizers, which are often prescribed by a GP when a woman is depressed, are addictive. They may actually exacerbate the problem of depression. They pass into breastmilk, so they make the baby sleepy, and feeding becomes hard work. There is another problem with tranquillizers. If a woman feels angry with her baby, and is likely to be physically violent, they may make her feel more out of control than she was before. It is as if in lifting her mood they push her foot off the brake pedal.

After a woman has been taking any drug for about a month she and her doctor should discuss whether it is the right drug for her, and whether the dose is right.

Psychotherapy

'There was a huge question-naire about my relationships and my sex life. I had to send it back before I got an appointment. I decided against it.'

If you decide that it would be a good idea to seek psychotherapy, it is wise to shop around and to take at least as much care in selecting a therapist as you would a childminder, or, for that matter, a hairdresser. This is very difficult when you have a new baby. Ask if you can have an initial meeting with the therapist to explore together whether this is the right arrangement, and the right person, for you. Trust your 'gut' feelings. You will want to be assured of confidentiality so that you can speak freely. You should not be expected to fill in forms with intimate personal details before having a meeting with the therapist, as is the case in some clinics.

If you are paying for counselling, you need to have a rough idea of how long sessions are likely to continue, and how much it will cost. What will happen if you have to cancel a session or are going on holiday? Think about whether you would prefer a woman therapist, perhaps one who has had children herself. Do you feel comfortable talking with someone who is of a different culture? Do you think they may have any stereotypes about you as a woman and a mother? Other questions to bear in mind are: What qualifications does the therapist have? What kind of training was involved? Are there any books or leaflets so that you can get an idea of the general therapeutic philosophy? If there is a waiting list, how long is it? Is childcare available?

When a woman is deeply depressed, she may be able to bear speaking to only one other trusted person. So check whether counselling will be one-to-one. Later on you may find a group very helpful, but this is not usually the best way to start.

Though a skilled and sensitive psychotherapist can give support by listening reflectively, and may be the only person who is not frightened by a woman's distress, psychoanalytic explanations after childbirth rarely take social conditions into account. They tend to be based on the theory that women regress to a more childlike state during pregnancy and in the first months after the baby is born. According to this, new mothers become less rational, more instinctual, and more

like babies themselves. Depression is perceived as the result of failure to work through earlier unresolved conflicts in the relationship with the patient's own parents.[7] Male therapists may take as the token of successful treatment the women's compliance with household and marital duties. One psychoanalyst reporting on a successful case describes how, after more than six months of psychotherapy, with sessions twice a week, a woman was cured and 'by this time she knew what hard work was involved in running a home and caring for a child, but she had come to find it satisfying'.[8]

Psychotherapy is not without risk. About 10 per cent of patients become worse with psychotherapy compared with people who have the same symptoms but who do not have any kind of therapy.[9] Around one in ten male therapists admits that he has had sex with his female patients.[10] Many more may have done so, but do not confess to the sexual victimization of women in this relationship of trust.

The psychological 'solution' is not the only one, and it may not be the right one for you. Two psychologists writing about their radical approach to psychology, say: 'As feminists, we oppose psychological explanations ... These translate political issues into private, individual concerns.'[11] They believe that psychology — talking about our 'inner child', for example — leads us to explain distress purely in terms of inner feelings and personal failures, and to ignore ways in which we should strive for political and social change.

Patrizia Romito, an Italian psychologist who is also a sociologist, suggests that both medical and psychoanalytic explanations assume that the cause of depression lies in the failure of some mechanism inside the woman, when in fact the most significant element is women's resistance to the oppressive social institution of motherhood.[12]

Social causes of unhappiness

If a woman who lived in a city under air attack from an enemy was fearful and anxious, or was depressed and listless in a country where thousands were starving, you would be unlikely to treat her for 'stress'. Of course she is under stress, but this is not what she needs to be treated for. You are more concerned to stop the war and to feed the hungry.

It is the same for women who are struggling to be good mothers in any society in which they are kept in virtual solitary confinement with young children for much of the time. Many are still loaded with the full burden of child-rearing and housework and without hope that anything will change in the future, except that one day the children will be 'off their hands', and they can clean, cook, and wash dishes for their husbands instead.

'Illness' is often the wrong word to use about a woman who is in distress. To call her 'ill' is to medicalize her condition. Someone who is unhappy because there is no money to feed the children and pay the electricity bill, or who is sexually abused, may derive some help from medication and psychotherapy, but it does not get to the root of the problem. There are practical things that need to be done, and ultimately the only solution is to be found in political, social, and economic change.

In India the traditional practice is often that a woman returns to her own home to have a baby and is looked after by her mother. In the countries of the developing world young people who would have had strong family support often move to a city, and families are fragmented. In the past women relatives and friends would all have come to help when a baby was born. Now women living in urban centres, in Africa and the Caribbean, for example, often become unhappy for the same reasons as women in the West—social isolation.

Women are labelled as suffering from postnatal depression when what they are is unhappy—and often for good reason. The labelling of unhappiness as depression fixes the cause firmly inside the woman herself. She becomes the 'patient' who has to be treated, often without any reference to the environment in which she lives, the people by whom she is surrounded, or her loneliness. These are also elements in depression, and, even if they do not 'cause' it, they certainly make it more severe. Ann Oakley, a sociologist who has studied maternal unhappiness, states that 'the medicalization of unhappiness as depression is one of the great disasters of the 20th century'.[13] For, when the social causes of unhappiness are ignored, nothing has to be done about them. The woman is supposed to change, but nothing around her need change.

A couple's relationship

Distress may come from a poor relationship with a partner. Sometimes he is violent and abusive. Often he simply does not understand. Most boys are still not brought up to be sensitive to and aware of women's major life experiences. They often bond emotionally with other men rather than women, and the two genders live in different worlds.

In targeting the woman as the patient who needs to be cured, attention is distracted from change that has to come from her male partner. If a woman cannot bear, or dare, to be angry with him, she may direct anger inward to herself, and it turns into depression. Counselling and psychotherapy is appropriate therefore only if it involves the partner, and perhaps other family members too. In recognition of this, family units have been set up in some areas where the whole family can come to be helped.

'He wasn't keen on coming, but once he realized he wasn't being criticized, he opened up. The therapist made us both feel safe.'

But a man may not see the need to do anything about it, and believe that since the woman is mentally ill it is she who ought to be treated, and it is nothing to do with him. It is often painful and humiliating for him to admit that he simply watched her sink into depression. It may be still more difficult for him to change his attitudes and behaviour so that she can be helped out of the depression. But this may be what she needs most of all.

Social isolation

Since the 1970s there has been evidence that there are many social causes of depression. They include lack of a supportive relationship with a partner, stressful life events such as the death of someone dear to you, unemployment, the loss of your mother in early childhood, and simply having children in the home. One major study revealed that 30 per cent of working-class mothers with a child under 6 years old suffered from depression, and another 20 per cent were very unhappy. One woman in three 'lived in such difficult circumstances that any extra threatening event could tip her into severe depression'.[14] In Western society many women with young children who become depressed are isolated from other adults, and have no close relationships. There is nobody with whom they can share the good and bad things in life, and talk openly about their feelings, nobody who helps them in practical ways when the going gets tough. They are socially isolated.

In my own research on crying babies I discovered that the women who were most unhappy were those who were alone with the baby for eight hours or more a day. Some were terribly afraid that they would let rip and hurt the baby. A few actually did. None of them had anybody to talk to about it.

We all need other people. We are validated by having our identity acknowledged by others. Children give us identity, too, but that is as *mothers*, not as autonomous adults. When a woman is cut off from other adults and adult concerns, she is socially isolated even if she has a crowd of little children at her knees.

Women are isolated if there is no good public transport and they do not have the use of a car. They are isolated when a partner works outside the home for ten hours a day, or brings work home and settles down to catch up on it with doors closed against children's noise. They are isolated if there is no extended family to give support, and when any relatives they do have live a long distance away. They are forced into isolation when there are no local leisure and recreational activities which welcome small children, and when breastfeeding outside the home is thought of as vaguely indecent.

They are isolated in countries where cold weather makes it difficult to take a baby outside the home. They are isolated where grandmothers have vanished because they are at work, are on holiday, or are themselves lonely in homes for the elderly.

Isolation, together with poverty, which makes it worse, is one of the primary causes of depression in women with young children. Being depressed because she is isolated has nothing to do with a woman's early infantile experience, her relationship with her mother, her emotional immaturity, or her hormones. She is depressed because the environment makes mothering an almost impossible task.

Mothers have to be amazingly adaptable and ready to switch attention at a moment's notice, to stimulate, soothe, guide, encourage, and comfort. That entails a dissolving of boundaries, a suspension of personal identity, in order to have empathy with the baby. This loss of identity can be shocking because it is so different from how all other adults function. In her study of early motherhood Amy Rossiter found that the loss of self does not just come from feeling gobbled up by your baby—although mothers often have thoughts like this—but because the social situations in which our identity is continuously acknowledged and reconstituted simply disappear.[15]

Depression of this kind is extremely rare in societies where everybody knows everybody else, in peasant cultures and other traditional societies where in times of crisis and transition there is always someone to turn to for help, and where family and neighbours give continuous support.

'The manager told me breastfeeding was not allowed except in the toilets.'

'It was such an effort to get ready to go out—boots, jacket, snowsuit, cap, gloves— that I gave up. Stuck in the house, I got still more miserable.'

We need to look for ways in which we can compensate for a culture in which mothers are forced into solitary confinement with their young children.

Breaking out of isolation

For any woman who is unhappy because she is socially isolated, there are things in her environment and close relationships that need to be changed. If this is the case for you, you probably know what they are, but it may seem impossible to alter anything. So do it step by step as self-confidence grows. Among the organizations listed at the end of the book are some in which you can meet other women who have coped with depression, or who have the empathy to understand how you are feeling even though it is not their personal experience. Women's networks like this give strong support when you are feeling isolated. You know that you have only to pick up a phone to talk with someone who will listen without passing judgement on you, and who gives the emotional support you need so that you can find the energy within yourself to cope.

When you are depressed, it is difficult to exert the energy to change anything. But if you can explore your ideas about what you might be able to do with someone who cares, you can probably find a course of action that would make a real difference. Here are some changes other women have made that they found helped them. Some of these may not feel right for you. Others may spark off ideas of your own. The list is not intended to be prescriptive—only to help your imagination come alive as to possible solutions.

Ask for help. When people enquire how a new mother is, she often says, 'Fine!' or makes a joke about sleepless nights and how busy she is, even if she is feeling awful. You can cut through the conventions and say instead, 'I'm terribly tired,' or 'I'm finding it hard to cope' and ask for practical help.

If they ask, 'Is there anything I can do?', take them seriously and answer, 'Yes please.' Ask for a casserole dish that only needs to be put in the oven for a meal. Or suggest they tackle the chaos in the kitchen, arrange for the drain to be unblocked, clean the fridge, take a load of washing to the launderette, do a week's shop for you, baby-sit for a couple of hours so that you can get some sleep, have your 3-year-old over to play with their children for the afternoon, or, if they have only twenty minutes to spare, give you a back rub.

Get out of the house every day early in the day. Since depression tends to hit worse early in the morning, this is the time to take preventive action.

See if you can get more mobility, the use of a car, teaming up with another woman who has one, or using public transport.

All babies sleep sometimes. You will have more energy if there is a chance to relax for a short while each day, even if it is only for half an hour. Sleep when the baby sleeps. If you cannot get to sleep it does not matter. Breathe slowly and relax. *Don't try and catch up with all the things you have not done.*

Have some exercise, best of all with a group who have regular meetings. When women get together in this way there is always an opportunity to make friends.

See your GP and say that you are unhappy. Ask to talk to someone who has time to listen.

Join a women's discussion group— one especially for new mothers, or any other in which you do things together which are not focused on babies. Shop around for one in which you feel at home.

As you start to feel better, consider joining a group of women who have experienced depression themselves, so that you can learn from and give support to each other. Some of these self-help organizations are listed at the back of the book.

If there is someone else to give a night feed you can express your milk and store it in the fridge, or use formula if you prefer, at least for a few nights or at weekends.

Make a simple outline plan for your day. Don't make it difficult for yourself by setting goals. Just work out something that helps you give shape to the day. Make sure that you have some space for *yourself,* and space for being together with at least one other adult with whom you feel at ease.

Find a baby-sitter you can trust, or explore possibilities of day care, so that you can get out without the baby for at least a short while.

Consider any options that present themselves of working part-time, or doing some creative work at home while someone else cares for the baby, even if only for an hour or two.

Explore possibilities of household help, someone to do the laundry, to cook a meal, or to look after older children, so that you can spend more time just with the baby.

None of these things can cure depression. But any of them may help you draw on your inner strength to find a way out of your unhappiness.

Getting over a difficult birth

For many women depression is linked with a difficult birth experience. This does not necessarily mean that the birth was especially painful or long, or that it was a complicated delivery or a Caesarean section. It means that, even if from a medical point of view it was a completely straightforward birth, a woman was unable to make informed choices between alternatives. This often happens when labour is induced and there is a great deal of high-tech intervention. Yet it is not so much the equipment that is used and the things that are done to a woman, as her sense of control over what is being done to her, that makes all the difference between a birth about which she feels triumphant and one about which she feels that she was completely under the control of other people—that she was just the body on the delivery table.

A common element in the experiences of women who find it very difficult to come to terms with the way they were treated during childbirth is that they were denied choice. They could not share in decision-making about what was done to them. They often felt emotionally blackmailed by being told that they must submit to procedures for the baby's sake, and that if the baby died or was mentally handicapped it would be their fault. They were disempowered. Many of these women look back on the birth as a violation, like sexual abuse. They say that they were raped.

'I felt assaulted and angry. I can't get over it. If a man had raped me I could at least have gone to the police.'

For anyone who has not experienced birth as disempowering the analogy between birth and rape may seem far-fetched. Yet there are many similarities in the way that the woman's body is forcibly penetrated without her consent, in the violence that often takes place, and how that the experience invades her thoughts and dreams long after the event.

She feels dirty, degraded, robbed of personal identity, and ashamed. She is terrified that it could happen again. She feels that she has been used and discarded. She is terribly alone, cut off from other women and from those nearest to her by the experience, and is often unable to make loving human contact with anyone. She may also suffer great physical pain from genital mutilation and may believe, with some justification, that her body will never be the same again.

In the days following the birth she is often deeply shocked and emotionally anaesthetized, unable to feel anything. Gradually numbness gives way to a sense of relief that she has survived. So there is often a time lag before she feels the full horror of the experience. This may last several months, and sometimes much longer. It may be difficult for her to find words to describe what she has been through. There does not seem to be the language for it.

She may find it almost impossible to make an official complaint because she is dazed, confused, and just wants to forget it and get back to 'normal'. Other people often urge her to put the experience behind her, and say things like, 'Count your blessings,' 'You must get things in perspective,' or, 'Put it behind you and get on with your life.'

Many women who have been through this kind of experience suffer panic attacks, agoraphobia, disturbing dreams, and sudden vivid memories which intrude on and poison their everyday lives and relationships with other people—most of all the relationship with a sexual partner. If they are able to grieve over the experience, and have support in doing this from understanding friends, they gradually come to terms with what happened. Otherwise the emotional disturbance they feel may last for months — or even years.

Sexual abuse

Women often suffer sexual abuse. American and British surveys reveal that at the lowest estimate 12 per cent, and at the highest 42 per cent, have been sexually abused as children. The way they are treated in childbirth often brings back keen memories of this abuse.[16] A woman may anticipate extreme pain in childbirth, and expect the baby to be deformed or to die, as a punishment for sexual sin. Sometimes the two scenes of rape and birth merge to become one in terrifying flashbacks and nightmares. They were prevented from moving. Their legs were forced apart, and they felt incredible pain as something was pushed deep inside them. It is not surprising that a pelvic examination can stimulate these intense feelings, too, and that 'some of the very rituals designed to desexualize the examination, such as lack of eye contact and isolated focus on the genitals, may actually reinforce links with previous experiences'.[17]

If you are distressed because of a birth in which all control was taken away from you and it feels as if you have been raped, perhaps this has brought back to you an earlier experience of sexual abuse. There are things you can do to work through your pain. When you feel very unhappy, it may seem an impossible task. Yet just lifting up the phone to call someone to whom you can talk about it, knowing that this person is not shocked by what you are saying, and understands, is a way of starting out on the journey of healing.

Empowering yourself

When women talk about ways in which they have coped with unhappiness, the important thing seems to be not what was done to them — where they were at the receiving end of care — as the things

that they felt able to do themselves. Sometimes these seemed very trivial at the time, but enabled them to begin to be in control of their lives. Here are some positive actions taken by women that they say helped them personally.

'She believed me. I didn't have to argue or explain. She just believed me. And she recognized how assaulted I feel.'

Sometimes a woman wrote a story of what happened to her, how she felt during the birth, and her emotions afterwards. Other women made paintings or drawings, told the story in clay, or sewed it on fabric. It seems that if you are able to do this, an idea is no longer simply festering inside you, but is out where other people can see it as a reality, too.

Women sometimes talk to a rape-crisis counsellor or someone who is willing to listen reflectively. Occasionally it is their birth educator or postnatal counsellor, someone else who works with a childbirth organization who is a mother herself, or a woman therapist. The list at the end of the book will give you an idea of organizations you can contact to find help.

Women who have had traumatic birth experiences can write a carefully worded official letter of complaint to the hospital, medical committee, or health authority responsible. They address it to the organization or committee of management, rather than writing to an individual, who could just file away their letter, and they keep copies of all correspondence. If you need help in finding out to whom you should write, or the way to write, ask your childbirth educator or a consumer organization that includes healthcare in its agenda. These organizations will also be able to advise you if you are thinking about litigation.

Some women join a consumer birth movement to improve care in childbirth; they canalize the energy that comes from their anger to help other women.

Some women who have gone on to have another baby have made the decision to have a homebirth with a midwife who is known to them. A good birth experience often heals the emotional wounds of a previous bad experience.

You can also look at the suggestions on pages 142–4 to see if any of the ideas listed there could help you.

Psychosis

'All I wanted to
do was die. I
remember
dumping all the
tablets I could
find in the house
down the toilet
because I was so
afraid I would
kill myself.'

When a woman is very disturbed, especially if there was a sudden onset, a psychiatrist may diagnose psychosis. One or two women in every thousand suffer a postnatal psychosis. Only one-third of women who become psychotic after birth will have had any obvious psychiatric problems before, but those who have suffered from manic depression previously are at greater risk.

The problem often starts in the first two weeks after birth with emotional chaos which is so severe that the woman is unable to sleep. Thinking becomes confused, and she has hallucinations and delusions.

She is restless, agitated, and panic-stricken. She may be recklessly cheerful as if 'high' on a drug. She may engage in obsessional rituals, like hand-washing or house-cleaning, that she believes she must do to ward off evil and prevent something dreadful happening to her or the baby. On the other hand, she may not realize that she has had a baby at all. She may blank out the baby's existence, believe that it belongs to someone else, or that it has died. It is as if the responsibility of having a baby is overwhelming—and she cannot face it. So it is simpler to erase the baby from her mind.

The vast majority of women recover completely. Many are admitted to a psychiatric hospital—the best are specialized mother and baby units. The average time of mental confusion is about eleven weeks, but sometimes it lasts longer. Treatment usually consists of antidepressants, antischizophrenic drugs, and tranquillizers, sometimes with ECT (electroconvulsive therapy) as well, often followed by counselling and family therapy.[18] When a woman has had a psychiatric breakdown of this kind there is a 50 per cent chance that it will not happen again after another birth.[19]

In the English city of Nottingham, where a special Motherhood and Mental Health Service has been set up, Dr Margaret Oakes devised a system of homecare in the early 1980s which is working well. As a result, only 40 per cent of disturbed women are admitted to hospital—and some of those only because this is what they prefer. Dr Oakes believes that spending a long time in hospital can impede progress, and a mother who is separated from her baby may find it difficult afterwards to feel that the child belongs to her.

Although it is often taken for granted that a mentally disturbed woman should not be with her baby, they can be kept together with one-to-one care.[20] It is too heavy a burden for a family to bear, but when a psychiatric nurse is assigned to give concentrated care for up to eight hours a day, and admission to hospital can be guaranteed the minute need arises, many women can be looked after successfully at home. The nurses in this scheme help a woman to build self-esteem, to cope with everyday life, and to enjoy her baby.

Any woman who is desperately unhappy needs strong support from a partner and from other women. A woman therapist who was a very good listener was told by one woman who had previously had the standard psychiatric treatment for psychosis, 'Psychotherapy is the first place in nine years that I have been asked what I feel rather than being told. The psychiatrist always asks my husband how I've been as if I'm not there. They treat my illness as his problem.'[21]

A woman who is mentally disturbed becomes cut off from other human beings. They tend to be embarrassed by her behaviour and confused thinking, and are often themselves very anxious and frightened too. Yet if she is to emerge from her suffering, she needs more than drugs. She needs loving human relationships that affirm her identity as a person and enable her gradually to become self-assured and positive, and begin to enjoy life again.

Your Baby's Personality

Babies used to be seen as mere bundles of reflexes until they gave their first 'social smile' at 5 to 6 weeks. It was believed that they had 'a life of vegetation' until then, and did not realize that their mothers existed apart from themselves. Only at this stage of development did they start to have rudimentary personality.

All you had to do was to ensure that a baby was adequately fed, clean, dry, and warm. Relationships were impossible. Communication from the baby consisted almost entirely of the message, 'I'm hungry.'

It was assumed that babies did not feel pain, or at least nothing like as much as adults. Newborn babies who required surgery were operated on without anaesthesia, and all babies had many painful things done to them in hospital, especially those who were pre-term or of low birth weight and who were in an intensive-care nursery. Doctors and nurses ignored signs that a baby was in pain, even when one managed to grab catheters and syringes and tried to push them away. Sadly, in many countries this is still the case. Mothers, of course, know their babies better, and realize that they feel discomfort and pain, and are often in acute physical distress. There seems to be a gulf between medical and mothers' views of babies. So doctors who do not have babies themselves, or who have babies but do not know them well, and get all their knowledge from medical textbooks, sometimes say things about babies which mothers know cannot be true.

Side by side with the idea that babies were not capable of feeling very much was a theory that you had to make sure that they did not get the 'better' of you. They needed firmness. As with training puppy dogs, you had to show them who was 'master'. It was easy to 'spoil' babies by giving them what they wanted, by picking them up and feeding them when they cried, for example.

Though Spock began to introduce his liberal ideas in books and articles in magazines for mothers published at the end of the 1950s and through the 1960s, the prevailing culture of childcare was still restrictive, dogmatic, and insensitive to babies' needs. Health professionals often treated them as objects to be managed, and advised mothers that infants should spend most of their time in a pram or cot, except when—from the age of 3 months—they were placed on a rug, with the nappy loosened to allow movement, for half an hour's 'kicking time'.

My first child was born then, and my book of 'mothercraft' (which was considered a progressive one) told me to put her in the pram from 10.30 a.m. until 1.30 p.m. and from 2.30 p.m. until 4.30 p.m. At this point she could have thirty minutes' 'mothering time', and after feeding was to be put to bed at 6.30 to sleep until the 10.00 p.m. feed. 'A comfortable, properly fed, healthy baby should sleep peacefully and regularly. If the sleeping is interrupted and poor, the baby cannot progress as it should.'[1] So if your baby did not conform to this routine she could suffer physically and mentally.

One of the most important things that happened in the Sixties may not have been the so-called sexual 'liberation' that came with the contraceptive pill as much as this new general awareness that children were people, too. With it, mothers developed confidence that they probably understood their babies better than anyone else. They began to think that, difficult as it often is to interpret the messages coming from a baby, and inconvenient as their desires and needs may be, perhaps babies know when they want to feed and sleep better than anyone else.

The backlash against babies

Yet even today there are adults who are highly suspicious of babies. In a quality Sunday newspaper a journalist recommended that babies should be taught early on not to be 'self-centred' and 'self-absorbed', and a mother could do this by not 'giving in' to their 'demands.' When her baby was a year old she lit a bonfire in the back garden and burnt all the baby books. She wrote: 'I had spent months dancing attendance on my baby ... She had no idea that there was an appropriate bedtime—no sense that human beings in civilised societies have set meal-times … A generation is growing up like little emperors … developing bad habits that can last a lifetime.' In this particular case the journalist found her baby's constant calls for attention intolerable because she wanted to 'be available' to her partner. The baby, she said, 'comes along and gets in the way'.[2]

About the same time a woman wrote in another newspaper, 'Even among the very young there are children who are simply bad. Some children show a savagery, even as babies, which is frightening.'[3]

So there are still highly conflicting attitudes to babies, and the drive to control and discipline them and make them fit into a timetable is strong for mothers who love their babies, but are frightened that they will take over their lives, and believe that to give a child what he wants is to spoil his character.

Yes, of course babies get angry sometimes and are utterly unreasonable, but to project on to the baby the destructive feelings that you have as an adult, and to think that a baby is threatening you, is to split off part of the self. Instead of facing up to the anger inside you and things that you hate about yourself, you see the baby as having these emotions and incorporating the badness that you cannot eradicate in yourself. Any adult who does this is in danger of treating the baby as an object against which it is acceptable to express the rage that is welling up inside. Parents owe it to babies not to be frightened of them, and not to retaliate against them. Babies need to know that they cannot destroy us, however angry they are. A father or mother who in their own childhood has not had that sense of security may be at risk of seeing a distressed baby as 'the enemy.'

Your talented baby

I look at babies in a very different way. I see them as exquisitely sentient creatures, capable of intense pleasure and pain, with senses open to light and dark, heat and cold, rough and smooth, silence and sound, and to harmony and disharmony expressed in our own actions and relationships. They are brilliant learners who absorb things about the world around them, and other human beings in it, faster than is possible for most of us at any stage later in life. Each baby is from the beginning a personality distinct from all others, with a great capacity for joy and for both receiving and giving love. Babies are lively communicators long before they say their first word.

Only twenty years ago nurses, even midwives, sometimes claimed that babies could not see or hear. It was one of the objections raised to mothers holding their babies in their arms in the delivery room, and having time to get to know them. 'What's the point? The baby can't see you.' Even if they could see, their eyes were tightly shut, like a

153

kitten's. The author of a British midwifery textbook dismissed the Leboyer approach to childbirth because, she claimed, babies had their eyes closed anyway, so they could not possibly look into their mothers' faces.[4]

A baby was treated like a manufactured article just off the assembly line. It had to be inspected, checked for quality, cleaned, and packaged, before being shown to the mother. Because the baby could not feel much, the skin was rubbed roughly. The spine was forcibly straightened and the body stretched in order to measure it. The baby was plonked in metal scales and weighed like a dead fish. It was tested to make sure that it did not have a dislocated hip by suddenly jerking the legs out and in. It was placed under the glare of bright, fluorescent lights. Because babies could not really hear, it did not matter if it were in a nursery where a dozen other babies were crying loudly, and if staff talked loudly, clattered instruments, and had the radio blaring away. Newborns were subjected to a barrage of noise. In some countries—as still happens in many US states—stinging liquid was squeezed into the eyes in case the mother had gonorrhoea, which could cause blindness in her baby. Then everything became blurred and misted over, and the baby screwed up its eyes in pain and closed them. In some countries babies are still held upside down and slapped at birth, to make sure they are breathing. In Moscow I have seen them taken straight from the delivery table to be held under the cold tap.

The baby's sensory awareness

The senses of babies are fully alive. They can see well, if only from a limited distance. They see best things which are 23 centimetres (9 inches) away—about the distance from your face as they lie in your arms. David Chamberlain, a psychologist who specializes in the behaviour of newborn babies and those who are still inside the uterus, comments that this is useful because babies need to see their parents, 'not read microfilm or freeway signs.'[5]

Babies who are awake and alert can, from birth onwards, protect their eyes from dazzling lights by squinting, screwing them up, or closing them. When lights are adjusted so that they are not dazzled, they scan the surroundings, searching for interesting shapes— dips and protuberances, circles and curves, the play of light and shade, and above all a human face. When your baby gazes at and searches your face, she is attracted especially to the bright shine of your eyes, and to your moving mouth as you talk. And babies can see colours and enjoy them.

Video experiments have shown that babies, even newborn babies, can sometimes imitate adult facial expressions. So if your baby is relaxed and alert and the right distance away from you, when you open your mouth or stick out your tongue, she may copy you. Though we

do not understand why, the baby obviously knows that she, too, has a mouth like yours, and can move it in the same way. If you look sad or worried your baby may look sad and worried, too. If you look surprised or happy, you may notice the same expression on your baby's face. As the baby gets older this can turn into a wonderful game.

Babies can follow a moving object with their eyes. If something interesting — your face, a rattle, a small teddy bear — is comfortably in their field of vision, and then is very slowly moved, they can follow it with their eyes. They make little movements of the hands, too, as if — having caught the interesting object with their eyes — they now want to reach, touch, and grasp it with their hands. It is the beginning of hand–eye co-ordination.

From birth babies can smell and taste keenly, probably as well as adults can. When only a few days old they are familiar with the special scent of their mother's milk, and can distinguish between different women's breast pads, and their own mother from other babies' mothers, because of her underarm odour.[6]

They hear perfectly. Newborn babies recognize, and concentrate on, stories that were read to them repeatedly while they were still inside the uterus.[7] They are especially sensitive to high-frequency sounds that adults may not even notice. If you had an ultrasound scan during pregnancy you were probably aware that your baby jumped around, though you could hear nothing. High, shrill sounds can be very disturbing for them. They hear more acutely than adults, and are especially receptive to changes in patterns of speech and in phonemes, the smallest units of speech. From the twentieth week of pregnancy they have been listening to sounds inside their mothers' bodies, and to their mothers' voices. 'Elaborate sound spectographs reveal that babies in the womb are taking language lessons,' David Chamberlain writes, 'literally learning the speech characteristics of their mothers.'[8]

Newborn babies cry when babies of the same age can be heard crying, but are not disturbed by white sound—a random whooshing sound — or by computer-simulated cries, a crying baby chimpanzee, or a crying five-month-old baby.[9]

Babies, of whatever age, are aware, expressive, and affected by their interaction with us. They are curious about everything, and are learning all the time. They actively communicate long before they can speak. They imitate our facial expressions and our actions. They are 'cognitive geniuses.'[10]

Moving freely   At birth a baby's muscle control is concentrated in the important area of the jaws, mouth, and throat, so that she can latch on to the breast, suck and swallow. At some point between 9 months and 18 months she has developed the enormously complex muscle co-ordination involved in walking. This co-ordination begins with the eyes, and movement of other limbs follows from the initial exploration and reaching out of the baby's eyes.

'At 10 months, she's started climbing. She loves crawling upstairs, and she climbs on everything that looks in any way climbable.'

A baby who is free to move, and who has the space in which to do so, moves in a rotating circle. If you unwrap your 3-week-old baby and place her naked on a rug on the floor, you will see that even at this early age she can wriggle round with a circular movement. Dr Montanaro, of the Montessori School in Rome, points out that usually, as babies become more mobile, we restrict their freedom of activity: 'They go from crib to infant-seat, baby carriage, push-chair, and play-pen.'[11] This is largely for reasons of safety, but also because mobile babies get under our feet, and when really on the move they can create chaos.

Yet movement is very important for babies, not only because they develop muscle tone and co-ordination in this way, but also because every time a baby swipes out at a mobile and makes it move, or shakes a bell and listens to it ring, or manages to travel to a stool and then succeeds in pulling himself up, he learns, 'I can make things change. I can do it for myself.' This is vital in building self-confidence and in stimulating the baby's ability to explore, to learn, and to achieve.

Concentrating

Babies have enormous powers of concentration. Watch a baby as one hand first brushes against the other in front of his face. Notice how he pauses, seems surprised, and tries to do it again, how he concentrates on this work of finding the hands. Watch carefully as he strives to bring them simultaneously within his field of vision and to touch one hand against the other. This develops into hand exploration, hand play, reaching for objects, grasping them, making them move, and producing sounds from them. The baby discovers that, with attention and co-ordinated action, he can make things change in his environment.

We should never interrupt a baby, or an older child, who is concentrating on a task in this way. It is important to avoid distracting a child, asking questions, giving praise, or even picking him up for a cuddle. For this is important work. We are witnessing the discovering, the concentration, learning, and striving, which can change the world.

In touch

In traditional cultures mothers touch their babies' bodies more often than is usual in the West. The touching seems to be of a different kind, too. It may be more intimate. Touch between you and your baby is an important part of your developing relationship. A mother may

recognize her baby just by touching the back of his hand. Research in Jerusalem shows that seven out of ten women who are blindfolded, and who have spent only an hour with their babies since birth, know them by touch and can select them out from a number of other babies.[12]

But it is not as simple as that. There are many other elements in touching, the most obvious of which is that it is a way of expressing tenderness and compassion, and is comforting to a distressed baby. When she is soothed by your touch, it confirms that you are a capable mother. When she is not soothed, you explore different ways of touching, and at last, when you come up with the right ones, you feel a sense of achievement. This validates you as a mother.

Touch is a way to communicate with a baby and for a baby to communicate with you. It is a pre-verbal language as important for human beings as it is for other mammals, but which many adults forget how to use. You relearn it with a baby, and it is a delight for you both.

Certain kinds of touch can stimulate the baby's body awareness in a positive way, and help muscle co-ordination and movement. Mothers in traditional cultures often massage their babies with oil, as they used

'Polly gets very hungry after her massage. She has a breastfeed. We have a lovely bath together. Then she falls into a deep sleep.'

to do in Europe, too.[13] Babies respond to massage in different ways. Sometimes they relax and almost fall asleep. Sometimes they join in actively, arms fluttering, legs kicking, as if in a dance. As you massage your baby, notice how he reacts, and the massage movements that he enjoys most.

When you massage your baby, it helps your hands to slide easily if you use a vegetable oil, such as almond oil. A drop of lavender aromatherapy oil added to it does not irritate delicate skin, is relaxing, and smells delicious.

A baby massage   Undress your baby in a warm room and sit on the ground with your knees bent up, the massage oil beside you, and your baby lying against your thighs facing you on her back. Pour a little oil in your hands. Start by caressing her body gently with the oil so as to distribute it and make her skin smooth and glistening.

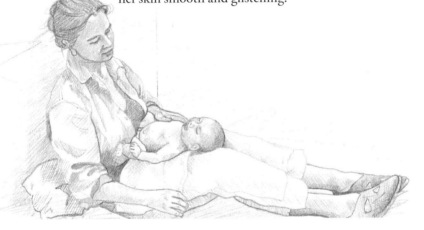

With the palms of your hands over her chest, stroke out and downwards to the sides of her body and then up again to her chest.

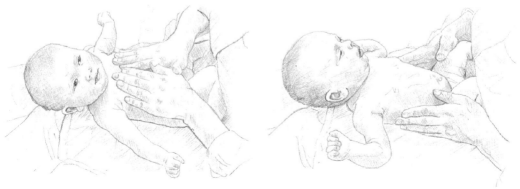

159

With the palms of your hands resting at either side of her pelvis, stroke up on to one shoulder, then down again to her pelvis, then up on to the other shoulder, and down again.

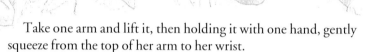

Take one arm and lift it, then holding it with one hand, gently squeeze from the top of her arm to her wrist.

Now do it again, but this time with a slight twist as well.

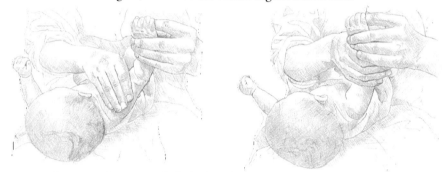

Press gently on your baby's thumb to open her hand and stroke forward over the baby's palm and out over the fingers. A young baby who still has the grasp reflex will clasp your hand. An older baby's hand will spread out. Repeat the arm and hand massage with the arm and hand on the opposite side.

Starting with one hand on your baby's thigh and the other underneath her arm on the same side, stroke downwards, one hand following on the other with a continuous movement.

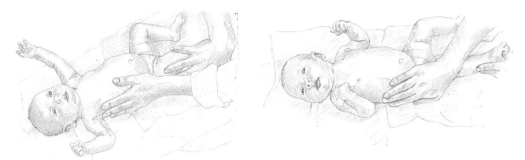

Massage across the baby's tummy to the other side, and then back again.

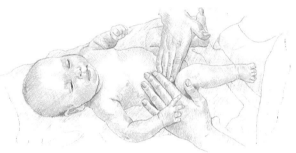

Draw the baby's feet closer to you, hold her legs up, and use your forearm to massage down her tummy to her knees and up again. Then do it with the other arm.

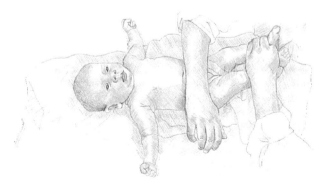

Doing first one leg and then the other, massage her legs and feet just as you have massaged her arms and hands.

Now turn your baby over on to her tummy, lying across your thighs. With one hand on the side farthest from you and the other over your baby's bottom, massage across her body with both hands up to her shoulders and then down again to her bottom.

With one hand on her bottom and the other at shoulder level, make firm strokes all down her back, starting from the shoulders.

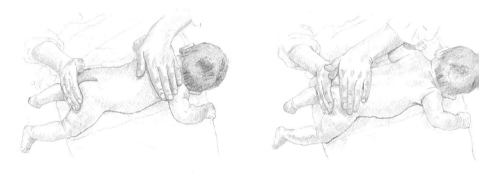

Then do the same thing with one hand holding her ankles and the other starting at her shoulders and moving right down over her legs.

Turn the baby over so that she lies on her back again, and massage her face very gently, avoiding her eyes. With your fingers over her forehead, stroke gently out and down to her ears.

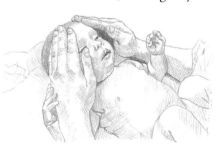
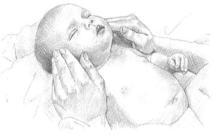

Then, with your fingers over her cheeks near her nose, stroke gently out and down to underneath her ears.

With your thumbs make light stroking movements from either side of her nose down to her chin. (This will not work with a baby under about three months, as she will think you are offering a feed, get very excited and start to root.)

While you do all this massage, talk or sing to your baby, and be aware of her responses. Be guided by her and continue the massage movements for as long as she enjoys them.

Physical closeness

Having your baby nestled in a carrier against your body may feel good to you both. Your arms and hands are free and your body balanced. But it is important to find one that is right for you, and when the baby grows heavier it is more comfortable to have him on your back than in a front pack. As you walk and work, the baby is soothed by your movements. A baby in a carrier — either on your back or facing outwards on your front — feels secure, has a good vantage-point to see what is going on, and, absorbs the surrounding culture in this way.

At night close body contact may enable a baby to sleep better than if he were isolated from you. Your breathing, heartbeat, body warmth, and physical presence help him feel safe. In traditional cultures all over the world babies sleep with their mothers at night. Once breastfeeding is well established you can feed the baby whenever he needs it without fully waking up.

The expectation that babies should sleep in social isolation is a recent, and unevaluated, cultural experiment. Solitary sleeping may not be the safest arrangement. It is normal in most societies for mothers and babies to sleep together, either in the same bed, or very close to each other. There is some evidence that a mother's movements during sleep, and the noises she makes, stimulate a baby's breathing.[14]

Many women say that they cannot sleep as soundly, because of the baby's little movements and noises, but sleep better than if they were straining their ears to listen for his crying, and worrying whether he were still breathing.

Play and touch

Reciprocal touch is one of the earliest ways of playing together. Mother and babies everywhere enjoy patting, licking, bouncing, sliding, tickling, nuzzling, and kissing.

Baby wearing

One way of getting to know a pre-term or low-birth-weight baby who has been nursed in a plastic box in an intensive-care nursery is to bind her to your body with cloth, so that she is in direct skin contact with you. You 'wear' your baby under loose clothing—a long shirt or tunic, for example.

This 'kangaroo' method first achieved publicity in a hospital in Colombia. Native South American mothers usually enfold their babies in a *ribozo* or similar strip of cloth. So this was not a new method, but the rediscovery of an age-old way of carrying and caring for babies.

In the San Juan Dios Hospital in Bogota, Colombia, it is used for many tiny pre-term babies, instead of putting them in incubators. In technically advanced countries neonatal intensive-care facilities usually provide greater opportunity of saving severely underweight and pre-term babies.[15] But as soon as your baby is discharged from hospital this can be helpful for both of you. It can start to make up for the separation you have had, and enable you to put behind you the anxiety that comes when a baby has had breathing problems and a fight for life.

When you treat your baby like a baby kangaroo who is still in the pouch, you give her the comfort of your constant presence. Your own body heat keeps the baby warm. It brings you in touch in such an intimate and loving way that it helps you cope with the guilt you probably felt in having pushed her out into the world too soon, or not nourishing her well enough inside your body. You can breastfeed while she is still tucked inside your clothing.

'She looked like a skinned rabbit. I was frightened to touch her. But as soon as she was out of the incubator and I could wear her, she became mine.'

Here is one way of 'wearing' a baby. It is described by a woman who lived for three years in a West African country where, as a new mother, she says she 'quickly adopted many of the culture's relaxed, efficient, and commonsense approaches to child care'.[16] West African mothers usually wear their babies on their backs so that their arms are free and they are unencumbered. This, however, is a way of carrying your baby nestled against your breasts. You need a piece of lightweight cotton cloth 1.8 metres (2 yards) long by 114 centimetres (45 inches) wide (if you are large, allow some extra). The cloth has to be long enough for you to tie a knot easily with the two ends. The front-cradling version of this is particularly suitable for a pre-term or low-birth-weight baby and any baby in the first six months of life. Sherri Saines calls it a 'heart-to-heart wrap'.

Tie the strip of cloth around your waist. Knot it firmly in front so that it forms a split skirt.

Rest your baby on your hip facing you. Lift the corner of cloth that hangs below the baby. Wrap it under the baby's armpits from back to front. Support the baby with your arm and, holding the wrapped corner with the same hand, reach for the other corner. Pull it over your shoulder from back to front.

Knot these two corners across your chest. The baby should be resting at hip level, with one foot tucked inside the cloth. The other can be outside it. You can cover a small baby inside the cloth so that the head is supported and only some hair and a few toes are showing. A bigger baby can get more of a view and one leg may protrude from the carrier.

When you want to take off your baby pouch, lean forward, cradle the baby's bottom with one hand, and untie both knots with the other. If the baby is still asleep, you can put her down inside the bundle.

Dreaming

You may have been told that babies cannot dream. There is evidence from research in perinatal psychology that newborn babies dream about half the time they are asleep.[17] They smile, quiver, squirm, pucker their faces, suck, breathe quickly, look surprised, scowl, chirp, grunt or lip-smack.

Babies dream even before birth. REM-dreaming-sleep, is first recorded on ultrasound at 23 weeks. After birth external stimulae, with feelings of hunger and satiation, distress and comfort, and pain and relief from pain, create patterns from what first is stimulatory confusion, and dreams become more complicated.

When your baby startles, jerks, wriggles or murmurs in her sleep it is not a sign that you should wake her up. It is important to respect a baby's dream life. Dreams should not be interrupted unless they are obviously distressing. They are a way of reliving, connecting, and patterning experiences. Dream-time is important for babies, just as it is for adults.

Sleep patterns

Babies can sleep under conditions which their parents would find impossible. They can catnap, like the very old and wake refreshed. They often sleep best with a background of regular, reassuring sound—people talking softly for instance. They have been used to the steady beat of their mother's heart and the sounds of her digestive system while they were still inside her body. Perhaps silence makes them feel lost and alone.

*'She loves Dan
playing his
guitar. They
spend most
evenings together
while I have a
bath and relax
after the busy
day.'*

If you are aware that certain sounds help your baby to sleep, you may want to record them and make a soothing tape. It can be the sound of a vacuum cleaner in the distance, the tumble drier, a ticking clock, waves crashing on the shore, the hum of traffic — even the lavatory cistern flushing over and over again.

Parents and grandparents all over the world sing lullabies to babies. When you are keyed up, you may find that singing helps you wind down, too. You can also make or buy a tape of music and songs to help a baby relax and sleep.[18]

Though books tell you that newborn babies sleep sixteen or eighteen hours out of the twenty-four, that a 3-month-old should sleep for fifteen hours, and a 6-month-old sleeps twelve hours through the night, your own baby may have very different ideas. You cannot *make* a baby sleep. Bear in mind that these figures are averages, and there is wide variation in the amount of sleep anyone needs, and the ways in which sleep is patterned.

It is often difficult for babies to drift down into sleep. They startle and wake again. You soothe them, and they have another go. Even when they are deeply asleep, they may suddenly surface and want to know that you are close, and that everything is all right. In the first six weeks they chirrup a bit and give odd little cries, but if undisturbed some will sink to sleep again after five to ten minutes. If they seem too restless to do this, rhythmic patting, rocking, or humming with your cheek close to theirs will often get them to sleep again.

In the first weeks it is hard for babies to wake and return to the real world, too. They often behave as if they are lost in a strange and frightening place, with monsters of hunger gnawing inside them. They need loving arms around them and the comfort of suckling.

Other mothers may tell you how their babies sleep, just as your mother and partner's mother may tell you how they got their babies to sleep. This is interesting, but your baby has his own personality, and his sleep needs and patterns are probably different. Avoid treating it as a competition as to who manages to achieve a more regularly sleeping or longer sleeping baby.

At around six weeks many babies get down to learning about the fascinating world around them with such a thrill of discovery that there are long periods when they refuse to go to sleep. Life is so exciting that your baby may be one of those who is agog to use all his senses to explore the exhilarating, dancing, reverberating world around, with its kaleidoscope of changing shapes and colours. When it comes to around five or six in the evening, his mind is buzzing, fizzling with excitement — and it has all been too much. It is impossible to settle to sleep. He has reached out with all his senses, has absorbed so much, that now he cannot calm down unless he is helped by your calm, loving presence. He needs the reassurance and comfort of your nearness, and a reduction of stimulus so that he can gradually detach himself from the heady excitement that comes with being awake.

A baby who behaves like this usually develops into a bright child. But it is exhausting for you. It helps if you create sleep rituals in the hour or so before you would like your baby to sleep: a leisurely warm bath in a softly lit room, an aromatherapy massage, rocking, and gentle lullabies are all worth trying.

When your baby cries

All babies cry to alert attention to their needs. If your baby starts to cry, especially in the evening, you will help her to be happier if you carry her against your body and give her the closeness and rhythmic stimulation that comes from this. There is evidence that this reduces crying, especially the kind that often starts when a baby is about six weeks old and makes evenings a misery. In a randomized control trial it was discovered that carrying babies for an extra two hours a day from three weeks onwards resulted in them crying less than babies who were not carried around like this.[19] You may be told that this is spoiling the baby. You may feel guilty that you are 'giving in'. But if the result is that you have a more contented child it is well worth doing. So it makes sense to ignore the well-meant warnings that your baby will become a 'dictator' and any admonitions you may receive to 'show the baby that you are in control'.

Some parents spend hours trying one thing after another to calm their crying babies. It happens especially towards the end of the day, when both they and the baby may be tired. It often goes on until late at night. People who have to listen to a crying baby feel emotionally torn to shreds. They may accuse each other of not being able to stop the baby crying. They may cry themselves. They may become violent. They may try to escape. The baby sounds as if he is being tortured, and they feel that they are being tortured by the baby.

One common reason why babies cry is that they are in physical pain from colic (indigestion) or hunger. That sounds as if it were easy to sort out. But often it is not. Hungry breastfed babies, for instance, may suck almost non-stop, and thus get a dilute milk which is high in lactose, and which causes further pain from colic. Both breastfed and formula-fed babies may suffer the pain that results from allergy to or intolerance of cow's milk protein. One in five babies who cry persistently is in pain for this reason — the breastfed babies because their mothers are drinking milk and eating dairy products.[20] If you are

169

breastfeeding, it is worth trying the effect of cutting out dairy foods for a while. If your baby is on formula, you could switch to a soy-based baby milk, though unfortunately some babies are allergic to soy protein, too. Fortunately, babies often grow out of this food intolerance in a matter of weeks.

Babies often cry because they feel lonely and lost. Pick them up and they stop immediately, only to start crying again when you put them down. It is as if they are saying that they need stimulation, movement, and human contact, even at times that are very inconvenient to you, because these are important parts of their development.[21] By the time they are 6 or 8 weeks old, babies start to cry because they are bored and desperately want something to happen. They are stuck in one position looking at the ceiling. No one is talking to them. They cannot yet entertain themselves by examining the interesting shapes, weights, and colours of playthings, and they may not yet have learnt even how to suck a soothing thumb. So the only thing left to do is to cry.

But babies cry because they are over-stimulated, too, and want to be able to rest in a quiet, shadowy room, though someone keeps on jiggling them about and trying to feed them because they are crying.[22] If you want to soothe a baby who is 'over-tired', there is a special knack of helping the baby to wind down. Rock gently, hum, sing softly and repetitively, pat the baby's bottom, for instance. It is difficult to do this if you yourself are wired up and anxious. So it often helps to put the baby down in another room with a loudly ticking clock, the rumble of a washing machine or dishwasher, or some other reassuring sound. (I do not understand why dishwashers and washing machines are sometimes advertised as being so quiet that a baby could sleep on them. Babies usually like a comforting background noise.)

Some babies cry because they have an immature nervous system. Some cry after a difficult birth. Though people acknowledge that a baby can be physically injured by birth, there is little understanding that birth may be difficult for a baby in other ways, too, and that a newborn baby is able to remember, learn, and express emotion. Those who do not acknowledge this deny babies their own experience of birth.[23]

It takes some time, anyway, for babies to adapt to a diurnal rhythm, to realize that night is different from day, and that we all want to sleep at night-time. Many babies understand this pretty well between their fourth and fifth month, but it may take many weeks of trial and error before they begin to sleep through the night.

However it feels to you at the time, babies *never* cry deliberately in order to irritate or attack you, to manipulate or defy you, or to accuse you of being a bad mother. They cry because of their own need. You can only discover that need by carefully observing and getting to know your baby.

It may help you find out how to comfort your baby if you keep a careful record of exactly when, for how long, and in what way she cries, and what occurred just before the crying started, and earlier in the day. So it is worth keeping a diary about your baby. Some of the best research about babies has been based on keeping diaries. Six days of diary-keeping usually yields enough information to work out how to help the baby.[24]

Babies who cry inconsolably often become much more peaceful and happy when they are about four months old. Sometimes it stops almost overnight.

The steps of a dance

As babies develop and interact with their mothers and fathers, they get better and better at synchronizing their behaviour with the expected behaviour of those caring for them. They expect certain things of us and may be bewildered if an adult looks different from usual, or behaves in a very different way. If a mother wears a mask over her face, or puts on glasses for the first time, for example, or is silent instead of talking to her baby, it can be frightening.

Babies mould themselves to the anticipated shape of the mother's body. They turn expectantly towards the breast as she starts to unbutton her shirt. They know by the sound of her footsteps and the familiar body movements who is coming toward them, even in the dark, as well as knowing her by scent, by the contours of her face and the play of light and shade on it, and the sound of her voice. If the father cares for the baby too, they quickly come to anticipate his appearance and behaviour, also. If there are other children in the family, they synchronize with and adapt to them as well.

Sometimes when a baby half wakes, hungry for a feed, it is as if a little animal is groping for the breast, fists clenched, eyes tightly shut, mouth open and rooting. You may feel shut out because your baby seems to need milk, not you. It is as if you are being treated like a milk machine. You may look down at your baby at the breast for the third time in an hour and think, 'Why am I doing this? It's boring.' On the other hand, the knowledge that you can satisfy this urgent need may bring you deep contentment. However anxious you were before you gave birth about whether you could be a good mother, now these worries disappear. You relax completely, as you listen to the steady rhythm of sucking, feel the closeness and receptiveness of your baby's body, and know that you are meeting another person's elemental need in a totally satisfying way.

At other times, when your baby is alert and wide-eyed, and wants to feed, it is as if she is actually asking for the breast, with bright eyes, eager face—almost as if she were talking to you. By the time she is 2 to 3 months old she pats, strokes, or pushes your breast with her hand, which is now open, rather than curled into a fist as it was in the first weeks. She looks up at you and gazes into your eyes. She nibbles or bites you, and smiles. Sometimes she protests, pushing her lower lip out as if sorry for herself. When contented, she coos, and the inflections in her voice are early signs of the speech patterns she is hearing around her, and of her readiness for conversation. She moves a hand to touch your face, rests it on your breast, or pops a finger in your mouth. She looks around, curious about things and people. She makes eye contact and grins. She discovers patterned fabric, a tassel or button, a picture to look at, the curve of a tumbler, the shine on a teapot, a fascinating corner of the table, and murmurs approval.

The times when the baby is relating to you and is alert and interested in the surroundings get longer and longer. You begin to enjoy your baby in more lively ways, and your baby enjoys you, drawing your attention towards what he wants you to notice, making it quite clear what he wants, and joining in games. Your sense of the baby's individual identity and strong character becomes more marked, and you get to know him more and more as a person.

Half-way through the first year when you hold your baby on your lap facing you upright, she jumps with a delighted sense of achievement. She concentrates on bold illustrations in a book held so that she can reach it, rubs the pictures, and discovers with surprise that she cannot pick things off the page. When she wakes she may lie waiting contentedly for a while, knowing that a feed is coming, playing with toes or fingers or a rattle, fascinated by a mobile hanging above the cot, or a bell suspended where it makes a sound when she waves her arms around or kicks it.

Now you no longer have to provide a split-second response to your baby's need of you. You can relax in the knowledge that, in spite of earlier doubts, you are doing well as a mother, and you and your baby are in synchrony. It is as if you both know the steps of a dance, and move to the same music.

Growing, exploring, and learning

Babies grow and develop at different rates. If you think of development as reaching 'milestones' of achievement, you will be proud when your baby is ahead of others, but are bound to be anxious if she seems behind. There is enormous variation in patterns of development and your baby may do these things months earlier or later than is suggested.[25]

It is very exciting when you see a baby doing something for the first time, and you have a terrific sense of achievement. You may feel that your baby is a genius. The baby picks up your delight, and this encourages her further. But there is another side to this. When a baby seems a bit behind, a mother often gets very anxious that there must be something wrong, and the anxiety may be conveyed to the baby, too. This happens especially with a first baby.

'At a childbirth class reunion when our babies were a year old every single one was walking except Alice. It was awful!'

About 1 month Can hold head up a little while. Gazes at objects suspended within her field of vision— 25 centimetres (10 inches) in front of her. If you hold an attractive shape at this distance in front of her and move it slowly right and left, she follows it with her eyes, concentrating on it until it passes out of her field of vision.

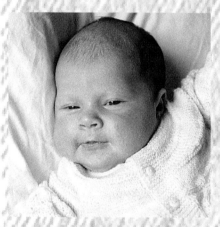

About 6 weeks When you hold the baby with hand under his tummy he can lift his head. If you hold his hands as he is lying on his back, and gently pull him upright, he is just beginning to hold his head up in line with his body. Discovers hands by touch. Likes looking at brightly coloured picture books. Smiles at you. Coos and gurgles.

About 3 months Swipes at objects in front of her with palm of hand. Mother-watching: follows your movements. Enjoys sitting up well supported. Back straight except for curve in sacro-lumbar spine (the small of the back). When he is lying on his back and you pull him up by his hands, his head stays in line with his body. When on his front he can control head movements, lift shoulders and upper chest off floor, leans on forearms, and looks about to crawl. Turns to the sound of your voice. Starts to play with fingers and hands, grasping

and examining them, and holding them in front of his face.

Enjoys exploring different textures with hands.

Holds a toy for a short while. If it makes a noise, looks at it as he holds it.

Finds it difficult to let things go, so usually drops them.

Kicks a lot.

Curious about everything.

Knows when is about to be fed or to have bath, and gets excited.

Laughs.

About 4 months Reaches for interesting objects: looks at hand, then at object, then hand moves. If she can't reach it, repeats this and continues until she gets it. She is teaching herself hand–eye co-ordination.

When mother's face is hidden, waits for it to reappear.

Recognizes best friends.

About 5 months Sits supported.

Likes splashing water.

May enjoy going in swimming pool if water warm and there are no noisy people around.

Explores objects and faces with fingers and mouth, and gets very excited.

Some babies are already wary of strangers at this age.

About 6 months May sit alone for a while, back straight. Likes sitting up to watch everything around. When on his back and you hold his hands, can almost pull himself up to sit.

Can now see as clearly as adult.

Rolls over from front to back. Kicks vigorously, on front and back. On front, may raise head and shoulders, push arms up, and rock backwards and forwards.

Extends arms to say 'Pick me up'.

Chews on fists and dribbles as first teeth come through. Two bottom front teeth often appear soon.

May sleep through the night.

Becomes frustrated when cannot get to things.

Giggles, shouts, and makes a lot of noise.

Plays with toes.

If you hold toy 23 centimetres (9 inches) in front of him, seizes it. Reaches, grasps, holds, lets go, transfers from one hand to other. Enjoys playthings, inspecting, manipulating, and turning them round, rotating wrist to do so—comparing, studying, and chewing them, and learning about shape, texture, volume, weight, colour, and sound.

May chew food he can grasp—e.g. rusk, apple. Anticipates your actions when you bathe and dress him. If you give tastes of solid food joins in to help.

About 7 months Rolls over from back to front, and may start rolling along a surface and right off it.

When held upright on firm surface jumps up and down on strong legs.

On front, can push up on to hands and knees. Makes pre-crawling movements; some babies do take off, and are surprised if they go backwards. Some babies start creeping now.

Make sure you have child-proof home: no

exposed electric sockets, trailing flexes, bottles, jars, glasses, pills, dangerous substances, knives, other pointed and sharp objects at child level. Ensure safety from hot liquids, stove, heaters, and fires.

Investigates everything in surroundings, by sight, sound, touch, and taste.

Knows name and turns to you when you say it.

May drink from feeding cup with both hands.

Enjoys finger food and stuffs it in with delight—and a lot of mess.

Throws things on floor when does not want them any longer, and repeats action to see what happens, often over and over again if you are willing to go on playing.

About 8 months Understands your different tones of voice.

In right mood, interacts well with another child.

Watches you with concentration and imitates things you do.

Wants to be part of the action—e.g. brushes hair like you.

Enjoys games which involve imitation: 'Now you do it. Now I do it.'

Grabs spoon when you are feeding him.

About 9 months Pokes fingers into everything.

Gazes at small things moving 3 metres (10 feet) away—e.g. ball being rolled.

Can make choices, has strong preferences—e.g. about food or the clothes he will wear today.

May enjoy water play of all kinds, knocking down bricks, playing with mirror, play-dough, plasticine, and sand, musical playthings and anything else that makes noise, and making marks on paper with wax crayons.

Helps turn pages of book as you read to him.

Enjoys pat-a-cake, peek-a-boo.

Says 'Mama' or something like it, and babbles constantly.

About 10 months May be able to feed herself.
On the move, one way or another.
Explores everything. Can open cupboards, pull
books off shelves, create chaos.
May be very clinging.
Grabs things from other children.
Waves goodbye.
May say 'All gone'.

About 11 months Knows names of people and
things—e.g. 'kittens', 'flower', 'shoes', 'book',
action words such as 'give', 'sit down', and
'where?'
May move rapidly now, crawling, creeping,
bottom-shuffling, or cruising crabwise round
furniture, holding on for support, or holding
your hand to keep balance.
Starts to climb.

About 12 months May stand alone. Then take
first steps alone, and fall. Tries again, and again,
and again,
May begin to show right-hand dominance.
Enjoys people- and animal-watching.
Knows exactly what she wants and makes it clear.
Points.
A more extensive understanding of the meaning
of words.
Nods to say 'yes'.
Can scribble with crayons.
Very sociable with people she knows well.
Alternates between moving away and exploring,
and coming back to you and wanting to be
cuddled.

There is huge variation in the ages at which babies do these things. If you are concerned about development, talk to your general practitioner or paediatrician.

Enjoys singing and movement games—e.g. 'row the boat.'
Can identify circle.
Very good at taking things to bits.
Enjoys looking at herself in mirror, and obviously realizes who she is.
Puts two bricks one on top of the other, and then knocks them over.
May have as many as eight teeth by now.

Your baby's pattern of development may be different from this. Most babies have phases when they seem to be developing very quickly, and others when nothing much seems to be happening. The important thing is to enjoy your baby exactly as she is now.

FEELINGS ABOUT YOUR BABY

As a woman emerges from the storm of labour, contraction following on contraction like waves crashing on the rocks, submerged in great whirlpools that seem to suck her down into their depths, and swims into the calm harbour that follows birth, a baby may come as an extraordinary surprise. When she is lost and tossed in the energy that swells up and envelops her body, it is easy to forget entirely that all this striving, this pain, these incredible sensations of pressure, stretching, pushing, bulging, opening, and at last swinging wide, are actually producing a baby.

So the first emotion that many women feel as they see and touch their babies is one of astonishment. 'It's a *baby*!'

What happens then depends on the setting in which birth takes place, and whether everyone is bustling to finish labour with rapid delivery of the placenta, clearing up, checking and weighing the baby, stitching up the mother, and processing them both through the hospital system, or whether there is a precious space for the mother and baby to get to know each other peacefully and without any rush.

Bonding

When the paediatricians Marshall Klaus and John Kennell first did research in the 1970s about how mothers fall in love with their babies and babies with their mothers, they introduced the term *bonding*.[1] Mothers have known all about that for thousands of years, of course.

But now it became medically respectable. Klaus and Kennell studied the conditions that were needed for bonding to take place spontaneously and easily. They looked at ways in which the hospital environment often made it difficult for mothers by separating them from their babies.

Their findings were gradually acknowledged, and many hospitals in Western countries changed their methods and incorporated 'bonding time' into their institutional practices. They even taught staff to watch mothers to see whether they were bonding successfully—the first examination in motherhood to be taken when a baby was about 5 minutes old.

As with all good ideas, once the idea of bonding became systematized, it was distorted. Administrators describing hospital policies said things like, 'We allow bonding between mother and infant,' 'We let the mother hold her baby for ten minutes before the patient is taken to the post-partum ward and the baby to the nursery.' Bonding was treated as an instant glue, the application of which had to be fitted into nurses' busy schedules. If the glue did not 'take', a monster mother might be produced, who would neglect, abuse, or reject her baby.

Mothers became anxious that they would not manage to bond. Some felt self-conscious and inept as they tried to bond under careful scrutiny. Those whose babies were taken away because they needed to be resuscitated, observed, or given special care in the nursery for a while felt threatened, because they had been told that it would be hard for them to bond afterwards. Sometimes mothers who had been through a difficult labour had babies plonked on their bodies, and were told they should put them to the breast, before they felt ready to touch and hold them. Mothers from Asian and other cultures traditionally expected women in the family to be there to tend the baby, care for them, and present them with a beautifully clean baby who had already been oiled, massaged, and cocooned in cloth. They sometimes felt humiliated and degraded when midwives insisted they held babies with mucous, vernix, and blood still sticking to them.

Then research was published that de-bunked bonding, and the pendulum of official thinking swung again.[2] Some hospital staff claimed that bonding had been disproved, and that they could go back to the old ways of taking babies off to the nursery and telling their mothers to go to sleep. Yet the Klaus and Kennell findings are still relevant. It was the way they were interpreted that was wrong. Adoptive mothers, mothers who have had Caesarean sections under general anaesthesia, those whose babies have been in intensive care, sometimes for weeks, and mothers who were unable to greet their babies because they were ill themselves, all know that instant bonding is not compulsory. But they were made to feel as if they must be exceptions to the rule. In fact, human mothers are not like goats and sheep, who reject their young if they are not able to smell and lick them immediately after birth. They are able to bond with their babies over a period of time, and do not have to do it instantly.

To claim that bonding has to take effect in ten minutes flat or you can never love your baby, never be a good mother, is like saying that unless you fall head over heels in love with someone you see for the first time in the ten minutes after meeting, it is impossible for you ever to love each other. People can know each other for weeks, months, sometimes years, and find over time that they are in love. It is the same with a baby. Love works mysteriously, and often deep below the levels of consciousness. It cannot be summoned by order. All we can do is to create the conditions in which love can be nurtured, and see what happens.

Klaus and Kennell had drawn attention to the appalling failure of the hospital system to provide a facilitating environment, to enable the mother to be with her baby for as long as and whenever she wished, and to breastfeed when the baby wanted it, instead of when hospital schedules dictated. They had alerted caregivers to the needs of the most vulnerable mothers—those whose babies were whisked off to a nursery, and were not allowed to sit in the nursery to gaze at, touch, stroke, and hold their babies.

They had pointed out how important it is for a mother to look into her baby's face and explore every detail of it, and that this is vital also for the mothers of babies who are in incubators. Their understanding and insight has revolutionized practice in hospitals all over the world.

Falling in and out of love with your baby

No mother loves her baby all the time. Or at least, though she knows that she belongs to the baby and the baby belongs to her, there are many occasions when she would like to escape from the bondage, because she feels that she cannot stand this angry, stubborn, unreasonable little creature any longer. Then, in the space of a minute, as the baby quietens and falls asleep, she is engulfed in passionate tenderness. Most mothers have times when they think, 'Why did I ever have this baby? It was the biggest mistake of my life'—and then feel dreadfully guilty about such thoughts, and cuddle the baby closer.

Your baby probably has similar conflicting feelings about you, though they are preverbal, and less sophisticated. You are often a goddess, and sometimes a witch. You are the fairy godmother who answers all desires with the twinkling of a wand, and also the wicked stepmother who puts poison in the apple. Fairy tales reflect children's fantasies about their mothers.

Some babies make it difficult to love them. It is as if the two personalities of the mother and the baby do not dovetail. Whereas a

mother may feel that she can understand one baby because she is rather like her, with another she may feel that she has a cuckoo in the nest. Sometimes, too, a woman who loathes things in herself that she thinks she can see in her baby's behaviour gets angry with the baby just as she is angry with herself. Some mothers find boys easier, others girls. Some are happiest with a big, bouncy, 'aggressive' baby.

Others like gentle, hesitant, pretty, clean little babies who let you do anything with them, mould themselves to your body, and are quietly responsive when you cuddle and play with them. Another woman finds that kind of baby difficult to stimulate, and worries that she is backward and will never develop independence. A woman may face a running battle with an assertive baby who knows what she wants and goes all out to get it. With twins, one baby may be considered 'easy' and the other 'difficult'—one active and outgoing and the other passive and receptive.

In the first few weeks of life you start to learn who your baby actually is, and adapt to the real developing person. Part of the excitement of that first year of life is finding the *otherness* of the baby, and building a relationship with someone who has a distinct personality of her own. It is often a stormy passage. But it is a great adventure for you both.

The act of birth is only one element in a longer process of locating the baby outside your body, outside yourself. This process continues through the years as the child grows and becomes more and more separate. The otherness of a baby is often a continual surprise—the funny things she does as she blinks, yawns, lifts an eyebrow, sneezes, burps, and gives a quick little half-smile in her sleep as if in response to some secret only she knows.

Mothers can gaze at their babies for a long, long time, observing minutely every little detail about them. Fathers who thought that babies would not be interesting until they could play together often discover for the first time the fascination of baby-watching.

As parents watch their baby, they are not only learning about her, but actively claiming her, making the baby part of the family, by identifying physical resemblances and behaviour which are like their own or other family members. 'He's got your chin.' 'Don't you think her fingers are like grandad's?' Grandparents do this too. 'That's just how you looked when you were a baby.' Adoptive parents look eagerly for signs of similarity, and are often delighted to point to physical features and elements in behaviour which are like their own.

It is a great game that is played in family after family. But part of it may also be identifying behaviour which is disliked. 'He's got a temper just like my father!', or, 'He gets whiney. I can't stand that. My sister used to whine the same way.' We tend to start identifying and labelling babies like this when they are only days old. This leads to expectations about how a baby will behave and assumptions which may be entirely erroneous.

Gender stereotypes

Gender stereotyping begins at birth, and means that boy and girl babies are treated differently. Boy babies are believed to be more vigorous and to kick more energetically, so even while the baby is inside the mother she may conclude that it must be a boy because it moves a great deal. A group of parents were asked to rate their newborn babies, all of whom were about the same weight and length, and healthy and vigorous, in terms of eighteen traits. The parents described girls as soft, fine featured, small, weak, and delicate, whereas boys were described as firm, large featured, well co-ordinated, alert, strong, and tough.[3]

In the 'Baby X' experiment, a 3-month-old baby wearing yellow was handed to students. Some were told that it was a girl, others a boy. They played with the baby in very different ways according to what they believed to be its gender.[4] In another experiment students were shown a videotape of a 9-month-old with playthings. They were asked to interpret the baby's emotions. Half the students were told it was a boy, the other half, a girl. The 'boy' was described as showing more pleasure and greater anger, whereas the girl was described as being afraid.[5]

In many cultures boys are given more food than girls. Research in Italy reveals that girls are suckled on average for twenty-five minutes, boys for forty-five minutes. Mothers wean girls three months earlier than boys.

Fathers often flirt with baby girls, while they treat sons as tough, enjoy rough and tumble play with them, and—at least potentially—see them as comrades, and even as fellow conspirators against the mother's wishes.

Feeding behaviour

The assumptions that we make about a baby play a large part in moulding that child's character. For just as in educational experiments some children in school perform better when teachers are informed that they are exceptionally bright (although, in fact, they are of average ability), so parents' fixed ideas about a baby are one of the most important elements in shaping the child's personality.[6]

Through the first six or nine months of a baby's life feeding lies at the centre of this. The way a baby feeds, what happens after a feed is given, and the baby's behaviour in the space between feeds, is at the heart of the complex feelings that mothers have about their babies.

In many ways they are assessed as being 'easy' or 'difficult' by their feeding behaviour. In the first months nothing rouses such strong emotions. This is because the baby's sleep–wake cycle is tied to it.

A baby only sleeps comfortably with a tummy that feels comfortably full and when she is not under attack by the raging tigers of hunger or colic. It would not matter if babies who were not sleeping lay and cooed and played with their fingers. But they have no idea how to soothe themselves until they are about 3 months old. Even when they get the knack, they do so for only a short time, and some never seem to discover the delights of solitude. They wake and howl, in desperate need for milk, solace, and human companionship. They gulp down milk, and some fight for it, struggling even as they gulp. Then their heads droop, eyes close—but before you can tiptoe away they are awake and howling again.

A mother who realizes that the milk she has given her baby has caused pain feels pity and helplessness, but she may also feel that she has a horrible, screaming, petty tyrant in her arms, who is accusing her of being a bad mother.

'She has a sixth sense. She is fast asleep and I get to the door and she starts to wake up again.'

If this happens, you may worry that you are rearing a child who will go on behaving in this uncontrolled, angry way—perhaps until adulthood. But research evidence suggests that a crying baby who is held close and cuddled is more likely by the end of the first year to become a secure, confident child who will play independently than one who is left to cry it out alone, and who is not comforted when she cries, whatever the reason for that crying appears to be.[7]

Whenever a baby is restless and fretful, other people are anxious to give advice and tell you what you are doing wrong. This usually makes you feel worse. If they interfere like this, you may feel a rush of protectiveness for the baby whom you hated only a moment before. As you pick her up for the twentieth time and she plugs on to your breast again, you feel allied together against a hostile world.

The second baby

By the time you have a second or third child you are much more relaxed, knowing that nothing catastrophic happens if you do not jump up at a baby's first cry, or if you keep your 5-month-old waiting a few minutes for a feed because, as you explain to him, you want to finish the ironing first. You know that babies do not *have* to be bathed every day. You are content to clothe them in hand-me-downs in place of the crisp gingham suits that your first baby wore.

Second-time mothers can afford to be slightly indulgent about the anxieties and alarms of first-time mothers: the time when the baby rolled off the bed, or scratched her ear and drew blood which you thought could be a brain haemorrhage, the first bruise or cut in the baby's delicate skin—and it was your fault it happened—the regurgitated milk which seemed at the time to be projectile vomiting, and the fright you had when you picked him up from his crib to discover him damp with sweat and fever. You and your baby are both survivors. A certain confidence comes with that. You realize that there is not one right way to bring up a baby—rather many different ways, and most work well.

You may ask yourself if this child is really easier than the first because he is a friendlier, more manageable, happier baby, or whether it is just that you are a more experienced, self-assured, and certainly more relaxed mother. Both may be true. There is no certain answer, because you and the baby are like the pod and the pea, the shell and the nut—so close-clasped that it is difficult to stand back and make any objective analysis of a relationship which, just as with the first baby, is growing and changing all the time.

A baby with a disability

It is hardest to make a link between the fantasies you had about your baby inside you and the one who is really yours when a baby has disabilities which affect both your own perception of the child as a whole person, and as a baby whom other people can respond to with pleasure.

Many pregnant women are assailed by fear that their baby will not be normal. It is one of the recurrent dreams of pregnancy, that you cannot create in the depths of your own body a baby who is perfect. 'The perfect child exceeds expectations. The imperfect child is not wholly unexpected.'[8]

There is shock, yes. But there is often a sense, too, that you have known this baby all along. This is your baby who developed inside you, and, in spite of handicap, the child belongs to you.

'I'm going to give this baby all the love I've got.'

For many women the difficult process then begins of coming to terms with fantasies about their own unworthiness in giving birth to a baby who has special needs, whether this is because he is frail and pre-term or because of some inherited disability or acquired illness. A stranger leans over the carry-cot about to coo at the baby, and you are aware of the tightening of her shoulders as she sees the large port-wine stain, the cleft lip, or that the baby has the slanting eyes and broad, flat face typical of Down's syndrome.

If the baby's condition is teratogenic — that is, if it developed as a result of conditions in the uterus — women especially blame themselves. They often feel abnormal and reproductively worthless. They search their memories, trying to think what they did wrong. Was it the slight fever over the weekend when I was about two months pregnant? Or the pain-killers I took for a headache? Or the party we went to when I drank rather too much? Or the stress I was under when Dad died? None of these things is likely to have produced disability. But we all struggle to find a cause, to pin-point it, and the result is that, just when a woman is faced with what may be one of the biggest challenges in her life — coping with a child who has disabilities — she tends to be overwhelmed by guilt. To have a continual sense of guilt is one of the biggest disabilities of all.

'I felt unclean inside. I had carried a baby who was handicapped even before I knew I was pregnant.'

[The mother of a baby with spina bifida]

A woman with a cerebral palsy baby often feels terribly guilty since she believes that the baby must have been short of oxygen because of something she did or did not do in labour. She may have made a birth plan in which she said she wished to give birth naturally, not to have electronic fetal monitoring, and to be free to move about. Cerebral palsy is rarely caused by oxygen deprivation during birth. Research in Australia reveals that only about 8 per cent of these babies are damaged during labour.[9] The damage is more likely to have occurred during

'He said she was brain-damaged. It went over my head — because I was so shocked.'

pregnancy. Sometimes doctors say nothing that absolves a woman from her terrible burden of guilt. They often do not tell her that research in Britain and in Dublin has shown that electronic fetal monitoring does not prevent cerebral palsy. Nor do any other of the high-tech interventions that have come into use since the 1970s. Though obstetric interventions have increased in variety and number, rates of cerebral palsy, instead of going down, have actually increased.

To be a mother is to bear another's pain in a way that you have never done before. When a baby suffers a chronic illness or has a disability, you live with that pain each day, and feel responsible for it.

The parents of a baby with a disability may spend much of the first year of the child's life consulting experts, and have frequent hospital visits as clinicians consider if they can help medically or surgically. The baby may be admitted for painful tests and assessments. Parents may have to face agonizing decisions about what is to be done.

It is often difficult to find out exactly what is happening and what the future will hold for your child. A mother often feels in limbo. Even when full and frank information is available, she may be unable to take it in, and need to hear it explained several times. Many paediatricians have chosen their work because they enjoy children and relate well to parents. In the team working with you there may be counsellors, social workers, and psychologists who are there to ensure that you are kept fully informed and that you have a part in all decision-making.

A woman whose baby had a metabolic illness which entailed being in hospital said, 'I can do all the day-feeding and bathing, and give Emily plenty of cuddles. Nobody breathes down my neck or mutters,

191

"She'll spoil her."' She felt confident to handle Emily's illness because she could stay in hospital with her baby, and was treated as the primary person responsible for her care. It is complicated to organize this when you have other children, of course, and you need reliable back-up help with them if you are to devote yourself to caring for your baby in hospital.

It is very difficult for women who, however confident and capable they were before the baby's birth, are made to feel that experts are the only ones able to care for and make decisions about the baby. As a result, they experience a learned helplessness. A GP who sat in on the clinics of doctors who specialized in the treatment of physically disabled children witnessed consultations like this:

'**Parent:** "I've got really depressed about this, doctor." (Clinician leafs through notes.)

Parent (louder): "I really have got very depressed about this, doctor." (Clinician continues to leaf through notes.)

Parent turns to husband: "In fact, I've got so depressed my doctor's put me on antidepressants, hasn't he, Dave?"

Clinician (after long interval): "Well, I'm afraid that the hospital won't allow me to guarantee that I personally will do the operation although I usually do." '[10]

You may find that the doctors you meet are never evasive and unapproachable like this. But it is wise to anticipate that you will encounter at least one who does not treat you as an equal, and rehearse in advance what you would want to say and do. Role-play with someone acting the part of the doctor is a useful tool to prepare for such encounters, and the stories that other parents of handicapped children tell may be able to help you work out how these difficult meetings may be conducted.

Talented doctors who are authorities in their field, and who may be brilliant surgeons, are not always good at human relations. They may not understand the anxiety of parents, and the practical difficulties of having a child with a severe disability. So you need to be assertive, to be pleasantly firm, repeating questions and requests to which you do not get satisfactory answers, and insist on being given reasonable time to discuss issues that concern you.

'I'd felt very isolated till then. It was such a relief meeting with these mothers and their babies.'

Linking up with other parents with babies who have the same condition can be a great help. In order to make sensible choices, and to plan ahead, you need masses of information, and to find out how other families cope. Self-help organizations often act as pressure groups to achieve appropriate care, equipment, and funding for children from the social services and government agencies. Your paediatrician can often introduce you to other mothers with babies like yours and tell you about such local groups. A list of self-help organizations is at the end of the book. You do not have to try and weather the storm alone.

The HIV-positive mother

The rate of HIV infection is increasing more rapidly among women and children than in any other sector of the population. Transmission to a baby usually occurs through the placenta. A woman who has learnt that she is HIV positive has especially complicated feelings, not only about her child, but often about her partner, too, and about her own future. There is also the constant dread that HIV may erupt into full-blown AIDS at any moment, that she will be unable to look after her baby because of AIDS-related diseases, and that she herself will die.

Around five HIV-positive mothers in every six will not have passed on the HIV virus to their babies. So there is a good chance that a baby will be healthy, but a woman cannot know this for certain until the child is 18 months old, because at birth a baby has maternal antibodies to HIV, and these remain present in the bloodstream until 10–18 months.

Any woman who lives in a country where bottle-feeding is safe because there is clean water, refrigeration, and regular supplies of formula which she can afford should probably decide against

breastfeeding. It is one of the ways in which the HIV virus can be transmitted, though this may rarely happen. It is very different for a woman who does not live in conditions in which bottle-feeding is safe. The risk to the baby of not breastfeeding is then higher than the risk of transmitting the virus.[11] There is also some evidence that, if a baby is already HIV positive, breastfeeding may provide partial protection against development of disease.

A mother who is bottle-feeding can hold her baby closely almost as she would when breastfeeding. An HIV-positive mother can kiss, stroke, and cuddle her baby, and give her child the fullness of love in the space of life they have together, however brief that may prove to be. Faced with the possibility of death, life becomes extra precious.

If you are HIV positive there are practical arrangements you can make which would ease some of the anxieties about what is going to happen to your baby. You can plan ahead with loved relatives or friends who will commit themselves to take responsibility for your child should you die. You can make sure that your baby gets to know and feels secure with this other mummy and daddy. There are now organizations in some countries which will put an HIV-positive mother in touch with potential foster and adoptive parents, who become part of the baby's life and are friends, and are ready to welcome a child into their own home if the mother becomes too ill to cope, or if she dies.

There is a terrible fear of AIDS, and anyone known to be HIV positive is often made to feel like a pariah, as if to touch someone could communicate the illness, whereas it is spread only by exchange of body fluids. Yet the AIDS epidemic is building bonds of love and caring through 'buddy schemes' and through the foster-mothering of HIV-positive and AIDS babies.

When a baby dies

First comes denial: 'It can't be. It isn't true.' You are numb. Then, with the realization that it is so, 'Why me? What have I done to deserve this? Why doesn't this happen to all those other mothers with their babies?' You may feel guilty for all the things you have done wrong, perhaps for not having loved enough, for not having noticed your baby's condition sooner, for not taking precautions that were possible. You blame yourself. It seems incredible that your baby is dying while other people continue their everyday lives, unaffected. You look out from your loneliness and suffering and see ordinary things happening. It is as if those people are in a different world. For, at its most intense, grief is imprisoning. There is no way of communicating with others. Yet at this time you need arms to hold you, someone who loves you to enfold you, even when you are so cold inside that you can no longer feel that the love is there.

Then you look for someone to blame: doctors, your partner, yourself, someone else. This is the beginning of bringing the pain outside you and into the open. It is part of grieving. But it disrupts human relationships, especially those with people who are closest to you. The death of a baby — even having a pre-term baby in intensive care — instead of bringing a couple closer together often has a disastrous effect on their relationship.[12] The divorce rate is high among these couples.

A bereaved father often lacks any emotional support or opportunity to express his pain. He feels treated as an appendage to the suffering woman. A doctor father whose 1-year-old son died writes, 'The sisterhood that was ready to help my wife was not matched by a brotherhood that was ready to help me.' Enquiries as to how he felt were usually made in corridors or other public places, like the one from a colleague who remarked that he was glad to see that he was 'over that little episode'. 'Support from men', this father observes, 'seems to be available only through a haze of alcohol.'[13]

If you know that your baby may die, it helps either to be with her if she is in hospital, or to have her at home so that she can die in peace, without all the catheters, electronic equipment, and other paraphernalia of the intensive-care unit. If you are in hospital and the time comes when it is clear that the baby is dying, it will help if you have discussed this beforehand with the doctors, so that your baby can be put in your arms and you can cuddle and talk to her, giving her all your love, as she dies. Your baby has made the journey through birth, and you were with her then. Now you can be with your baby on this other journey out of life.

One mother who gave birth to a baby with anencephaly (with little or no brain) cared for him at home until he died. She said, 'He loved his skin being stroked and would smile whenever someone bent over him or spoke to him. He would also follow the person with his eyes. Because we knew that we wouldn't have him for long, we gave him as much love as we could, and we have memories that we will treasure.'

A study by a woman paediatrician who gives women the choice of caring for their dying babies at home or in hospital reveals that the babies at home live longer than those in hospital, and that the parents of those whose babies stayed in hospital were sadder on looking back at their experiences, and thought that their baby's life had been of poor quality. Those who cared for their babies at home in their terminal illness felt more positively about their child's life. She writes, 'When expectation of life is reduced to days, weeks, or months, it becomes more rather than less important to give the parents and child time together. Terminal care, even for babies, should include care for the whole person not merely for the physical state.'[14]

If you have other children, let them share in the grieving and express it in their own ways. Many adults look back on a death that occurred in the family during their own childhood feeling that they were shut out of it. They often still find it difficult to come to terms with the loss of someone they love because they were marginalized and isolated. While adults grieved openly, children were not supposed to understand or to feel anything. Sometimes they were simply told that a sister had gone on a long journey, was 'with Jesus', 'in heaven', or 'asleep'. As a result,

they were afraid that God or Jesus would snatch them away, that if they let themselves go to sleep they might never wake up, and that if their mother or father went on a journey, they might not come back.[15]

Sudden Infant Death

Death from SIDS—the sudden infant death syndrome—or, more simply, cot death, is one for which no parent can be emotionally prepared. SIDS is the largest single cause of death in babies older than 2 weeks in the first year of life. One in five hundred babies dies like this quietly and unexpectedly. If a baby is sick and gradually fades away, or a tiny, pre-term baby lies for days or weeks gasping for breath, there is opportunity for everyone to adjust to the idea of that child's death. SIDS is more like a traffic accident. Here is an apparently healthy baby struck down without a sound. Then the body has to be formally identified and statements must be made to the police. It is the *shock* of bereavement which is an overwhelming fact when you lose a baby like this.

Since official advice in the UK has been to place babies sleeping on their backs, or on their sides with a rolled towel to prevent them turning face down, to breastfeed exclusively for the first six months, to ensure that babies do not overheat, and never to smoke in a room where a baby is, deaths from SIDS have been halved.

Yet sudden infant death is still mysterious. This is why mothers are often blamed—for ignoring signs of a cold, for letting the baby get overheated or chilled, for having a baby sleep in the same bed. Sometimes they are even accused of deliberately suffocating their babies. Occasionally an older child, trying to come to terms with the loss of a baby brother or sister and angry that the mother did not keep the baby alive, turns a knife in the wound, as did a 3-year-old who asked, 'Why didn't you look after our baby? Why did you let him die?'

Mothers blame themselves for not noticing, for not being right there with the baby. They feel terribly shut out because death occurred without their awareness. Perhaps they were watching TV, sleeping peacefully, or talking on the phone. A doctor whose 10-week-old son was dead when she went to pick him up from his cot for the early evening feed writes bitterly about the way in which professionals told her, over and over again, not to feel guilty: 'It is about as effective as telling a child who has broken a leg not to think about it, while constantly reminding him of his injury by saying, "Now, your leg doesn't really hurt, does it?"' She comments on how friends avoided her, even crossing the road to escape from having to speak. Others repeatedly asked, 'Are you getting over it?'—implying that the disaster was no more serious than a minor ailment, like a cold.

When a woman goes out, people ask, 'Where's the baby today then?' She needs someone with her who can help her have the strength to answer that question. Otherwise she may not be able to face going out at all. She needs day-to-day practical support, and in the depths of her grief she may need help completing even the simplest household tasks.

Parents whose babies have died this way often get together to support, console, and help each other to go on living. Here are people who understand because they have been through the same nightmare that proved to be reality. You can find addresses of organizations which will let you know about local groups at the end of the book.

Men often do not want to join such groups, as they are afraid they will give way to grief and appear weak in front of strangers. Their way of coping with grieving—like some women's—may be to plunge themselves into work or some other activity that keeps them busy. No two individuals grieve in exactly the same way.

The emotions a mother has about her baby—a baby who is well and happy, one who is in pain or ill, a baby who has died, too—are among the strongest feelings any human being can ever have. Intense feelings experienced in the past are not merely memories. After a long passage of years she can still feel the physical impact of the most powerful of these emotions: the rush of warm milk to her breasts as her baby cries, the knot in her stomach as she rushes to see if the baby has come to harm, the flush of pleasure in skin touching skin as she holds the baby in her arms, and her longing for her baby when they were forcibly separated.

Being a mother is not just a matter of having a baby to care for, taking on new tasks and responsibilities, and juggling your time in complicated ways. To become a mother is to be shaped by strong emotions which carve into your personality and determine how you see the world, and your relationships with other people, for the rest of your life.

BECOMING A FATHER

'My job is
demanding. I
contribute to the
family through
my work. There
are a lot of times
when I think my
wife ought to
deal with the
kids, because I
am tired.'

A woman usually becomes a mother because she has given birth. The biological process of parturition identifies her as a mother. A man becomes a father not because of a biological act — the ejaculation of semen —but because he acknowledges paternal responsibility for the baby. It is an act of awareness and of will, rather than biology. For some men there is a long emotional journey before they really feel themselves to be fathers.

As with marriage, and the stag-party on the eve of the wedding, the birth of a baby may be treated as an occasion for a drink all round with 'the boys'. The new father is expected to celebrate with other men and so reinforce male bonding.

Because traditionally the father is expected to be out at work, it is assumed that mothers will deal with the day-to-day care of the baby. The father can help, and is praised when he does so. But it is not for him a duty—rather a playing with different aspects of being a male in what is essentially female territory.

If a father is seen caring for a baby on his own—carrying the baby in a sling against his chest as he shops at the supermarket, for example, or wheeling a pram in the park—he may be perceived as slightly deviant. Although he may be praised by women for attempting tasks which are inconsistent with the dominant male role, he is often treated with some suspicion, too.

Many couples are now questioning the conventional role of the father. They are exploring ways of sharing parenthood. But they confront obstacles erected by a society which organizes work so that men are seen as providers, rather than participants in family life, and are expected to go home for leisure and relaxation, rather than to take on the work of being fully involved fathers. Though in Sweden fathers can have eighteen months of paternity leave, and have a statutory right to time off to be with a sick child, in most countries fatherhood is not supposed to interfere with work. Men often take on more commitments outside the home after the birth of the baby than they had before, because of the extra financial responsibilities.

It is difficult for men to be more involved with their babies, too, when the only role models they have may be those of their own fathers, who usually left baby care to their wives, whose only interaction with the child was as stimulating and playful outsiders or as disciplinarians, and who often found it difficult to express their emotions.

'I'm sure my father loved me, but he couldn't show it.'

Fathers in other cultures

In many traditional societies the transition to fatherhood is patterned by ritual emphasizing the father's bond with the baby. A man's responsibilities to his wife and child are stressed by ceremonial acts of commitment. The West lacks ceremonies like this.

The father is often the one who has to protect the baby from unseen evil influences which could threaten the child's life, and does so by observing taboos after birth. In North America the Yurok father must keep strict food taboos, and his diet is very limited until the dangerous transitional period is over.

In some cultures the father has a duty to nourish the baby's soul, just as the mother nourishes the child's body with milk. In Ghana a father who does not accept his spiritual responsibilities is likely to be blamed if his baby becomes ill or dies. In South Africa, too, the father must make sacrifices to the ancestor gods on the baby's behalf. If a Hopi baby dies, it is thought to be because the parents have quarrelled or the father was unfaithful. Everyone realizes that babies may catch a disease, but they would not do so if the home was happy.

Among the Mbuti pygmies it is the father's knife or arrowhead that cuts the umbilical cord. After the birth a man usually stays at home for up to two months, proudly carrying the baby around whenever he gets the chance.[1] This happens because there, as in many cultures, the father, together with his wife, is in a state of ritual pollution following childbirth. He cannot work outside the home, hunt, fish, or tend his garden.

The Manus father cares for the displaced older child when a new baby is born. Though this happens with fathers in the West, too, it is often difficult for them because they have commitments in the workplace, which may be distant from the home, and these are not modified just because a baby has been born. The Manus father, however, can concentrate on this task because he must be separated ritually from the other men with whom he usually works. As a result a strong link is forged between the older child and the father.[2]

There are wide variations in the way that fathers behave in traditional societies. But anthropologists have obviously been surprised at just how gentle and caring as fathers men can be in some societies in which no one has read any childcare books. Men in the West are often denied opportunities to be close to their babies, and to enjoy fatherhood.

Making the transition to fatherhood

It helps if you discuss together the kind of mother and father you would like to be. You can ask yourselves if you want to be the same kind of parents as your own mother and father. A man often sees that his own father missed out on the tender, intimate aspects of a relationship with a baby, and that he never learnt how to give the ordinary, everyday care such as changing nappies that babies need.

The transition to fatherhood is easier when a man can take time off to be with his partner and baby in what I call a 'Babymoon'.[3] A couple lay in food and other necessities, lock the door, and go to bed with their baby for a few days. Many couples have written to me saying that, though it was difficult to organize, it was well worth doing, and that this time together was precious to them. You can make this part of your birth plan, letting the midwife, grandparents, and close friends and family know in advance that you are doing it. One reason why it is important is that the man, too, needs a chance to get to know the baby. He needs to be able to do this at least intermittently in the months following, as well, because the baby is developing and changing every week.

Getting to know a baby is not just a matter of holding a clean, smiling, fed one, but a baby who needs changing, who is crying, who will not go to sleep, and who has a runny nose and a fever. It means knowing how to soothe and comfort as well as how to excite and delight, how to make hurt places better, how to tap into a baby's mood and find a rhythm and pace which is right for her at that time. And it entails doing all the mundane, repetitive tasks connected with babies, like wiping spills, tidying rooms, and clearing up the chaos that they create in the home.

Men often find this daunting. They feel they might be no good at these jobs. They are aware of other things that need doing urgently,

other priorities. When you feel you are not in control, and that what you are doing is part of someone else's scenario, the temptation is to half-do things and leave the person you think is in real control to complete the work. Sometimes men demand detailed instructions of such complexity that it is quicker to do a job yourself.

Roberta Israeloff,[4] writing about the transition to parenthood and her relationship with her husband David, describes a scene in which she asks him to change the baby. He declines because he says, 'You know Ben so much better than I do.' 'This knowledge, I reminded David, wasn't mystically implanted with me, but acquired through long, hard work.' He then intellectualizes the task and seems to her to make very heavy weather of it. He watches her change Ben's nappy and takes notes—'twenty-one steps'.

Women often feel they should be handling their men better. But it is not a personal defect—rather a sign of how a society organized largely by and for men, sees women's work as mothers as second-rate, tedious, and far less important than men's work.

A baby in the home entails extra housework. It is not only a question of caring for the child. When the first baby is born to a couple

who previously shared cleaning and cooking it usually heralds the introduction of a very different relationship. They revert to the old male–female division of labour. This suits some couples well. The woman does the housework and childcare, while the man helps occasionally with dish-washing and shopping, though 'shopping' may mean driving her to the supermarket and letting her get on with it. For many men house-cleaning, washing clothes and ironing are still out of the question. In his study of the impact of parenthood on men Charlie Lewis shows that fathers are usually assistants, not partners, and often rather unreliable ones. When a hundred men were asked how much they contributed to making their babies' meals once they were having solids, six did so regularly, twenty-eight did so more than once a week, the rest hardly ever. Forty had rarely or never changed a nappy, fifty-three had never cared for the baby by themselves, and sixty-two had never, or rarely, given the baby a bath. Even if the mother works outside the home, 37 per cent of these fathers did not change even one nappy a day.[5]

'There's about half an hour when there's just Oliver and me, before Dawn gets up. I call this our "special time".'

The traditional male role restricts men to being mediators between the outside world and the mother and baby. So women are often very surprised when their men get involved, show that they care, and are capable of being tender, sensitive, and skilled in looking after the baby. It often comes as a shock that a male partner can do this at all. A woman begins to see new aspects of his personality. It is then a growing point in a relationship, which acquires new depths of intimacy as the man expresses his love through the baby.

Fathers often do things in different ways from mothers. Babies can cope with this. A man does not have to bath a baby in exactly the same way as his partner, provided his way works and is safe. If he is watched

all the time he may be self-conscious and clumsy because his performance is being judged. He needs time alone with the baby to find out by trial and error what works best.

Powerful emotions

'I was in a daze. I couldn't take it in. I felt completely numb.'

'I sold my motor-bike and bought a car. I was a bit of a tearaway. Being a father makes you grow up.'

Becoming a father often brings a flood of emotions for which a man is unprepared. The first is simply shock. He cannot absorb all that is happening, the bustle of activity, his own emotions about the birth, and, above all, the reality of the baby and his new status as a father. Suddenly the whole world seems different. Ordinary landmarks have shifted. Relationships have changed irrevocably. Everything is topsy-turvy. He has lost control.

A man who feels like this may retreat from the scene of action. He withdraws because he needs time to assimilate everything, and to come to terms with his conflicting emotions.

Yet the birth of a first child is also the point at which a man at last feels grown-up. He now sees himself as an adult who has the right to step into his father's shoes.

This is not the case in all societies. In cultures that have been rooted in slavery, for example, a man is unlikely to accept responsibility for the first child he fathers. He escapes from commitment, leaving the woman with the baby. She cares for it with the help of her mother, or hands it over to her mother to rear because she must go out to work to support the grandmother and the baby. In the Caribbean the time preceding or just after the birth of a child is often that when a male consort is most likely to 'run'. The woman tries to make him 'response' for the child with a regular payment, but often fails. Only when a man is willing to 'response' for a child he has fathered does he begin to settle down. That is his transition to adulthood.[6]

A man's new feeling of maturity may bring with it flashes of regret for a lost youth, grieving for loss of the self, and concern about, as one man put it, becoming 'middle-aged, middle-class, with money in the bank', and re-enacting what he sees as his own father's boring, unachieving life.

But with this there is the positive sense that he can shoulder responsibility, be relied on to give the support that his partner and child need, and is a man among other men. It is similar to the pride men feel in a traditional East African society on being initiated into the warrior-age set.

When a man spends time caring for the baby, and the baby gives some indication that she knows him—stops crying, listens to his voice, turns her head towards him, gazes into his eyes, or reaches out with eager arms as he comes through the door—this sense of personal achievement and maturity is reinforced.

'I like knowing that he depends on me, trusts me. That's made me more mature.'

Feeling trapped

On the other hand, a man is often anxious about losing his freedom. A couple may have jogged along, each doing his or her own thing, with few boundaries or restraints in their relationship. There was little need to plan ahead or to programme their lives. They could enjoy each other without interruption, have fun, do things on the spur of the moment, and part to go in opposite directions when it was more convenient. They could even decide to split up without having to consider the effect on anyone else.

'I get irritated. The baby always has to be seen to first. There's no spontaneity any more.'

Now a baby is here, and there is a new person to consider; not just *any* person, but a vulnerable human being who depends on her parents for being fed, protected from danger, and her very survival—one whom they dare not forget for a moment.

Because the baby has grown inside the woman's body, and in the last months of pregnancy has made its presence felt with energetic insistency, the mother has been well prepared over a nine-month time span. So she is more likely than the man to understand that a baby takes over your life and changes it.

A prospective father often hopes to continue much as before. Of course, he thinks, they will have to organize themselves with the baby in mind. He realizes that babies need to be looked after. He may put a lot of energy into making a nursery that looks like a pretty container in which he thinks that they can place the baby, and then close the door. In constructing the nursery, couples sometimes seem to be expressing a hope that it will be possible to box in the baby so that it does not disrupt their lives.

After the birth, it is obvious that the baby has no defined territory, but is *everywhere*. The baby and baby things seem to ooze everywhere in physical space. There is no corner of a home where a man may not encounter a rattle, small garments drying, a nappy (clean or soiled), a pram or stroller, a bootee, a shawl.

More threatening still is the way in which the baby's existence takes over his partner's thinking, and how he cannot make plans without being pulled back to focus on what the baby needs, how this will affect the baby, and what they will do with the baby. As a result, he may feel resentment, anger, and then guilt at his resentment and anger.

Envy

'I felt redundant and alone.'

'Sometimes I can quiet him when she can't because she's so stressed.'

Freud believed that all little girls want a penis, and grow up feeling wounded because they do not possess one. Mothers, however, know that little boys often feel deprived when they are told that they cannot grow babies inside them, will never be able to give birth, and cannot breastfeed.

A man may envy a woman's reproductive power and the way in which she can nurture with her body. During pregnancy he sees her swell like a ripe fruit, the outward sign that her uterus is invisibly nurturing the developing baby. If he is present at the birth, he witnesses an astonishing energy, and her strength and courage. He watches as she cradles her baby in her arms, all her attention centred on the bright eyes, the soft hair, and the firm plumpness of the newborn. Then she puts her baby to the breast and feeds, as if by magic, with her body.

A man may be jealous of the woman's special intimate relationship with her baby. He feels no longer wanted, outcast from intimacy, and deprived of the mothering that formed an important part of the way in which they loved each other before the arrival of the baby. Sometimes he feels frustrated and angry. He may vie with his partner for the baby's attention.

Perhaps it is with such men in mind that an American firm has produced the Baby Bonder. This is a pair of simulated breasts filled with warm water which can be slung round a man's neck. It holds milk bottles so that he can feed the baby from soft, breast-like containers suspended over his chest. The marketing of such a product fails to recognize that a father's interaction with a baby does not have to mimic the mother's. The baby benefits from different relationships, each with its own special qualities. It is not a question of providing simulated latex breasts, but of giving a baby your time, responding to his needs, enjoying him, and offering unconditional love.

The mother and baby are sometimes described in the breastfeeding literature as 'the nursing couple'. This encapsulates how a man may see the relationship. Here is a new couple, in a deeply intimate relationship from which he is excluded. When he returns to work, has to get to the office on time, is expected to function effectively in a world which ignores the needs of families, he may feel even more shut out from a love relationship which is flourishing in his absence.

Many women who stay at home to care for the baby try to prepare a welcoming scene to which the man returns in the evening. They struggle to make time to get washed and dressed, to have a meal ready, the house tidy, and time to talk together. The woman's anxiety

'I used to hold him against my bare chest and talk to him, tell him that I was his Dad, and what a super kid he was. He'd go quiet and listen.'

'I used to hold him against my bare chest and talk to him, tell him that I was his Dad, and what a super kid he was. He'd go quiet and listen.'

The revelation of tenderness

'I was afraid to hold her. Rather like precious glass. I was frightened I'd damage her.'

mounts as breastfeeds, nappy changes, and crying spells pile up to interfere with these plans. The baby senses the tension, starts to fuss, and spends the whole evening crying.

There can be no clearer message to a man that his help is needed when he comes back to find a woman dropping from tiredness and a baby who is crying non-stop unless picked up, patted, soothed, rocked, walked with, and sung to.

This is when he can discover the range and depth of his nurturing ability. Far from being a threat to the couple's relationship, it may build a new bridge of understanding.

A new father, especially a man who has not held his baby immediately after birth, is often overwhelmed by a sense of the baby's frailty. He is anxious that he will do the wrong thing—drop or bruise him. He may feel that handling the baby is 'women's business'. He does not realize that the first-time mother, too, is anxious in exactly the same way, and fears that she may drop, drown, or smother her baby. He may think that his masculinity is an impenetrable barrier to knowledge about babies. Many men have been brought up to believe that a woman instinctively understands what to do with a baby.

This sense of incompetence is reinforced when he is given anxious instructions about how to hold the baby, when women smile condescendingly at his efforts, or when the baby starts to cry as he is put in his arms.

Any man who feels that other people have expertise which he does not possess is likely to retreat from baby care because he has no role to play, and feels useless and clumsy. In spite of advertisements showing hunky young men cuddling babies, frolicking with toddlers on the seashore, or sleeping with a contented baby lying peacefully against a hairy chest, the taboo on tenderness still forms one of the main themes in the rearing of boys and in men's images of themselves. It leads some men to escape from caring for their babies because they fear their own power to damage and destroy.

Paradoxically, sometimes when birth is complicated or there are medical problems with the baby, a man slips more easily into a positive role as carer. When a baby has been born by Caesarean section, for example, and he holds his child while the woman is still unable to cuddle him because she is under general anaesthesia, or cannot move her arm because it is fixed to an intravenous drip, he may make that transition to tenderness more smoothly than when the baby goes straight to the woman's arms.

Equally, when a baby is sent to the intensive-care nursery, and he is

the one who visits and holds him, because the mother has not yet had the help she needs to go to see her baby, he may find it easier to express tenderness, and to feel that the baby belongs to him. Perhaps this is partly because he feels that he is in charge.

The poet Vernon Scammell tells how he went to the hospital nursery to meet his newborn son who had a severe abnormality of the central nervous system. The child had a meningocele on the back of his head (a protrusion through the skull of membranes covering the brain, forming a cyst filled with cerebrospinal fluid). Images had been invading his mind of 'human monsters'. He was afraid he would make a fool of himself and faint when he saw the baby. Instead, 'I felt a surge of relief that was instantly followed by a drench of pure joy and wonder at the beauty of the child. I have never seen anything so beautiful. He lay on one side with his eyes closed, and the tiny features looked at once exquisitely carved yet tenderly human like the head of one of those babies you see in fifteenth-century Flemish paintings.' He describes the love that flooded through him. Then he went to the postnatal ward and his wife introduced him to the other twin, a healthy boy who was lying beside her. He glanced at him, but he was just 'an ordinary baby.'[7]

Men undervalue the love they can give and the compassion and sensitivity of which they are capable. 'Boys don't cry . . .' 'Don't be a sissie.' They need an opportunity to realize that their tenderness is acknowledged and validated by others. This often only happens when the woman is ill, cannot cope, or is occupied with other things. Many men never discover their own tenderness, so never develop the skills of nurturing.

Engrossed in the baby

A new father often discovers that the baby pulls his attention like a magnet. Though there are men who stay emotionally detached, many are surprised by the strength of this preoccupation with the baby. Some never experience it, because it is possible only when a man makes time in his life for the baby, and can let this emotional awakening take place without trying to stifle or escape from it. It may be important for a father to have this powerful involvement if a couple are to survive together the stresses of the first postnatal years, when their relationship is challenged as never before.

Martin Greenberg, a psychiatrist who also draws on his own experience as a father, describes different elements in the bond that links an involved father with his baby.[8]

'I look at her and think, "She's mine. I made her. I did that. I'm a father."'

The baby is visually appealing. He feels that his child is more attractive than other babies.

He enjoys holding and cuddling the baby. Fathers often comment on the smoothness and softness of the baby's skin, 'like a peach' or 'velvety'.

He can describe in minute detail the baby's characteristics, her eyes, chin, nose, ears, hands, feet, and hair. His baby is distinctive and memorable, unlike other people's babies.

He is astonished by the baby's perfection in miniature.

He feels drawn to the baby, wants to see and touch his child, and to check that she is all right.

He is elated. Men describe how they feel 'stoned,' 'on cloud nine'. His self-esteem is enhanced. He feels bigger, stronger, more capable, more important.

The baby as a mirror

The discovery of his child can open up a man to discover new aspects of himself. 'It is as if the birth of the child leads to his own birth as a father as well as his maturation into a more complete human being.'[9]

Men are surprised by the strength of the feelings. 'The child is a mirror, repeatedly bringing the man face to face with his own emotions.'[10] The rage a baby expresses reflects his own anger. The child's longing for the comfort of the mother's breast expresses a

yearning he, too, feels. The fear and loneliness that overwhelm a baby who is not picked up and soothed expresses the panic of being outcast that he has also experienced.

The intensity of these emotions, most of all the love he receives from the baby, often comes as if it were an unexpected gift from the child.

He discovers that babies are fun, too. There is enormous pleasure to be found in inventing games to play together, tickling and producing laughter, and bringing toys and picture books that make her eyes go wide in wonder.

For an older man this is a rejuvenating experience, one which he may have missed out on in a previous relationship. Men who have second families often behave very differently with a new brood, and become for the first time fully participant fathers. It is hard for the wife of a first marriage, who may have struggled alone to bring up the children with a man who thought it was enough to provide financially for his family, and there was no need to be further involved, to see that her ex-husband has become, after all, a good father.

But it has its threatening side. For these emotions are not all positive. A man may be astonished at how much anger he feels at a baby who is being difficult or who cries inconsolably. He may be surprised at the concern he feels that his baby might not like him, and his sense of personal inadequacy when the baby wants her mother, not her father; surprised, too, at the fear that overwhelms him when the baby is ill, and the anxiety he feels about what life may hold for his child, and about the future of the world.

Building a special relationship

Fathers say that these are the things that help them create a special relationship with their babies.

Get up when the baby needs attention at night. Walk with her, soothe her, give her a bottle of expressed breastmilk or formula if your partner wants to sleep through occasionally.

Carry the baby in a front- or back-pack when you go for walks and clean the house. The baby enjoys the closeness and the swinging movement.

Sing and tell stories to your baby—nonsense rhymes, silly stories, anything. He will love the sound of your voice and be a rapt listener.

*'He'd wake in
the morning and
say, "Well, he
slept right
through then!"
Did he hell? I
was up five
times, and he
just snored
through it. I
couldn't help
feeling resentful.'*

Sleep with your baby, in a bed that is wide enough for all three, where the baby has his own space and does not get overheated. If your bed is not large enough, a big mattress on the floor may work well. (There is evidence, however, that if you smoke, this interferes with the baby's breathing, so it makes sense never to smoke in the baby's presence and to ensure that he sleeps in a smoke-free zone.)[11]

Become expert at changing, bathing, dressing, and undressing your baby.

Learn how to decode the meaning of your baby's cries. This comes with experience. You may be able to differentiate between the shrill cry of pain, the abrupt call for attention, the vigorous cry of hunger, and the almost musical cry of tiredness.

Realize that a baby is hard work. Most men think they do more housework, more regularly, than they do. Clear up and clean as you go along. This is not an optional extra. Don't merely help. Take responsibility. Then you both have more time to enjoy your baby.

*'Having a baby
has made me
think about
myself, what I
can give him,
and what I'm
doing with my
life.'*

Babies disrupt your life amazingly. It is difficult to believe that such a small human being can bring so much chaos, involve so much hard work, and produce such emotional turmoil for both parents. Babies shatter complacency. They reveal your identity as you never knew yourself before. They force you to see the world in a new way. They produce a fresh challenge every day. They provide stimulus and opportunity for men to change their lives and become human beings able to care, and to nurture.

CHANGING RELATIONSHIPS

A baby is born. Suddenly your first baby becomes an older sibling, mothers turn into grandmothers and fathers to grandfathers, sisters become aunts, brothers uncles, friendships form and old ones dissolve, and you are parents. There is little choice about it. The birth of a baby signals 'all change'.

Shifts in role and status as you become a mother entail changes in relationships, too. People see you as different. You see yourself and them in altered ways. And ways in which you behave towards each other are transformed, sometimes dramatically, sometimes subtly.

Only with people who are not aware that you have had a child are things likely to be the same. Even then, your altered self-perception and new focus of attention mean that you see them in a different light.

Some people totally ignore the fact that you have been through the amazing experience of birth, that you are now a mother, and your whole life has changed. You may find this irritating. Many women want to talk about their birth experience and the baby. When work colleagues and other people make polite remarks but are obviously bored by the subject, and treat you as if you have merely had a brief hospital stay, trivializing the birth as if it were equivalent to having your appendix removed, you may feel that they are rejecting an experience which is very important in your life, and that this is a way of dismissing you.

'They expected me to be the same as before, and went on talking office politics.'

Turning into 'Mum'

The company dinner was the first time we were out together without the baby. All they spoke to me about was the baby—and I was the personnel officer.'

The biggest switch in relationships comes with those who now see you exclusively in a maternal role. Sometimes it is as if your previous self has never existed. This has implications for what they expect of your thinking, level of intelligence, conversational interests, work, and main concerns.

The effect of this identity change probably has most impact on professional and business women.

Increasing numbers of women are delaying child-bearing until they are over 35. Many of them have careers. During the 1980s the birth-rate among women aged 35–9 in England and Wales rose by 44 per cent. In the United States it went up by 41 per cent and fell by 19 per cent among those in their early twenties. In the past many women over 35, and even over 40, had babies, but they were the last ones in large families, whereas now they are often first babies.

Within a few hours of giving birth someone is bound to call you 'Mum' or 'Mummy'. They may not even address you directly, but talk to the baby about his 'Mum'. You have suddenly become someone totally different. Magazines, newspapers, and TV advertisements will give you an idea of what you are meant to be. Images of the 'good mother' are all around — the one who sacrifices herself for her children, who mops the kitchen floor spotlessly clean, whose washing on the line is whiter than the woman's next door, who prepares nutritious meals for delightful kiddies, who hug her with joy when presented with their favourite food. Mum is there to put the right ointment on a scratch and the gentlest soap on a baby's delicate skin. Though we laugh at these images, they are pervasive in the culture, and derive from still older images of mothers baking bread, scrubbing floors, bottling preserves, and nursing the sick.

Mum is instinctive rather than cerebral. As well as cuddling babies, she likes wiping bottoms, blowing noses, clearing away messes, tackling all forms of dirt in order to protect her babies — and finds this deeply fulfilling. She has the satisfaction of having achieved what every woman wants.

Mums tend babies, putting food in at one end and clearing up what comes out of the other. They lug around a mass of paraphernalia that even the smallest child requires for its servicing. They often look more like beasts of burden than women.

A mum's clothing bears witness to her role. It tends to be streaked and stained with regurgitated milk, mashed prunes, cereal, and fruit juice. When she buys a new shirt, she tries to get something in roughly these colours, the battle fatigues of motherhood.

However busy she is, she ensures that her partner feels good about himself and that having babies does not in any way deprive him of attention. 'Every woman should make sure', a male doctor says in his book of advice to mothers, 'that the new member of the family does not mean that her husband has less of her love, time and affection.'[1] Many women struggle to do this, but discover that it is as if they have not one but two babies in the house who need looking after.

You and your partner

We have seen already that it can be difficult for men to adjust to parenthood. The cataclysm of changes occurs independently of gender, however. Even when a man is not afraid to enter the female world of love and personal commitment, when he enjoys the baby, is sensitive to and aware of the woman's needs, and takes his full share in parenting, there is a dramatic change of scene and tempo. With a lesbian couple, there is a similar scene change, bringing opportunities for growth, but also new challenges to the relationship. It is the same when a couple adopt a baby, too. This is not simply to do with the psycho-biological impact of motherhood, with the woman's endocrine system or with lactation. It is just as likely to occur when parents take over a baby who has been born to a surrogate mother. And it happens however well a couple have prepared for parenthood, and when they have read books and attended classes. What preparation can do, however, is to help them identify problems, communicate with each other better, and enjoy the good times more.

'I don't believe anyone can prepare you for parenthood. We had good preparation for the birth but it was a shambles afterwards.'

With the birth of a baby, profound changes take place in a couple's relationship. These may push them apart from each other and eventually destroy the relationship; but they also present opportunities for growth and maturation.

Settling down or breaking away?

Before you have a baby, you may have done little long-term planning. Once the baby has arrived there is no way you can avoid planning ahead. Even a trip to the shops entails working out whether the baby is likely to be asleep or awake, if she needs changing first, whether her clothing is suitable for the weather, and when she will need to be fed. There are major decisions to be made about where to live, jobs, income — which with the birth of a child may be seriously reduced, at least for a time — childcare and schooling, and intangible things such as shared and conflicting values, religion, and convictions about child-rearing. With the birth of a boy the issue of circumcision is hotly discussed by many couples, for example. Some African couples may have different views about female 'circumcision' (in reality not circumcision at all, but excision of part or all of the girl's clitoris and labia), and each may

219

also face conflicts with older family members. There are family allegiances and questions of ethnicity, social class, and even citizenship which may become matters of dispute, especially for couples of mixed race or religion and those of different nationalities. Unless it is taken for granted that one partner is going to be at home with the child while the other works outside, a couple also need to discuss the time that each can give to housework, the baby and earning an income.

Having to think ahead reshapes a couple's lives. A relationship that throve on novelty, surprise, and flexibility may not flourish when there has to be forward-planning and if there are social pressures to conform to a set pattern. Perhaps a couple's parents express their satisfaction with the new arrangements as the younger people 'settle down'. Sometimes this sets off alarm signals: 'Are we going to get like our parents?' For a young couple in a relationship that started off as part of a bold gesture of freedom and independence from parental control it may seem that it is turning into an almost identical printout of their own parents' marriage.

'He has no idea of how my day has been. He comes in and asks "What's for dinner?" He can't understand why I don't find time for things he thinks are important.'

'Where did yesterday go?'

Though the birth of a child sometimes widens the gulf between a man or woman and parents who disapprove of the relationship because the chosen partner is considered unsuitable, it may resign the older couples to the inevitable. This often happens with mixed-race couples, for example. Grandparents begin to take an interest in the baby, and a bridge of communication is formed. But once they become involved they may also communicate concern for the child and anxiety about his future, which can be very irritating.

On the other hand, when an older couple have been together for a while before having a baby, the scene may be very different. They may have an ordered pattern of existence, which is now reduced to chaos. If both are employed, they depend on this framework for efficiency at work and in running the home. When a woman has her first child in her late thirties, this smooth organization has often been necessary to

221

achieve career goals. She may depend on a similar time-and-motion system to juggle child and career in the future, too. The upheaval that a baby brings shocks her and destroys self-confidence. Days merge into nights, night into day, time is unstructured. 'How is it that I am still in a dressing gown at midday? How can we make an evening meal when there is nothing in the fridge because there's been no time to shop? How can I concentrate with the baby crying like that? How can I make that meeting on time? Is there a clean shirt? Did you call your mother … ring the plumber … check the car tyres … pay the phone bill?' It can seem as if you have lost control of your life and that the baby is wrecking your relationship.

Fresh focus　　There is a dramatic shift of focus when a baby is born, although it often does not occur equally for each partner. It switches from outside to inside the home, from career goals and relationships with colleagues at work to concern about and interest in the baby's development, and often to the building of new relationships with women who have babies of a similar age. The outcome for many women is a kind of 'islanding'. It is as if an ocean lies between the intimacy of the family unit and everything that is going on in the world outside, including former social and work contacts. It can be traversed, but the journey takes amazing effort and a deliberate shift of attention which it is difficult to make.

　　This islanding is not necessarily unpleasant and unsought after. Many couples revel in it, and are so involved in their nesting that they do not regret the loss of previous relationships and interests. It often happens only for the mother, however. The partner who is working outside comes back to the home at the end of the day and introduces a gust of the outside world which she welcomes, or which leaves her feeling totally cut-off. If the one who is employed is disengaged from everything that is going on at home, this split becomes a split in their relationship, which may grow wider as the mother becomes more child-centred and increasingly isolated. A woman may enjoy her desert-island retreat for a while, but be anxious that she will never make contact with the 'real' world again.

A new home　　Many couples move house shortly before or after a baby is born, often to a neighbourhood they do not know, distant from former friends, and they have to equip a new home and make it a running concern. The move may have been essential because they did not have room for a baby in their original home, or there were tenancy rules about not having children. There seem to be a thousand things that have to be done.

There are positive aspects to this, the excitement of working together and discussing choices, trying out colours and shapes of furniture and fittings, looking at pattern books, shopping—all the pleasures of 'nest-building', drawing a couple closer in shared activities. But it can be financially draining and, because it consumes time and energy, it introduces fresh stresses in the relationship of a couple who are already finding that a baby is enormously hard work. If the mother is loaded with the bulk of this responsibility, it is bound to contribute to the fatigue that she feels through that first year. Shortage of sleep, anxiety about the baby, and the emotional helter-skelter on which she is often caught, combine with nest-building to make her chronically exhausted.

Discipline and dependency: topics of dispute

Agreements or disagreements about child-rearing, spoken or unspoken, form the undertow of many discussions between couples from the time that a baby is about 6 months old, in conversations between mothers and their own mothers and partners' mothers, and with friends who have children of about the same age. Talking with parents and grandmothers, and watching them interact with their

223

babies and young children in many different countries, I have been impressed with how often two issues seem to dominate: discipline and freedom, and independence and dependency.

Mothers of 4-year-olds often say that they want them to 'fit in', to be well behaved and obedient, and not to 'show them up'.[2] Some see it as important not to inculcate blind obedience and want to explain things and reason with them. Others want instantaneous obedience. These concerns start to be important to parents in the first year of the baby's life, too. There may be conflicts between them, and with their own parents, about matters of discipline.

The age at which adults think children should exercise self-discipline varies in different cultures and between individuals. Traditionally in China a child was thought capable of knowing right from wrong when he or she could carry a bowl full of liquid without spilling it. Behaviourist psychologists and paediatricians of the 1920s and 1930s taught that mothers should discipline babies from birth, so that good behaviour became a conditioned reflex. Truby King and other paediatricians strongly believed that babies had to be trained to sleep when they should, not to cry, to take milk at set hours and for set periods, and that cuddle and play should be limited to a half hour of mothering at a regular time each day. More recently Spock, Bowlby, Brazelton, and Leach have emphasized the importance of flexibility, sensitivity, getting 'in tune' with a baby, respecting the child's own rhythms, and recognizing 'the child's status as an individual with rights and feelings that are worthy of respect'.[3]

Most mothers probably veer between these two child-rearing philosophies. They try to follow the second, and then, when they get panic-stricken because it seems that their baby does not fit any known human pattern, or because they are desperate to carve some space for themselves out of the unremitting twenty-four hours of child-centred care, they turn to the older method. One thing that can be said with certainty is that the realities of mothering do not allow philosophical consistency. A partner who is less involved in childcare may not realize this.

Another area of conflict is the degree of dependence or independence that can be expected of a child at different ages. In contemporary North America, Britain, and Australia, for example, the emphasis is upon getting through babyhood as quickly as possible and producing an independent child. In many other cultures, Indian and Mediterranean societies, for example, far less emphasis is put on independence, and the link to the mother is stressed not only for children, but for adults, too. Whereas an English middle-class mother

'I want my child to make choices, not just do things because I say so.'

'That baby's running rings round her. She picks him up the moment he whimpers. She's making a rod for her back.'

may turn to a dummy only as a last resort for a crying baby, in one small *pharmacia* in Italy I counted sixteen kinds of dummy on a shelf, together with clips to keep them permanently available to the baby. Outside in the piazza each baby wheeled by in a stroller had a dummy stuck in its mouth. In Spain children of 3 and 4 years old often suck dummies while shopping with their mothers.

British and American mothers tend to be embarrassed if a child is 'clingy', and pleased when a baby starts to reach out to other children and to socialize. In Britain, to say of a toddler that 'he's a mother's boy' is a criticism of the mother's success at child-rearing, while in Mediterranean countries it is taken as approval of the close bond between mother and child.

These are not only culture contrasts. Within the same culture partners often have different ideas about the extent to which their child should be independent, and there are also generational differences between parents and their own parents.

These moral concepts and assumptions are in place long before the baby is born, but may become an issue in the first twelve months of the baby's life, and continue as matters of dispute all the time that children are in the home, and often beyond.[4]

Where do we go from here?

Whatever your own scenario as a couple, it helps to talk about your personal beliefs and expectations together. Avoid accusations. You may be perfectly entitled to accuse your partner, but—though head-on conflict sometimes clears the air—it will not help you find solutions. Do not ascribe motives or interpret the meaning of the other person's behaviour. Say only, 'I feel …' and then be honest about how you feel. No one can deny your feelings, though they may question the way you interpret the facts. Then you can go on to ask, 'What can we do about this?' and find joint solutions.

Talk with other couples, too, especially those in a similar situation. Postnatal discussion parenthood groups offer a forum for exploring and clarifying problems in relationships. There are groups for those with disabilities, groups in community and cultural centres, churches and other places of worship, lesbian mothers' groups and marriage-guidance associations. A glance through the list of helpful organizations at the back of the book may give you some ideas. You may not want conventional coffee mornings and get-togethers where the talk is all about babies' physical and mental development, comparing your own with other babies. If nothing exists that seems right for you, consider forming a group of friends—couples you met in childbirth classes, for example—and meeting in each other's homes.

You and your mother

To become a mother is to displace your own mother, who now becomes a grandmother.

Perhaps you think that you can never be as good as your own mother, or be able to devote as much time to your children. If you work outside the home or have commitments other than being a housewife and mother, you may have memories of her always there ready with food, clean clothing, and time to listen, which make you feel you are bound to fail, and she may represent an impossibly high standard.

Becoming a grandmother gives a woman an opportunity to remember and relive a time in her life when she was happy, and she may really enjoy this—especially since it provides the pleasures without the twenty-four-hour responsibility. This is a good basis for a positive relationship with your mother.

But this transition may not happen smoothly. The change from being a daughter to being a mother yourself may occur so swiftly that the older woman, especially if it is a first grandchild, is afraid that you cannot possibly know how to care for a baby. She may express anxiety in frequent check-ups to discover what is happening—phone calls and visits—and by giving unasked-for advice. Or she may be anxious not to interfere, and attempt to do this as casually as possibly, with a nonchalance that she does not feel.

Many first-time mothers are determined to do things differently from their own mothers. They feel in competition with them, driven to show that they can manage not only just as well, but better. They read magazine articles and books, and they get advice from the clinic and suggestions from contemporaries, that give information which is at odds with the older woman's advice. But this is not just a matter of following professional and published advice. They also take what they remember of their childhood, together with observations of how other mothers behave with children, and construct their own stories of how they want to be with their children.

Even if your ideas are very different from your mother's, conflict is not inevitable. It will help if she reads some of the books and articles that you find useful, and you then discuss them together. If you have a positive relationship with your mother, and she is flexible and interested, you can share together pleasure in the changes in child-rearing practices that have taken place.

Women now in their fifties and sixties were often subjected to authoritarian instruction about child-rearing. They were taught that they should not pick up their babies when they cried or the child would be 'spoiled', and that if they rewarded a distressed baby by giving her

'I had to feed you by the clock. It was a strict schedule. Mothers weren't supposed to cheat. But it upset me to leave you crying. And I often sneaked in a top-up.'

attention she would never learn self-control. Because mothers of this generation were often given very bad advice about breastfeeding—that a baby should only be fed every four hours, for example—the babies often failed to gain weight, and the mothers lost their milk and did not succeed in breastfeeding. As a result, they felt guilty about this failure, and sometimes very humiliated.

When their daughters and daughters-in-law have babies they see that everything has changed. Instead of having to listen to their crying babies, and steel themselves not to pick them up, the younger women can keep their babies close and cuddle them without believing that they are ruining their children's characters. When the baby is allowed to lead the way with breastfeeding the mother is also much more likely to have a plentiful milk supply, and so enjoy breastfeeding.

An older woman may feel some envy for a younger mother who can follow her instincts instead of sticking to rules, and who does not feel guilty about the dust under the beds and the sink full of dirty dishes, because she believes it is more important to spend time with her baby. If it is like this with your mother or mother-in-law, it may help if you ask her about her experience as a mother and try to understand how it was for her. This can be part of a process of healing the pain that she has carried with her through the years.

When your mother is coming to visit, especially if these visits are few and far between, you probably want everything to be perfect, the baby contented, and the atmosphere welcoming. This is the time when things go wrong. Perhaps the baby picks up your tension. Anyway, instead of sleeping, he fusses and cries, with the result that you cannot get on with cooking and tidying the house. Plan ahead if you can, with preparation completed the day before, so that you are relaxed and can spend time with your baby. To be honest, this may not work either. Remind yourself that your life is different from your mother's. You may be under pressures with which she did not have to cope. Even if you were fairly well organized when she came to visit before you had the baby, there has been a complete scene change, and things cannot be the same now.

Sometimes the older woman is anxious that her son or her son-in-law is taking on too much in the home, so she becomes protective about him, and worries that his career or health will suffer. She may have an idealized vision of him as a good husband and father. She compares the work he is putting in with the comfort and peace at home that she struggled to ensure her own husband had.

'I can't stand it. She keeps on calling him "my baby". He isn't. He's ours.'

This, too, needs talking about, and it is better to discuss such matters *before* accusations build up, when you can still be relaxed about expressing your ideas. If you and your partner have thought this through, and agree that you want to share parenthood as fully as possible, you can plan a joint strategy in explaining your convictions to his mother, and helping her to see that you are enjoying being parents.

If the older woman is unhappy, perhaps because she is lonely, has a stressful relationship with her partner, or feels dissatisfied with her life, she may seek fulfilment through the new baby, and become possessive. Then she visits too often, indulges the baby with toys that he does not need, and sweets that are bad for him.

Consider working out a pattern of visiting with which you are happy—only Sundays or a meal once a week, perhaps, and laying down firm ground rules about presents and things that the baby is allowed to eat. If you do not approve of chocolate and sweets, for example, suggest apples and bananas. If the house is full of soft toys, talk with her about your baby's next stage of development, and the kind of playthings which would be helpful at this stage.

When you face problems with your baby and learn how to be a better mother through trial and error, building on your mistakes, you also begin to understand the difficulties that faced your mother, and see how hard it was for her. As adults we sometimes have stored up deep inside us anger against our mothers. Now you can come closer together in understanding. A woman has to be able to forgive her mother for being less than perfect.[5]

But often a grandmother is so preoccupied and busy with her own life, or geographically so far away, that she is not around when you have a baby. Or your mother may have died. Perhaps you miss her desperately and want her to be there so that you can show her your baby and have her approval and support. You may feel that the baby is somehow a reincarnation of your mother. When this happens, the baby is denied an identity of her own and a mother does not relate to her as a person in her own right. It can be lonely when there is no mother, and when your growing relationship with her as you have babies comes to a full stop.

Sometimes a partner's mother fills that gap wonderfully. On the other hand, she may be the last person who can take your mother's place, and you resent the fact that she is alive while your own mother is dead. It may be difficult to acknowledge the anger you feel, but you

need to do so if you are to open yourself to understand the older woman's vulnerability and to be friends with her.

There may also be conflict between your two families. Some cultures offer ritualized ways of handling stresses between families: between a mother and her parents, and between her own parents and her in-laws. In France there is the three-generation family get-together for Sunday lunch in a restaurant. In Japan the tradition has been that a woman goes back to her mother's home for the birth of a baby. The grandparents all meet at the maternal grandmother's home when the baby is about 7 days old. When the baby is first taken to the shrine a month after birth, both grandmothers should also be present. Then there is a shared meal with celebratory *sake* (rice wine). The father's family formally thank the mother's family for looking after the new baby till now, and the mother's family thank the father's for lending the baby to them. After a hundred days a further ceremony takes place at the shrine, which also involves both sets of grandparents. Everyone knows the correct rules of behaviour, and it is a matter of carrying them out, instead of worrying whether one grandmother will feel slighted if you invite the other, or how often you should ask them for a meal.[6]

Ritualized behaviour can support individuals and groups through difficult transitions in life. When there are stresses in relationships, at least potentially, you may be able to devise your own ritual get-togethers and celebrations that help oil the wheels of family relationships.

Friends

Friendships often change when you have a baby. Some friends disappear altogether, but you make new ones.

Women friends who do not have babies are probably living a completely different life from you, so you no longer have much in common. It may be difficult to organize yourself to join in leisure activities that you used to share, because you have no spare time, there are transport problems, and many things you used to do together—going out to eat, playing a game of tennis, swimming—make no provision for babies, or there are even official statements that they are not allowed. You cannot take a baby to the theatre, cinema, a football match, a concert, or the bingo hall. But you may not be so keen on doing these things anyway because your interests have changed.

When you are home-bound, you may feel envious of the freedom and flexibility in the lives of friends who are not parents. It is difficult for people who have never had babies to realize how restrictive life can get, and the almost superhuman feats of organization that are required to get out and to be at places on time. They may be unwilling to make concessions and give the help and encouragement you need to join in, and you feel shut out. The resentment you feel may drive a further wedge between you.

Friends may be envious of you, too. A woman who has not found a person with whom she wants to share her life, although she wants a baby, one who has been trying to conceive for a long time or whose partner is adamant that they should not start a family yet, or a woman who has had a series of miscarriages, may find it painful to be with friends who have babies. So you drift apart.

In some women's groups there are few mothers, and women who are active in feminist politics and direct action may not expect mothers to turn up with babies. Though they welcome you when you can put in an appearance and if the baby is quiet, it is difficult for them to understand that your life has changed and that the baby is now your top priority. If the baby is a boy they may be highly sensitive to and critical of any aggressive or violent behaviour, and you feel that they are blaming you. It is difficult for friendships to survive given such attitudes of moral disapproval and judgement.

Relationships are likely to change with male friends, too. Some men are rather embarrassed by the presence of a baby, especially when you are breastfeeding, or if they think you might. Or they do not *expect* you to stay friends once you are a mother. They label you as a 'Mum', and that makes you out of bounds.

A woman with physical disabilities may get completely housebound. She needs transport, help with the baby, good support from the social services of a kind that is determined by her, rather than her caregivers, and the extra financial resources to adapt to life as a mother with a disability. She—more than any other mother—is anxious to show that, however slow and difficult it is for her, she can take care of her baby. Having the baby enables her to make new friends. When she is out with her baby, other people may make contact with her through the baby, although if she is in a wheelchair, they may not believe it can be hers.

Babies always have a way of bringing people together. Women who would never have approached you before, speak to you at the supermarket check-out, on the bus, in the park, or at the clinic; or that you start chatting to someone with a baby of about the same age.

Some new friends may be older women who remember what it was like to have a young baby, and who may be missing their own

'She never thinks of anything but the baby. That's all she can talk about. It's terribly boring.'

'My sister lost her baby. We used to be very close. But now she can't bear to see me with my baby.'

'I have MS and, because I am on crutches or in a wheelchair, I am socially excluded. I can't get to places where other mothers meet.'

231

grandchildren. Others are women like you who are feeling isolated and are keen to make friends with other mothers.

The displaced baby

With the birth of a new baby, an older child is displaced. Jealousy is natural, whatever you do to avoid it. Psychologists who observed pairs of siblings over a two-hour period recorded on average four conflict episodes each hour. Their mothers often asked, 'Do other people's children squabble as much as mine do?'[7] If you have more than two children, you may have to multiply this by three or four.

A first-born who is 2 or 3 years old does not really understand what a baby is. He thought a baby would be someone to play with. Other people may have said, 'You'll be able to play with your little brother or sister.' It turns out that whenever he runs his truck over the baby or bounces a ball near her face, people shout, 'Don't hurt the baby!' 'Keep away from the baby!'

The first-born may think that you have got this baby because he has been naughty and you are going to get rid of him. Once you imagine the thoughts that may be in a small child's mind, regressive and disruptive behaviour is understandable, and you can handle it with more sympathy. If there are two or more children in the family, the

*'I can remember.
I felt betrayed.'*

older ones realize that having a new baby does not mean that they are rejected. But one who has been until now an only child may have fears of punishment and replacement which are difficult for adults to comprehend because they may no longer remember how it was.

Children of a single parent may have had their mothers—or sometimes their fathers—all to themselves. If the parent then starts a new relationship, which is followed by a baby, they may feel very threatened. They have to accept first a new adult who takes up the loved parent's time and attention, and now a new sibling who seals the relationship and becomes the centre around which the family revolves.

A 20-year-old wrote about her feelings when her mother had a child after a nineteen-year gap. On hearing her mother was pregnant she was horrified and blurted out, 'Will you still love me best?' 'How could I explain the pangs of jealousy, the resentment towards this unborn usurper, the terror that somehow the creation of this new family would leave me, the child of the previous marriage, out in the cold?' Her mother tried to get her interested. 'I realized that exclusion was not going to be the problem. Even worse, they seemed to want me to be *involved.*'[8] The baby was born pre-term and ill. She visited him in the intensive-care nursery. He was 'unbelievingly tiny and frail. The feelings that swamped me were shockingly protective. He was, after all, my brother.'

He is 3 now, and she is glad that she does not live at home and have to share her things with him, but quite annoyed that he talks about her boyfriend more than he does about her, so plans to bribe him with *Thomas the Tank Engine.*

The emotional journey she describes is one which much younger displaced siblings experience, too, from intense feelings of rejection and the shock of awareness that they are no longer to be the centre of the mother's world, to realization that they are still loved, bonding with the baby, and concerns to earn the baby's love.

Signs of resentment may not occur immediately the baby is born. But by the time a 10-month-old knocks over a 3-year-old's carefully constructed tower of blocks or Lego plane, it is almost impossible to avoid it.

Some of the great advantages of homebirth are that a small child is not separated from her mother, birth becomes a normal part of family life rather than an illness that needs hospital treatment, and the older child meets and bonds with the baby when the newborn is still in an awake, alert state after an undrugged birth.

Women who have given birth at home often comment on this and treasure the memories of their older children's first meeting with the baby. A mother whose 4-year-old was present at the birth described how her daughter lent over and kissed the baby as soon as his head was born, while the body was still inside.

'I say "No" and physically restrain him and turn it into a cuddle. There are no two ways about it. Violence is **out***.'*

You make it easier for the ex-baby if you foresee situations in which the newcomer is likely to be the focus of admiration, and defuse jealousy by giving the older child extra attention and things to look forward to at these times, assuring him of your love. Be firm about protecting the baby from harm. Explain that you would not have allowed anyone to hurt him when he was a baby. The older child will feel very guilty if by intention or 'accident' he harms the baby. He needs protecting from his own aggressive behaviour, just as a baby needs to be protected from the consequences of it.

Some psychologists advise against intervening in conflicts between siblings, believing that this adds fuel to the flames. But conflicts provide an opportunity for basic teaching about human rights and responsibilities, consideration for others, and caring for those who are weaker. When a mother reasons with a child, she is teaching social rules in a situation where it has vivid meaning for the child. It is not just a matter of controlling the older child's jealousy. If she discusses behaviour in this way, she acknowledges her child as a social and moral being. This contributes to further social development. A psychologist who observed mothers' and siblings' interaction comments that 'mothers' treatment of conflicts between siblings, far from separating the children and resolving conflicts for them, as psychologists have assumed, served to establish and define the child's position in relation to one another'.[9]

'He seemed a giant, almost gross, compared with the delicacy of the baby.'

You cannot treat any two children equally. Babies' needs are different from those of toddlers and older children. What you can do is to respond to each child's needs and wishes in a sensitive way. When a baby is born, even a 2-year-old may seem relatively grown-up, and you find yourself demanding too much from a child who is virtually a baby herself.

When you are feeding the baby, sit down with the older child too, and give her your concentrated attention. (All mothers know how to concentrate on two things at once.) One small child drew a picture of her mother as an octopus with four pairs of hands—all fully occupied. Keep a stock of playthings and books in a special cupboard which comes out only when the baby is being fed. Then each feed is a pleasure to which the older child looks forward, when she can select favourite toys and picture books which you enjoy together.

You will not be able to give as much time to the older child as you did before. But the ex-baby needs more attention, not less, as he tries to cope with feelings of anger and jealousy. It is a huge help to have other loving adults whom the ex-baby knows well, and this is a point where your partner's commitment, and your parents' too if they are around, is invaluable. Make regular time for playing and reading together, for baking sessions in which dough can be pummelled and anger taken out on an inanimate substance, for enacting puppet plays with scenes of family life in which there are a mother and baby and real feelings can be expressed, and for getting out of the house and into an exciting world that is waiting to be explored—trips to a pond, the park, the wildlife centre. The older sibling may develop new skills with startling rapidity. It is as if the birth of the baby stimulates and frees her to move forward.

Regressive behaviour

On the other hand, your older child may refuse to leave your side. Many children regress to earlier baby ways as they try to cope with the arrival of a new baby. Sleep disturbances, baby-talk, thumb-sucking, and outbreaks of uncontrolled rage are common. A previously potty-trained 2-year-old may go back into nappies for a while. It is better to accept this with goodwill than to have constant battles about bed-wetting or making messes. They may want to drink out of a bottle when they can manage perfectly well with a cup, or breastfeed when they stopped months ago.

The younger the ex-baby, the more likely she is to get upset when you go out of a room, and to want to be cuddled in one arm while you feed the baby the other side. The child is not being awkward deliberately. This disturbed behaviour comes from an acute sense of loss.

Imagine that your partner brought home another woman who would be part of your family from now on. People came to admire and coo over her, and said how beautiful she was. He lay on the bed cuddling her much of the time. She did not even have to feed herself. He was right there ready to put food into her mouth. She slept a lot, and you were told to keep quiet and not disturb her. When she was not sleeping she was either crying, eating, or being cuddled. He told you to be gentle with her because she was precious. You must not poke her eyes out. But you could help look after her. He did not spend much time with you any more because he was busy, and she woke up and demanded attention in the night, too, so he was tired and cross. She did all sorts of things you were not allowed to do, often made a dreadful noise, and was smelly and dirty. But *everyone* loved her.

No wonder the displaced sibling is bewildered and feels crowded out. Though it is often helpful to emphasize how grown-up and responsible the older child is now—'You can have your own bed'—this quickly turns into a weapon used against the child: 'You're too big to suck at mummy's breast/have a bottle/wear nappies.'

It works best to be relaxed about regressive behaviour and to accept it as more or less inevitable. Why shouldn't the older child breastfeed or drink from a bottle? It will not matter if she is in nappies again for a while. A displaced sibling needs assurance of your love, and also to know that you understand and accept her anger and loneliness.

You can talk about how you felt as a child when a baby brother or sister was born, and make up stories in which the central character is a child with a new baby in the house. Many picture books are published that deal with this subject for 2- or 3-year-olds.

Describe what your older child was like as a baby, too, how you

'He holds on to my legs so I can't walk. He's under my feet in the kitchen. I can't even go and pee without him.'

237

looked after him, your feelings as parents, what you did when he cried, and about his development—when he first smiled, started to walk, could splash in the pool, and sat at the table with the grown-ups to eat. Make a picture book together of him in his baby days and showing how he grew big and clever. In this way you trace the child's developmental history and express your pleasure in it.

Instead of telling a child that she must behave in a more grown-up way, do things which are appropriate for her age, which the baby would obviously not be able to do. Any evidence of the advantages of growing up must come from a child's pride of achievement, manual dexterity, physical power and mobility, and making things and playing in ways which the baby cannot. The baby cannot catch a ball, or climb into a treehouse, or go to the pantomime. He is too young to enjoy fireworks or to make a snowman.

You help a child to grow *through* jealousy when you accept that it is normal, show your delight in his activities and achievements, and reinforce his self-confidence.

Older siblings are great educators; the older child can teach the baby things she can do herself. Talking or singing, winding up a musical box, playing peek-a-boo and other games are all ways in which an older child can draw on her own repertoire of skills and enjoy the baby. Praise from you, and your evident pleasure in the baby's responsiveness—'Look, she turns when she hears your voice … she's smiling at you … she likes you doing that'— reinforces the older child's relationship with the baby.

The mother alone

Single-parent families have doubled in Britain in the last twenty years. Close on 20 per cent of all families are now headed by a solo parent—and it is usually a mother.[10]

In spite of this, women with children who are not living with a man are often lumped together as if they were in one social category, 'the single mother'. They are perceived as a social problem, and described as if they were socially disadvantaged and feckless teenagers with no knowledge of contraception.

For many teenage mothers, regardless of the circumstances of conception, the experience of pregnancy and childbirth in which they can make choices between alternatives and are helped to develop self-confidence can be empowering. They are not merely 'victims', or even 'survivors.' Motherhood is a great educational and maturational experience which may teach a great deal more than was ever learnt in school.

The term 'single mother' includes women whose partnership has been broken during pregnancy or after birth by the man walking out on them, those whose partners have died, women of all ages who have conceived accidentally and, for different reasons, have made the decision not to terminate the pregnancy, women who, after much thought and planning, have decided that it is best to go it alone, lesbian women in partnerships who have decided on self-insemination or who have children from a previous relationship, unmarried women who have been raped and have gone on to bear the child, and women in cultures where it is accepted that a woman bears a child who is brought up with the help of her mother, as in many Afro-Caribbean societies. These women have little in common except the fact of their pregnancies.

The main problem for many mothers alone is not the absence of a man but shortage of money, for they tend to be in the lowest income brackets. In Britain eight out of ten are dependent on state financial aid. In any country where there is poverty, they are among the poorest of all.

A woman alone, without someone to love and support her—without anyone who cares—has special needs as a mother. To be on your own as you pass through this amazing transition, and take on the responsibilities of parenthood, is to face an overwhelming task. Yet many women have done it, and often more easily than those living with men who pose yet another problem because they are violent, drink heavily, compete with the baby for mothering, or simply lack understanding of what the woman is going through.

A parent alone, and any woman who does not have emotional support and practical help from her partner, needs a good support network. One who has no close friend—someone with whom she can

'For me the worst things about being a single parent are the isolation, constant money problems—and knowing that mothering has no status.'

240

talk freely—has a still greater chance of unhappiness. Brown's and Harris's research on the social origins of depression revealed that a major element in unhappiness was the lack of an intimate, confiding relationship. Easy, spontaneous communication with someone who will give time to listen, who understands and values you, helps put the stresses of motherhood in perspective.[11]

When a woman does not have this, it is important to get out of the house and do something quite different from mothering, even if that is only for a few hours a week. Lack of paid employment is another important factor in the build-up of depression in women with young children. A woman who does not have a close relationship reduces the chances of being depressed by half if she has a job.[12] This in itself depends on having good childcare on which she can rely. A strong support network is vital if you are to enjoy your baby and feel good about yourself.

SEX

Some women feel sexually recharged and long to make love within days of giving birth. Others find that it takes much longer than this to be fully aroused—sometimes so long that they are anxious that they will never be able to recreate a happy and spontaneous sexual relationship. In the meantime all they want to do is to get some sleep before the baby wakes again. One study revealed that out of twenty-five babies of mothers who were keeping their sexual diaries, twelve were still waking for a night feed at six months. Their mothers started intercourse later than mothers of babies who slept through.[1] Yet, even when a baby begins to sleep through the night, all your energy, creative imagination, and emotions may be focused on mothering for most of that first year after birth.

'Body fat, soft, tired—relationship with husband terrible—baby crying.'

Many women are anxious about or afraid of intercourse because they are in pain, they are weak and worn out, or they hate how their bodies look and feel after having a baby. It is as if they have been unsexed. Following a Caesarean birth, abdominal tenderness may make a woman shrink from any vigorous love-making, whether or not it involves genital sex, because she feels so vulnerable.

The way you feel about sex in those postnatal weeks and months depends very much on the kind of birth experience you had, whether birth caused physical damage, as well as your feelings about yourself as a mother and how your partner sees you in this new role, how you feel about your partner, how tired you both are, your partner's emotional response to the birth of the baby, and the way you are both experiencing the major life transformation of becoming parents.

Some women cannot enjoy genital sex so long as they are breastfeeding. They feel that their bodies are dedicated to their babies, and raised prolactin levels during lactation may enhance this feeling.[2]

A new mother may feel it important to keep distinct in her mind sensations when breastfeeding her baby and those she experiences in her sexual relationship. For women who are incest survivors this is urgently necessary. One woman described how when her husband put his mouth to her breast she reacted violently and slapped him. 'My breasts are part of my motherhood, and it feels like mixing sex with motherhood … it feels like incest,' she explained. 'I need a firm boundary.' She goes on to say 'To enjoy healthy sexuality, survivors must be able to make rules, set limits, and define "safe space".'[3]

There is no norm for sexual behaviour, no goals to which you ought to strive, just as there can be no recipe for sexual fulfilment.

When birth is an enriching and satisfying experience and takes place in an intimate, peaceful setting, it may be a celebration of a couple's love. This is most likely to happen with a home-birth, in a birth centre, or in one of the small but growing number of hospitals where caregivers honour a woman's autonomy, create an emotionally supportive environment, avoid unnecessary interventions, and know how to stand back and allow the rhythm and power of the birth passion to be expressed through the woman's body.[4] The depth of emotion felt after the baby is born sometimes leads quite naturally to love-making within days of birth.

After a birth in which no injury has occurred and when a woman has felt in harmony with her body and enjoyed the excitement of labour, once bleeding has stopped there is no *physical* reason why she should not have sex whenever she wishes. But it must be entirely up to her. The important things are that she should be aroused, and that her lover should be gentle and considerate, and accept that she may not want penetration.

But most births are not like that. Many women are shocked and physically damaged by birth, especially when they have their first baby. Love-making is the last thing on their minds as they try to handle the outrage they feel, and to struggle through the painful post-partum days and weeks. They seek relief from perineal pain and backache, and want comfort, tenderness, understanding, and a stretch of undisturbed sleep, rather than sex.

Medical research into sex after childbirth reveals little about

'I feel my breasts belong to the baby. I don't like him touching or sucking them, though I used to love it.'

'I wanted him to love my swollen breasts. But he was revolted.'

'Love-making started labour. She was born two and half hours after. We made love five nights later. That was wonderful, too.'

244

women's feelings. Categories of respondents are listed who 'resume intercourse' within the first, second, third, or fourth month, or later. They may be asked to indicate whether it was 'painless', 'rather painful', or 'painful', or to rate 'comfort' and 'discomfort' on a graded numerical scale. They are not asked whether they wanted intercourse in the first place, or how they felt about it afterwards. Nor are we told anything about foreplay, the position in which it took place, whether the woman experienced orgasm, and, if she had pain, whether this was on penetration or later. Most research takes it for granted that sex equals intercourse. This ignores lesbian women's experiences, those of heterosexual women who do not like penetration, and of women who satisfy themselves without a partner.

After a bad birth, when a woman is likely to be feeling very negative about her body, she may submit to intercourse because she is anxious that her man will otherwise feel rejected and unloved, that he will turn to another woman, or because she thinks it is her duty. But many women try to avoid it for the first two or three months. They feel exhausted. They dread it because they are in pain. They are frightened that the episiotomy or Caesarean wound will split open. They cannot imagine that they will ever want to make love again. They are worried about conceiving, and dread the thought of having to go through all this another time. For some, intercourse entails re-experiencing an act of violence perpetrated on them by those who delivered the baby. Even women who are highly aroused may start to make love and then discover that it hurts far too much to continue.

Men and sex after birth

'My husband finds breast-feeding irritating. He often works 120 hours a week and wants me to himself when he's at home.'

Men's attitudes to sex after birth vary widely. Some demand their 'rights', whether or not a woman is feeling aroused. Others keep their distance because their religion teaches that she is polluted by birth or in a sacred condition which rules out any sexual contact. Some are jealous of the baby. Some cannot tolerate witnessing the baby at the breast. A man may see the woman's body as maternal, not sexual. It belongs to the baby. Others are deeply and passionately moved by birth, and enjoy the woman's new softness and openness.

Some are turned off by having witnessed birth in which there was obstetric intervention, and are frightened of injuring the woman, especially if they have watched an episiotomy and its repair.

It is often not realized how much a traumatic birth experience can affect a partner who is present, too. It need not have been an obstetrically complicated birth—but simply one in which the woman was treated as if she were part of a factory process to produce a baby.

A father writing about a birth experience six years earlier says, 'There are still times … when we do not feel comfortable with each other and our sexuality, or our confidence with each other as lovers.… It has taken all those years of soul searching, stress, talking into the night, and many, many tears on both sides to reach some kind of continuous and enjoyable sex life.'[5] He describes how his wife used the baby as 'a protective screen'. 'We circled each other like wary cats, and we both dreaded going to bed for about six months because we knew there would be tears and frustration, and so much sadness.' He felt under great pressure to be capable and strong, but needed support himself. It was only later that he came to understand that he had been responsible for many of the difficulties they encountered because he expected his partner to have sex a regular number of times a week, and to experience orgasm, and they both felt they had failed when it did not work out like this.

But this was not the only problem. For his wife the birth had been like a rape. She had lost confidence in herself, and every time they made love sex brought a flood of feelings about being abused and violated, so she could not bear her partner to touch her.

Traditionally in many cultures sexual intercourse is prohibited for forty days after birth.[6] Mexican women, for example, are not supposed to have intercourse until after they have menstruated following a forty-one-day period from birth.[7] These religious and cultural prohibitions often have the strength of taboo. It is believed that there will be automatic divine punishment in the form of illness, infertility, or death if the prohibition is broken. The baby may be reclaimed by the ancestor spirits, and the man may become impotent or his penis wither and drop off. It is also often thought that intercourse while a woman is lactating poisons the milk. This was the case in the sixteenth and seventeenth centuries in England, and is a pattern in many traditional cultures.

As customs change and old taboos are rejected in societies all over the world, women are exposed to risk, including that of infection while the inner lining of the uterus and vaginal tissues are especially vulnerable, in ways that they never were before. Often there is nothing to stop a man insisting on intercourse whether or not the woman feels like it, and virtually raping her. When tissues are damaged by forced penetration, a woman is most at risk of acquiring the AIDS virus and other sexually transmitted diseases. Women are also exposed to the risk of conceiving again within a few weeks of childbirth, and when breastfeeding is replaced by artificial feeding, any contraceptive effect of lactation is lost.

Vaginal moisture

The usual lubrication of the vagina does not return till some weeks after birth. In the meantime you feel dry, although some natural lubricant will be released when you are aroused. Tissues which are rubbed become sore. Additional lubrication can be provided by using a dissolving vaginal gel, obtainable from the chemist, which you or your partner smooth in as part of love-making.

You can help the release of your natural lubricant and enhance sexual arousal if you or your lover gently massage round and just inside your vagina and down over the root of your clitoris with very light, feathery strokes.

'Sex was not painfree until seven months after the birth. Then we made up for lost time!'

Notice exactly where you like this stroking to take place and what kind of touch feels best, *and tell your partner.* After childbirth a lover needs to rediscover your body. It will have changed, so nothing should be taken for granted. Sexual techniques have to be developed and adapted. The kind of touch that excited you before you were pregnant may have been different from that which you liked in early pregnancy, and different again from what you wanted in the weeks just before the baby was due. Now you may long for a special kind of touching and holding which your partner is not aware that you seek. Touching and movements that you enjoyed before feel awkward, uncomfortable, or painful, or simply leave you cold.

You do not have to go into great anatomical detail. Nor do you require medical or Latin words to communicate about this. All you need say is 'Yes' or 'No', and make the kind of appreciative sounds that help your partner learn about and get in tune with your no-longer-pregnant body.

247

If you are aware that you have little natural lubrication, avoid having a bath before making love, as this will dry your tissues further. If you like massage, it may help you relax and develop sensate focus on your body. Suggest places where you like to be massaged and concentrate all your attention on the area being stroked. It may be the backs of your knees, your neck, your inside arms, your feet, bottom, or sides. Once you have created sensate focus in this way, your vagina is much more likely to be plump, soft, and moist.

Penetrative sex should never occur unless and until you are in this aroused state.

The root of the clitoris

The clitoris, rather than the vagina, is a woman's main sexual organ, and it needs stimulation if a woman is to be highly aroused.

But it is a great mistake to think that the it is a magic button which only needs to be pressed to trigger ecstasy. Constant rubbing of the visible part of the clitoris, that sticks up like a little rounded plant shoot or a pea between the upper folds of the labia and beneath the curved mound formed by the pubic bone, can be extremely irritating. An anxious lover may spend a long time exerting friction against this tiny organ hoping that, like Aladdin rubbing the lamp, the effect will be magic. Unfortunately it does not work like that. The exquisitely sensitive part of the clitoris which responds to pressure and to friction cannot be seen. It lies deeper down and is the *root* of the clitoris.

It has been said that sex consists of 'friction and fantasies'.[8] But it all depends what kind of fantasies a woman has, and where the friction takes place. Often fantasies that flood into a woman's mind after childbirth turn out to be destructive, and friction exerted by an over-zealous lover is applied in the wrong place.

Interrupted sex

There is more than one kind of 'coitus interruptus'. Even when you both long for sex and enjoy it, babies have an uncanny knack of waking up and wanting to be fed just as you get started. This is one of the hazards of love-making after childbirth. It is almost as if they have a sixth sense, pick up the energy that is flowing through you, and become alert and curious.

So feed the baby a short while before you make love whenever possible. That will give you the greatest chance of a free hour. You can put the baby in another room or behind a screen, and even playing soft music as a sound-screen may be enough to keep the baby settled.

When your breasts are full with milk you may find it quite difficult to move easily during love-making. Any pressure against breasts is painful, milk leaks as your partner strokes them, and when you have an orgasm it spurts out. Since oxytocin is the hormone of love and floods into your bloodstream when you are sexually aroused and when you breastfeed, this is entirely natural. Keep a face towel or nappy handy so that you can grab it and stem the flood. If you apply firm pressure with your fore-arms against the sides of your breasts, the milk flow will slow down and stop.

Birth and sexual empowering

Some women who have not really enjoyed sex before they had a baby start to feel more positive about their sexuality, and become more sexually aware, after a good birth experience. It is as if they have suddenly discovered what their bodies can do. Their male partners who shared in the birth experience, and who did not merely observe, have a new respect for their vibrant energy and power in birth-giving. Instead of the old male–female game of dominance and submission, they find a sharing and tenderness, a depth of feeling, which is a new element in their relationship. The whole rhythm of the sexual dance changes. The man becomes more caring, gentle, and oriented to her needs and wishes.

The male idea of the vagina is an organ that accepts and contains the penis. In fact, the latin word *vagina* means 'a sheath', and through the ages male doctors who have written books about women's bodies have described how it receives and holds, as if it were simply a receptacle waiting to be filled. Even William Masters, in many ways the father of sex therapy, who writes about the female orgasm with great understanding, talks about 'the vaginal barrel', as if it were a gun waiting to be loaded by a man.[9]

In giving birth a woman often discovers the female knowledge that the vagina can be powerful and active. A penis becomes erect, ejaculates, then goes down. The vagina can do a good deal more. It not only receives, takes in, and encloses, but can actively open up, like the great, fleshy petals of a peony, to give birth. When you are with a woman who has no obstetric intervention, and is able to give birth in an unhurried way, the gentle fanning and spreading out of vaginal and perineal tissues can be seen at the height of each powerful expulsive contraction. As the baby's head is pressed down and through the vagina with each strong tightening of her uterus, and then retracts between contractions, she may experience a rippling movement in the muscles around her vagina which creates a wave-like rhythm that is similar to psycho-sexual arousal. In my books about childbirth I describe this as 'the birth passion'.[10]

For such women their bodies may suddenly be revealed to them in a new way, and some are able to express their love and longing, and to experience intense and satisfying pleasure in sex with a partner, for the first time in their lives.

Sex after stitches

It can be frightening to start making love again after you have been cut or torn and then stitched up. In the week or so after having the baby you were probably in pain as you emptied your bowels and bladder, and when you walked in the first few days the only way of doing so was to waddle. When you wear jeans the crotch seam rubs the sore, tender area where the wound was, and you may feel you will never again have sufficient room for a partner's penis, or even a finger. You just don't want to be touched.

'I had an image of an enormous, gaping wound. I felt his penis entering me would open me up again.'

The medical term for painful intercourse is dyspareunia. Women who have had natural tears tend to have intercourse a month or so earlier than those who have had episiotomies. In my own study of women's experiences of episiotomies, 40 per cent of women who had natural tears said that intercourse was never painful after childbirth, compared with only 21 per cent of those who had episiotomies. Many of these women had not even wanted to try to have sexual intercourse until two or three months after the birth. Nineteen per cent of those who were subjected to episiotomies said intercourse hurt for longer than three months, compared with 11 per cent of those who had tears.[11]

'My body felt so abused. It didn't seem like my own any more.'

When a woman can at last face the idea of penetration, intercourse may still turn out to be painful, and she has to go about it very slowly and tentatively, with the assurance that her partner will wait or stop altogether if she says so. She needs to be able to trust her partner not to

*'Each time we
attempted
intercourse we
had to stop.
Attempts became
fewer because of
fear of failure.'*

get over-excited and start thrusting, and to be sensitively aware of how she is feeling.

Although you may recoil from doing so, because you are anxious about what you will discover, many women find it helps if they use a mirror to see how their stitches look and exactly where they are. At first the area around may still be swollen and puffy. This oedema always occurs after injury, and is part of the body's way of protecting and healing itself. The more sensitive the area where injury occurs, the more oedema you will have. If you are having problems with stitches, look back at the section on episiotomy in Chapter 4. Until they have dissolved or been removed, stitches look enormous and ugly, and you feel as if you are sitting on thorns. They make you feel that this part of your body has become a medical specimen and does not belong to you any more. After they come out, have another look in the mirror and explore the area with finger-tip touch. Sometimes a stitch that should have dissolved or been removed has become embedded in scar tissue. You can see it as a black or green line like a splinter. It feels like this, too. Contact your midwife or doctor, because it must be nicked out. You will feel enormous relief after this has been done.

Feel the edge of the scar. There should not be any pus issuing from it and the tissue around it ought not to be inflamed. Sometimes there is infection which needs to be treated with antibiotics. When an episiotomy damages nerve endings, there is a particular spot that a woman cannot bear to be touched, and the pain she experiences is rather like toothache, and very localized. Healing may take months.

This is your body and it is important that you know and understand it. Your vagina is not just an opening for penetration. Nor is it simply a passage through which a baby has to be pushed. It is a living, feeling part of you which you now need to reclaim.

When you feel you have come to know your perineum, vulva, vagina, and clitoris by touch, you can then take your lover's hand in yours and trace the same area, explaining where it feels good to be touched, where it hurts, where you feel neutral about touch, and what kind of caress is best for you. In some places where it is painful to rub, just cupping a protecting hand over the tender area may help you feel secure. In other parts light stroking feels fine, where deep massage would be painful.[12]

The most common problem is that women feel they have been stitched too tightly—the result of over-zealous, intricate embroidery, often performed on tissues that are already oedematous. In British hospitals midwifery staff sometimes avoid waking doctors on call during the night, so stitches are not put in until the morning, or several

hours after the birth. Infection is a well-known complication of episiotomy, and it is much more likely to occur if suturing is delayed beyond half an hour or so.

Many doctors do not know much about sex after childbirth. A male doctor may base his thinking about the subject on a couple of statistical papers in medical journals and how his own wife behaved, and make tentative generalizations from this.

There is little about painful intercourse in the obstetric literature. Though its frequency is often recorded, it is not described in detail, and we do not learn what couples actually did, and when and where women experienced pain. Perhaps because of this, doctors' views tend to be no more informed than lay people's. Many women feel that they cannot ask their doctors about sexual difficulties.[13] Even if they do, some doctors tell a woman she should expect pain after having a baby, and that this is how all new mothers feel. It is not true. Some advise a woman to put up with the pain of intercourse and to go *through* it. They believe that intercourse is bound to get more comfortable if she does this. They seem to be suggesting forceful stretching of the vagina.

'He didn't want to hurt me and I didn't want to let him down.'

252

This is treating a woman as if she were simply a container for a penis. Anyway, it is not the real problem. The tissues of the vagina will fan out and become moist and receptive if a woman is sufficiently aroused, and only then. Love-making should never be reduced to being like the forceful pushing of a digit into the tight finger of a new glove.

Some doctors assert that episiotomy ought to improve sexual functioning after childbirth because it prevents stretching of connective tissues of the vulva, though they produce no evidence to support this. One obstetrician made the claim that episiotomy 'ensures the restoration of conjugal as well as anatomic normalcy'.[14] It would be extraordinary if having a woman's sexual organs cut with scissors ensured 'conjugal normalcy' for any couple. Other doctors go so far as to assert that vaginal delivery permanently impairs normal coitus, and therefore advise Caesarean section. Apparently this is one of the reasons why Brazil now has a Caesarean-section rate in some parts of the country of over 50 per cent.[15]

After episiotomy many women feel a lump of tender, tight tissue at the base of their vagina. If this is how it is with you, avoid pressure or friction against it by tilting yourself so that, if your lover enters your vagina, this occurs at an angle which avoids the painful area. A pile of pillows is useful. You may want one under your bottom or pelvis. Or you may want to lie in a position supported by pillows where you can enjoy manual stimulation, or in which the penis produces friction against the upper edge of your vagina and the root of your clitoris instead, which is not only more comfortable, but more exciting.

You may also find that you can relax and enjoy sex more if you are the active partner, and your lover follows your lead. You can use your pelvic-floor muscles to draw your lover inside, instead of feeling that your body is being invaded.

Some women have pain deep inside the vagina. This occurs when cervical ligaments have been torn or when a laceration has extended inside the vagina. Deep penetration may then be incredibly painful, and should not be attempted until you have healed completely.

However, most women for whom intercourse is painful say that it is pain *on entry* that puts them off the whole idea. If penetration is gentle, with extra lubrication, they feel much more comfortable beyond that point, unless they are being rushed. Ask your lover to slide in gently, and then just wait until you indicate from the kisses you make inside with your pelvic-floor muscles that you want to go on. It is often surprising how, once your lover's finger or penis is inside, and you feel safe, pain disappears and you begin to enjoy love-making.

Positions

The 'missionary position,' with your partner on top, is often uncomfortable after having a baby. Your lactating breasts are full, tender, and aching, so you cannot bear pressure on them. If you have had a perineal wound, pressure and friction against your lower vagina and posterior vaginal wall may be very painful. If you have a Caesarean scar, you cannot tolerate pressure against your abdomen.

A woman is often anxious that she will be hurt if her partner shifts position thoughtlessly or becomes over-excited. So she holds herself rigid, ready to protect these most vulnerable parts of her body. She needs to be in control so that she can feel secure.

So the time after having a baby is a good one in which to explore different ways of making love and to experiment with different positions. Ones in which you are free to move your pelvis are usually best: kneeling on top of or crouching over your partner, or lying with your back to your lover in a 'cupped-spoon' position.

Fantasies and flashbacks

Fantasy often plays an important part in sexual arousal. You are not just a body in a rumpled bed, in a room where windows are streaky and stained, and where the number seven bus rumbles by and you can hear next door's TV turned up too loud. Instead you are making love in a bluebell wood where sunlight filters through beech leaves, or are isolated on sand dunes where the only sound comes from waves washing on the shore and the call of seabirds.

But the trouble with letting your imagination have free play is that many women have had bad sexual experiences. If anyone has abused their power over you as a child or adult, or if you felt powerless in childbirth, and were strapped down and physically mutilated, ugly, destructive fantasies may flood in and take the happy experience from you. So you close your mind to thoughts and keep sex at the level of the physical. This works for a woman if she is vigorously sexual and readily aroused, as people often are in their teens and twenties, or when starting out on an exciting new relationship. But if sex holds no novelty, and has become a repetitive act, perhaps performed at high speed, or at times when a woman is weary or anxious, at the end of a day filled with housework, a crying baby, shopping for and making meals, dirty dishes, dirty nappies, and she has a throbbing, aching perineum, the faintest suggestion of sex may leave her feeling completely cold.

After a pregnancy and birth in which you have been disempowered, you may feel that your body no longer belongs to you. Some women have switched off from the waist down, detaching themselves from all feeling.

The positions in which you usually have intercourse may give you vivid and painful flashbacks to labour and delivery—being examined roughly by a doctor, having your waters broken, manœuvres in which an attempt was made to dilate the cervix further or to rotate the baby's head, having your legs hauled up into stirrups for a forceps delivery, being given an episiotomy, and the ordeal of suturing afterwards. Flashbacks are more than memories. They are like an intense re-enacting of an event in the past, and produce physical symptoms. They may change your breathing, your galvanic skin response, muscle tension, pulse rate, and blood pressure.

When you lie on your back with your legs apart you may feel cold and sick, break out in a sweat, and tremble. If you are held down in any way by your partner's weight or cannot move your limbs, or if he looks at your genitals and pokes and prods as if a doctor were doing a pelvic examination, not only is your sexual arousal instantly switched off, but you may find yourself pushing him away or crying helplessly.

Flashbacks come without warning. Sometimes they also bring memories of being sexually abused as a child. Instead of a flashback to a specific birth event, they are mixed, distorted images.

If you have had a bad birth experience and realize that this is happening to you, you may want to seek help from a rape crisis

'I had programmed myself to feel detached with great success. Cancelling the program after the birth was far more difficult.'

'Whenever he touched my vagina I thought of the birth, doctors, examinations, and got very upset.'

counsellor. In many towns there is a rape crisis helpline. You can talk anonymously on the phone to a woman who understands what you are going through. An alternative is to arrange face-to-face counselling, either through rape crisis or with a woman sex therapist.

Vaginismus

Vaginismus is a medical term to describe a condition in which muscles around the vagina go into spasm and snap shut, sometimes so tightly that intercourse is impossible. It is painful for the woman, and seems to a man the ultimate rejection. After childbirth these muscles have been stretched by the passage of the baby between them, and have often been cut with an episiotomy, so true vaginismus is unlikely. But they still may tighten involuntarily and resist entry. This adds to the pain that the woman is experiencing anyway following suturing of the perineum as her partner tries to penetrate. Many women suffer from muscle spasms like this that are not severe enough to prevent penetration if a man is determined, but which make intercourse painful. To label a woman who does not want penetration as suffering from a disease called 'vaginismus' is rather like saying that someone who gags on being forced to eat snails or oysters, must have a malfunction of the throat muscles. When a woman experiences vaginal spasm, her body is simply saying that she does not want penetration. It is not a disease. It may be considered a disability, but a disability, in effect, for the man, rather than the woman, for she often loves her partner and likes making love, but does not want full intercourse. It is not her fault, and the man needs to change *his* behaviour more than the woman needs therapy.

Gynaecologists may treat vaginismus first by getting the male partner to put on surgical gloves and conduct a vaginal examination under the doctor's direction, with the woman draped and her legs in lithotomy stirrups. The husband is 'encouraged to demonstrate to his and his wife's satisfaction the severity of the involuntary constriction ring in the outer third of the vagina'.[16] Once they are home again, 'the actual dilation of the vaginal outlet is initiated and conducted by the husband with the wife's physical co-operation', using graded dilators to convince the woman that her vagina has room for an erect penis. This may be followed with exercises to change the conditioned reflex and stimulate the muscles to respond with vaginal readiness for intercourse. It is often combined with exercises in general relaxation. Psychotherapy may, too, be used as an adjunct to this physical treatment. These crude methods of 'cure', which Masters and Johnson claim are 100 per cent successful, are offensive to many women.

Spasm of the muscles around the vagina may also be the body's reaction to sexual abuse. A woman has often repressed the memory of this experience. But her body remembers. It is another kind of flashback. Vaginal spasm can occur after a difficult birth, too, one in which a woman has felt at the mercy of people investigating, manipulating, or mutilating her genitals, causing pain, and forcing the baby from her body. Like other flashbacks, it may relate to both birth and earlier sexual abuse.

If you cannot bear penetration, and your muscles are going into a state of contraction, you may want to talk about it with a woman therapist—someone who understands what the after-effects of episiotomy may be, and who does not equate love-making with penetration and intercourse. It is probably wise to decline therapy from a man. Refuse any help offered that is not the kind you require. Addresses of organizations that offer sexual counselling are included in the list at the back of the book.

Ovulation

Ovulation, hence the possibility of conception, is unlikely to occur again for several weeks after childbirth, but you cannot be sure of this. If a woman is breastfeeding freely without restrictions, and the baby is having no other food or fluids, she may not ovulate until feeds are spaced out in a roughly four-hourly pattern, or the baby is sleeping through most of the night. Breastfeeding is an unreliable form of contraception, however, especially in a society where women have more than ample food.

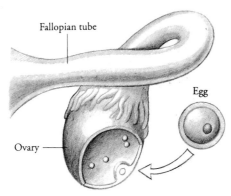

Egg ripening in the ovary

Ripe egg travelling down the Fallopian tube

The ripening of an ovum takes place *before* a woman has her first period following childbirth. A small bud shape swells up on one of her ovaries, and then breaks free and is sucked into her fallopian tube. This is ovulation, and if she has unprotected intercourse in the next few days she may conceive.

So it is wise to think about your chosen method of birth control as soon as possible after the baby. The method you used before may not be the best for you now.

Contraception

Until your periods return, and are coming in a regular rhythm, it is best not to use the contraceptive pill. It is also best to avoid pushing any barrier contraceptive inside you if you have had injury to your perineum, vagina, or cervix until it has completely healed. Bear in mind that, unless you are breastfeeding freely and fully, ovulation may return within a few weeks of childbirth. But with unrestricted breastfeeding that includes at least one night feed, and if your periods do not start again, there is a 98 per cent chance that you will not conceive within the first six months.[17] Other practical choices in the early months are between non-penetrative sex, a man pulling out before ejaculation—which is very risky—and using a condom.

Male and female condoms

There is such a wide range of condoms that are used as sheaths for the penis that it is impractical to describe them here, But it is worth noting that latex can be painful against sore tissues unless you use a generous dollop of water-based lubrication (not oil).

Femidom

The female condom was first introduced in 1991. It consists of a soft, flexibly fitting polyurethane sheath, approximately 15 centimetres long and 7 centimetres in diameter, which fits into your vagina and covers your labia.[18] It is sold pre-lubricated. In the United States there are two kinds, one which consists of a tube-like pouch that is held in place by straps that loop around the woman's thighs, and the other more like a child's sock, the same as the British version.

Chances of conception when using the female condom are estimated to be about the same as those when using the male condom. With careful use, two women in one hundred become pregnant. With careless use, two in fifteen get pregnant.

'A condom is fun. There are so many different sorts now.'

'I like the fact that it's under my control, and there are no harmful side-effects.'

The sponge

'It's soft and easy to insert, with the dimple over the cervix.'

The diaphragm or cap

Diaphragm

'I like the diaphragm because I can use it during my period, too.'

The pill

'The pill is right for me. I have freedom and spontaneity, and that's important.'

As you become more comfortable, you may want to explore other possibilities. There is the contraceptive sponge, which contains spermicide. You slip it in before intercourse and leave it in place for at least six hours afterwards. Using it carefully, nine women in a hundred become pregnant. Using it carelessly, as many as nine in twenty-five conceive.

Sponge

If you used a diaphragm or cap with spermicide before your pregnancy, you will probably need a different size after you have given birth, and also if you lose a lot of weight. With this kind of contraception, you introduce a soft latex dome into which you have inserted spermicide and lubrication, sliding it deep inside your vagina and over your cervix. You need to learn exactly how to insert it. Again, it needs to be left in for six hours after intercourse. Unfortunately the rubber of which a diaphragm is made and the spermicide used can both cause irritation, and women using diaphragms are at risk of cystitis, probably because the rim rubs against the neck of the bladder. Chances of conception are eight in one hundred with careful use, two in fifteen if you are careless. Some women find that the cap is less messy and more comfortable than the larger diaphragm. But sometimes it is difficult to introduce the cap because it is too short or too long for your cervix, or is just not the right shape for your particular cervix.[19]

Once back to your normal menstrual rhythm, you may want to consider the contraceptive pill. The combined pill—a mixture of oestrogen and progestogen — is contra-indicated for any woman who smokes, and, if you are breastfeeding, it is wiser to select a low-dose pill anyway. This is the progestogen-only or mini-pill. When you first go on it, your milk supply may be reduced for a few days. But even if you take it for two years, and breastfeed during that time, the baby would absorb the equivalent of only one pill by the end of it.[20] The progestogen-only pill should be taken within three hours of the same time each day. If by mistake you miss a day, take two the next day. Less than one in a hundred women conceive while on the pill, though, if you are careless in its use and skip days, there is a one in four chance that you become pregnant on the progestogen-only pill, and a one in seven chance on the combined pill. Many women are concerned about the possible long-term effects on health of absorbing artificial hormones day in, day out. Results of research are conflicting, some even suggesting a positive effect.

The IUD

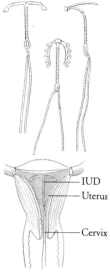

IUD
Uterus

Cervix

Various types of IUD

The intra-uterine device or coil is a plastic or copper loop or squiggle, about the size of a delicate earring, that is inserted by a doctor and, with any luck, stays in place until you want to have another baby, or for five years. It is usually taken out then to check that everything is all right. It is best to insert it during ovulation because it is simpler to put in then, and usually less painful. Following childbirth, it should not be inserted until the muscle walls of the uterus are thick and resilient again, because otherwise there is a risk that it may perforate the uterus. Many women who have never had a baby eject the IUD—the uterus contracts and it drops out—but after they have had a baby they are more likely to retain it. A side-effect of having an IUD inserted is an increased risk of pelvic inflammatory disease. Sometimes this leads to an ectopic (tubal) pregnancy. The woman then has to have an emergency operation to remove a section of her fallopian tube. Inflammation often results in infertility. Women may also get heavy bleeding and backache. An IUD may also get lost inside, and you do not know whether or not it has dropped out. Some women become pregnant with it still inside them, and are offered abortion, since having a foreign body inside the uterus during pregnancy increases the chance of miscarriage and pre-term labour. The chance of pregnancy is less than one in a hundred. A new hormone-releasing IUD may be coming on the market which can be kept in place for at least seven years. It has a low ectopic-pregnancy rate, makes periods lighter, and offers protection against pelvic inflammatory disease.[21]

Periodic abstinence

This is sometimes called 'natural family planning' or 'the rhythm method'. It is often favoured by Catholics. It entails being able to identify ovulation and to avoid intercourse around that time. There are different variations to this approach: the calendar method, the basal-body-temperature method, the cervical-mucus method and the sympto-thermal method.

To use the calendar method you have to calculate your 'safe' period by working out the length of your menstrual cycle for at least six months. Only then can you estimate when ovulation occurs. The basal-body-temperature method enables you to estimate this more accurately. You have to take your temperature with a thermometer every morning before getting up. Ovulation results in a slight temperature rise over a three-day period. The cervical-mucus method used to be called the Billings method. Mucus gets thin and stretchy, like raw egg white, with ovulation. After ovulation it becomes stickier and thick again. You need to stretch your mucus between your thumb and first finger to assess its condition. The sympto-thermal method

'I like the natural method because there are no health hazards and I'm not stuffing my body with chemicals.'

uses a combination of these different techniques. Because it is difficult to know exactly when the fertile period occurs, with the different 'natural' methods you may have to abstain through most of the menstrual cycle, so it requires high motivation from both partners.

With the cervical-mucus method 25 per cent of women get pregnant within a year, and with the sympto-thermal method nearly 20 per cent. It is vitally important to get detailed instruction from a nurse or doctor who is skilled in teaching these ways of birth control. Although there are many problems with them, they do have the advantage of enabling you to develop fertility awareness and to learn about your body. This is useful if you want to conceive. Some couples use a combination of this approach to birth control and a barrier method during the fertile period.[22]

There are other methods, involving hormone injections and implants, and new male methods of contraception, in the process of development and experiment. Many have undesirable side-effects. If this all sounds rather depressing, it is because there is no perfect method of birth control, and no one method that suits all couples.

If you had a good sexual relationship before you had the baby, all the evidence suggests that you will rediscover it, or build a relationship even more exciting and fulfilling, after the birth. But this usually does not happen immediately. For the majority of couples it takes at least six months to adjust. They have to adapt to new rhythms of love-making, new perceptions of each other, the woman's changed body, and having awareness of the baby in the forefront of their minds.

When a woman has had episiotomy and suturing of the perineum it may, unless she is lucky, take the better part of the first year after childbirth before she is completely unselfconscious and no longer on her guard about love-making. During these months she may not want penetration and intercourse. But she can enjoy other ways of love-making if she knows that her partner does not consider this merely 'foreplay' and a prelude to intercourse. In the year after childbirth a couple can take the opportunity to expand their repertoire of love-making skills, and to understand each other's bodies with deeper intimacy.

In this way the challenges of sex after childbirth bring new opportunities in their relationship, stimulate more open communication, and draw them closer together.

Coming Up for Air

The first year after birth is for many first-time mothers like an uncharted sea. However many books you read, however much help you receive, it is for each woman an adventure that is uniquely hers.

A new human being emerged from your body, and in the twinkling of an eye your whole life changed. It may have been frightening at first, but you really had no choice but to dive deep into this experience—like a swimmer discovering an underwater world with forms and colours that were startling and miraculous. You may have felt very out of touch with land, distant from all fixed certainties, from the usual realities of your life as it was before the baby came. At times you have had to push against strong currents, even, perhaps, to battle with monsters. This intense and vivid experience has increased your capacity for both suffering and joy; perhaps it has also given you awareness of your own inner power.

Now, towards the end of that first year, you come up for air, assess what you are doing, connect up all the images you have formed of yourself as a mother and of the pattern of your relationship with your baby, and plan for the future.

Whatever mistakes you have made, however critical you are of yourself as a mother, however difficult it has all been, you are a survivor. Celebrate this!

Space for yourself

When your life is shaken up like a kaleidoscope you are likely to feel dazed. Moreover, a newborn baby knows nothing of civilization, good manners, the limits that should be put to the demands made on a mother. At first the baby cannot even differentiate night from day. And if he is hungry and lonely and empty he wants to be fed *now*. Babies are never merely little bundles lying in a cot. They come into the world urgent, seeking, insistent, and bursting with tumultuous energy. A baby attracts like a magnet our deepest concern, our anxiety, our longing to fulfil a helpless being's raw and urgent need, and to see him secure and satisfied. A baby takes over your life.

At the same time a woman is struggling to create pattern out of chaos, to find a framework, to fit in other responsibilities, and to keep *everyone* happy. Becoming a mother is for many women like being caught up in a whirlwind.

Then a time comes when you seek to ground yourself, to stand back and consider your own needs. Motherhood is inherently stressful. But now you think about how you are handling stress and whether you are employing the most effective means of dealing with it. Skills in stress management are among the most vital skills in being a mother.

Mothers develop all sorts of ways of handling stress as part of their survival strategy. With some it is a gin and tonic at 7.00 p.m., a cigarette mid-morning, or collapsing in the evening in front of the TV set. With others it is a jog before breakfast, a natter with friends, playing in a string quartet, or dropping the children off at mother's to have a browse round the shops.

Only you can assess what works best, given your life and the pressures on you. But there are ways of trying to cope with stress which do nothing to contribute to your energy, or which—like smoking—make you ill and knock a few years off your life. There are others that help you feel positive about yourself and contribute to a sense of well-being.

We all know what we *should* do. Every woman's glossy magazine is full of exhortations to slim down, snap to, and get ourselves together. Many mothers of small children do not take kindly to this bossiness. Instead, they are experts at muddling through, compromising, meeting the challenge of the moment, and being infinitely adaptable. They are good at the things that never bring first prizes: soothing hurt places better, strategic distraction when a crawling baby is bound for the electricity socket, knowing when to let a baby explore and concentrate on discovering new things to touch, hear, see and do, when to reach out to hold a baby to calm her fear and insecurity, when to move forward and when to stand back, when to cuddle and when to let go.

'I lock myself in the bathroom and go off in a dream for quarter of an hour.'

'I go and swim. Mum looks after the baby.'

264

Yet most women seem to feel that they are not being good enough mothers, and there are times when they are overwhelmed by guilt.[1] They come in for a lot of criticism from people close to them, casual observers and the media. One of the most important elements in learning how to handle stress is valuing yourself.

Stress management

Breast feeding

Breastfeeding—when it is going well—is an excellent way of managing stress, both because natural opiates , which help you relax, are released in your bloodstream as the milk flows, and because you have the satisfaction of seeing the baby blooming on your milk. When breastfeeds come round every few hours, they ensure that you sit down, leave the dirty dishes, and have time for yourself and your baby.

Instant relaxation

Another simple way of quickly entering a peaceful state and regaining energy—something like that described in the old Quaker phrase 'centring down'—is to give a long breath out, drop your shoulders, and relax. It is amazing how it can stop you saying things you wish afterwards that you had never said and doing things you wish you had never done. The simple act of breathing out and letting your shoulders drop 'grounds' you. It is much better than counting to ten or biting your lip in mounting tension.

Focused breathing

Focused breathing is a development of this. For instant relaxation, breathe out, drop your shoulders and relax, and then let breath flow in through your nostrils again, without forcing it. When you are ready, give another long breath out, listening to the sound of your breathing. Focus on the feeling and the sound of breath going out, and pause for a moment while the desire to breathe in comes, and then breath flows in through the nostrils, your ribs swing out, and your abdominal wall presses up. There is another slight pause, and then a wave of breath flows away again.

If your baby is crying you can do this as you stroke down the baby's back with each long breath out, so that you give comfort to your baby at the same time that you are helping yourself with focused breathing. Or you can slowly pat your baby's bottom as you breathe out, or rock, with her in your arms, while you breathe out and in.

Ten-minute yoga

If there is a chance to close your bedroom door, you can do simple breathing and stretching yoga exercises. They can be done in the office or kitchen, too, and with other people, but you need to be able to concentrate. The philosophy behind this form of yoga is that you increase and regulate your vital energy in a harmonious flow through your body. You release tension, build up energy, and breathe more fully and deeply. The important thing is to keep your mind in the present moment and to concentrate on the breathing and your physical sensations. A study in Oxford that compared relaxation, visualization techniques, and yoga revealed that Pranayama yoga, as taught by Sissel Fowler, an experienced yoga teacher, was more effective in increasing mental and physical energy and feelings of alertness than relaxation or visualization.[2]

Start by sitting on the floor or on a chair with your back straight. Relax and listen to your breathing. Notice the movement of breathing in your lower abdomen, which, according to this yoga system, is your centre of gravity. Breathing in and out through the nose, concentrate on the breath out and let the breath in take care of itself. Allow time for a pause each time after you have breathed in.

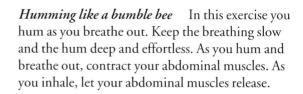

Humming like a bumble bee   In this exercise you hum as you breathe out. Keep the breathing slow and the hum deep and effortless. As you hum and breathe out, contract your abdominal muscles. As you inhale, let your abdominal muscles release.

Contracting the pelvic-floor muscles   You are already familiar with this from postnatal exercises. Pull the muscles around your vagina and perineum up inside you, breathing in as you do so. Then release and breathe out simultaneously. Be aware of what is happening inside your abdomen.

The tiptoe stretch   Stand and stretch out your arms vigorously, first on one side, then the other, stretching up on to the balls of your feet as you do so. When you stretch, allow grunts to come. Again, feel what is happening in your abdomen.

Chest expansion twist   Still standing, clasp your hands behind your body. Lift your chest and squeeze your shoulder blades together. Rotate to the right and exhale with the breath out, making the sound 'Ha'. Let the breath come in again and as you do so return to your starting position. Now twist to the other side in the same way. Continue doing this from side to side five to seven times.

The half moon   Stand with your hands clasped behind your head and bend sideways on a soft 'Ha' breath out. As your lungs fill again, return to the starting position. Do this from side to side five to ten times.

Shoulder shrugging   Running on the spot, shake your shoulders loose, and as you breathe out make the sound 'A-a-a'.

Arm circles   Draw a circle with your right arm from front to back, following your hand with your eyes. Inhale as your arm rises and exhale as your arm goes down and behind you. As you breathe out make an 'O-oo' sound. After you have done this five to seven times, reverse the movement. Then do it on the other side.

These simple yoga exercises have the great advantage that they can be done sitting at a desk, standing in the kitchen, or anywhere where there is enough room to swing your arms. Babies also find it great entertainment.

Head, shoulder, and foot massage

Anyone with strong and sensitive hands should be good at massage. Head, shoulder, and foot massage can be done without needing to take off any clothes, and releases tension instantly. It can even be done with your baby on your lap or at the breast.

Scalp massage   With the fingertips of both hands, your helper makes small circular movements travelling slowly over the scalp, moving the flesh on the bone. He then changes the movement slightly by using one hand to cradle the forehead while the other makes the same circular movements over the back of your head.

Neck and shoulder massage   If there is a chance to loosen the clothing around your neck this massage will be more effective. Your helper lifts your hair up and with the palms of both hands strokes from the base of your skull down over your neck with flowing movements outwards over your shoulders and down the outside of your arms as far as your elbows.

Now your helper spreads fingers over the front of your shoulders and massages with thumbs in the little valleys at either side of your spine.

Then the thumbs move out in a circular motion over the shoulder blades.
Guide your helper's hand to where the massage feels best.

Foot massage   You sit on a low chair while your helper sits on the floor. Rest your feet on a cushion in your helper's lap. The massage starts with a flowing movement of both hands from just above your ankles down your feet, along the soles as far as the toes, and up over the top again, keeping a continuous movement.

Now your helper grasps one ankle with both hands and uses a squeezing movement of each hand down either side of your ankle and over your heel so that your foot wobbles. The squeezing movement is continued down to your toes.

Your helper massages the other foot in the same way, and continues massaging your feet alternately. Now your helper puts both thumbs under the ball of one foot, resting the fingers above your foot, and applies pressure with the thumbs with a small circular movement.

Then the other foot is massaged in the same way. This massage continues until both feet are relaxed.

Solo head and foot massage   You will find that you can do scalp and foot massage when you are on your own, adapting the techniques slightly—a speedy pick-me-up that will leave you feeling refreshed and energized.

Taking pressure off your baby   Often the cause of your stressed state is that the baby is distressed. Parents' favourite stress treatments for babies and young children include:

Feed the child without delay.

Whatever time of the day it is, climb into bed with your child and giving him your undivided attention—talking to him, tell him a story, listening to music, cuddle him.

Either put the child in a bath or get into the bath with him. It may turn out to be either a relaxing or a lively bath. Lively baths need buckets, waterfalls, plastic containers, water pistols, pingpong balls, funnels and other water toys. For a relaxing bath you may want to draw the curtains, light a candle, and play soft music.

Get out of the house and into the fresh air—visit the ducks, play in the park, watch older children on the jungle gym.

If it is bed-time, soothing, rocking, stroking, massaging, singing, or humming, help a child wind down and eventually fall asleep. Dim the lights, and reduce all extraneous stimuli.

If a baby is fractious and overtired but will not settle, try putting her in the car seat and going for a drive. If she is likely to wake up when you lift her out, either move her in her car seat very carefully so as not to disturb her, or relax in the car with a book or some sewing, or take the opportunity of a sleep yourself.

Sharing the load

Many mothers do the equivalent of two full-time jobs without pay. They are on call twenty-four hours in the twenty-four, and are the first person anyone turns to when something goes wrong. As one woman puts it, 'I'm always doing the job of mothering, even while I am doing other jobs, or things for myself. I would estimate that I am actively mothering for at least half of my waking hours, and some of my sleeping hours as well.' She has kept a record of what she is doing each hour, and it turns out that her work in the house takes forty-two hours a week *without counting childcare*. If a child is ill, she easily works more than a hundred hours a week.[3]

Sometimes a new father cannot imagine why his partner seems unable to get through the most basic chores while he is out of the house. To him it looks as if she has been doing virtually nothing all day. Meanwhile she can hardly find time to have a bath, eat, or dress. She gets more and more tired, and resentful of a partner who does not understand the time that caring for a baby takes.

If a man is unemployed, even though he is around all the time, he may have no idea of jobs that have to be fitted into the day. Many men

271

feel humiliated by unemployment and leave housework and childcare to women, because to take responsibility for domestic concerns would threaten their male identity further. Others would like to help but have never learnt how to do tasks which the woman could do with one hand tied behind her back—if she had time. So each partner feels angry and resentful.

Whether or not there are stresses like this between you, it may help to get together to sort out your workload, and decide who is to be responsible for different tasks, so that it is fairly distributed.[4] Some women do not feel that they can attempt this kind of discussion because it will turn into a confrontation, and lead to further stress. Other couples find it really useful. It may be that it is better to face up to the difficulties now rather than allow a build-up of mutual resentment in the future.

You can discuss exactly what commitments you have and what else you would like to fit in, and the time they are likely to take each day or week. Sometimes you have to do two things at once, though chores may take longer then. Women are often expert at this. Men may find this doubling up more difficult because they are not accustomed to it.

If either of you is studying, include the time this takes. Work outside the home often entails further work at home, too. If you have family commitments which mean that you are looking after a parent or other relative, this ought to be added, too. If you have other children, decide who is going to take them out, give support for their homework, and get them to and from out-of-school activities. If you have twins, a child with a disability, or a non-sleeping baby, or if you yourself have a disability, discuss how to divide all the extra tasks. If you have hobbies or other activities you want to do for which you want to make time, bear these in mind as well.

Working mothers

There is no doubt about it: all mothers are working mothers. But for those juggling paid work and work at home childcare arrangements are central to their lives. These must operate smoothly or schedules are disrupted, appointments and deadlines missed, and the child, mother, and family suffer as a result. If you send your child to a day-care centre, the personal relationships involved may be minimal, and you never really get to know the people who are looking after your child. This is one of the great disadvantages of day care, and you may want to go out of your way to foster relationships with the carers. The relationship with the carer is central to a woman's efficiency at work and to the child's happiness.

Women who are high achievers in professional and business life

usually have to be careful not to take the nursery into the boardroom. They make complicated arrangements to split their two lives. For whereas work can impinge on the home, domestic concerns must never be allowed to impinge on the workplace. The price of almost any successful woman's achievement is that she has to copy men. A man is not expected to turn up late at a committee meeting with the excuse that his baby is feverish. It is more acceptable to say that the train was delayed or he could find nowhere to park. So this is what women often have to do, too. When women in the public eye do not copy male behaviour, they are often criticized. A British TV personality whose baby could be heard enjoying a breastfeed during a radio interview, and a Member of Parliament who fed her hungry baby in the House of Commons, were both accused in the press of flaunting motherhood and making an indecent display of their lactating breasts. There is great

resentment of women who do not rigidly separate their role as mothers from their role in the workplace.

There is some evidence from research in the United States that employed mothers who are breastfeeding may have more help from managers than from many work colleagues—especially from managers who have either breastfed themselves, or whose wives breastfed. Women who keep up their milk supply usually pump or express milk in their lunch breaks. There are often hostile reactions to this, including jealousy that a woman can continue to be employed while breastfeeding. This research suggests that it happens most often in office and school settings. Women who have successfully continued breastfeeding say that the most important things are support from management and colleagues, being able to get a day off when necessary without too much hassle, and, when the place of employment is not too distant from the baby, having an opportunity to feed the baby during workbreaks.[5]

Back to work?

You may have to make practical arrangements for childcare long before you come to the end of this first year. Your job is waiting for you; you cannot extend maternity leave any further; you depend on your income for keeping up the mortgage or simply to make ends meet. Or perhaps you believe that it is important to be with your child during these important early years, and you are prepared to cut your standard of living so that you can be a full-time mother.

'I don't want to dump my baby on anyone else. For me, this time at home with the baby is precious.'

Many women have no choice but to work outside the home. In Britain it is still assumed by government, businesses, administrations, and many schools, that every child has two parents, one of whom is the breadwinner, while the other is available for childcare. Yet thousands of families need two incomes. The issue of childcare is urgent. Three out of five women go back to work within a year of having a baby. Even then, the cost of care leaves them with little extra income.

Today women are the main breadwinners in many parts of Britain. Seventy per cent of married women between the ages of 16 and 59 are in the workforce. Twenty years ago 60 per cent of the workforce was male. Now it is only 51 per cent.[6] Almost half these women work part-time, and they all tend to be in low-paid, low-skilled jobs, often the sorts of jobs that men are not prepared to accept. For women's earnings remain significantly below those of men in spite of equal opportunities legislation. These working mothers bring in the only income for many homes in areas where unemployment is high, and if it were not for their earnings the number of families in poverty would treble.

'I've put my career on hold. This time will never come back again.'

'A baby knows when you are resentful, frustrated, and angry. I'm a much better mother when I've had a break from the baby.'

'My husband's unemployed and we need the money. I don't have any choice.'

But women work outside the home for many other reasons. It may be the only way in which they can keep some control over their lives, and look forward to a future beyond child-raising. 'Women are not in employment just because they cannot find a man to earn "a family wage." They work because they want to; because they want to earn a living for themselves; because they want to use their abilities and their education; because they want adult company. And because they know they cannot rely on marriage for life-time financial security.'[7]

In Australia, for instance, the man is the sole breadwinner in only 32 per cent of families. More than half of all women aged between 16 and 65 are in the workforce. As in Britain, women who can add something to the family income, even if only from part-time work, are under great pressure to get back to work, not least from their employers, as soon as they can after having a baby.

You may be longing to get back to work, torn in two about it, or hate leaving your baby. It may be what you thought you wanted, but now you feel strongly that you should be with your baby. Becoming a mother often changes priorities. It can be a terrible deprivation to miss out on the many 'firsts' of your baby's life, the first time he rolls over, pulls himself up to standing, walks, the first time he says 'Mamma', or 'dog', the first time he waves 'bye-bye'. You may feel cheated when he does these things 'for' another person who is looking after him, not you. It is hard not to be jealous of someone who looks after your child, and to resent the love that he gives her. Childcare is not a clear-cut practical issue. Though there are many important practical considerations, it involves deep and often disturbing emotions.

Childcare

No country in Europe has adequate childcare facilities financed by the state. Even the most generous, Denmark, provides for only about half of all families. France and Belgium follow in the league table, with provision for 20 per cent. In Britain, places for only 2–3 per cent of children under 3 are available in publicly financed nurseries. So everywhere women are forced to choose between staying at home and juggling arrangements for care which are often temporary and sub-standard.

Childcare is not necessarily a second-best option. When it is good, it offers a child an enriched social environment, stimulation, and friendships with other children and adults. It enlarges the child's world and enhances experience. Research in Sweden shows that children who have been in day-care centres before their first birthday are assessed as having grown into teenagers with more social confidence than those cared for exclusively by their mothers until they started school.[8]

Ninety per cent of British women with children under 4 depend on relatives for childcare. This may be what most of them want, but there is little choice. The vast majority of these women cannot afford nannies, and even when day-care centres, nurseries, and childminders can be found, they have to do a juggling act to get the child to and from the place of care.

You may have already worked out your priorities concerning childcare. Under-twos seem to flourish best in a one-to-one relationship with not more than two or three carers, including you. Babies attach themselves to a loved person, and it is important that, if your child is in a nursery, there is a single individual who has primary responsibility for him. When this works well, the child becomes deeply attached to her, and she in turn loves the child. The depth of attachment may be such that the mother feels that she is missing out on the relationship and cannot help sometimes being jealous of the closeness between child and carer. But this bond between them shows that the relationship is working. One of the sad things about nurseries in Communist Russia was that, when babies were dropped off as their mothers went to work, there was no single person whom they could love and be loved by, and each baby was just one of a well-organized, expertly disciplined crowd.

There is a lot to be said for arranging care of a baby under 15 months in your own or someone else's home. If it cannot be in your own home, it should if possible be not more than a ten-minute distance from your home or place of work. In this way you provide security and constancy, and avoid long journeys, often in bad weather, with a sleepy or sleeping child, or one whom you think may be going down with a cold.

If the only practical arrangement is for your baby to be cared for in someone else's home, once your child is 8 or 9 months old there are some advantages in having a minder who has one or two other children as well. He can develop relationships with other children, yet have the individualized attention that comes from being part of a small family.

The interview　　When you interview a possible childminder or nanny, you will need ample time for discussion together so that you can really feel what kind of person she is. For some time to come she will be one of the most important people in your life, and this is not a relationship to start out on lightly. You will want to know why she started this work, what the other children for whom she has cared are like, which age group she enjoys most, and to get an idea of her values and philosophy of care. Find out about her previous experience and how long she has been doing this kind of work. If she has children herself, ask about them and show interest in her as a person.

Always ask for two references, preferably from people for whom she has done similar work. If anything about her makes you feel uncomfortable, even if you cannot explain how, trust your feelings.

If you are thinking of taking your child to someone else's home, you should expect to be able to meet her children, her partner, and anyone else who might be around and be involved with your child. So ask, 'Who else is at home in the day-time? When can I meet them?'

If she is coming to work in your own home, sort out whether she will be doing any housework. If you want her to do some, make sure that she knows that the baby is her priority, not the vacuuming. Ask open-ended questions rather than ones which draw a simple 'Yes' or 'No', or which suggest the answer you might prefer. 'What do you do when a baby does not settle to sleep?', and, 'How do you cope with a child who is upset when the mother leaves?' are better questions than asking, 'You don't leave a baby to cry, do you?'

It is a good idea to have your baby with you as you chat so that you get an impression of how she is with him, and how he reacts to her. If he is at a crawling or walking stage, put him down and see what happens. Give them a chance to get to know each other.

As you talk, watch how she treats children. If it is during her working time, be prepared to break off the conversation so that she attends to them. How does she talk to them? Is she really interested in and fond of them? Does she show patience, consideration, and respect for children? How do they respond to her? Is she lively, energetic, and resourceful enough to handle several at once?

Remember to sort out what will happen if she is ill or your child is ill, and discuss arrangements for holidays—hers and yours.

If you are thinking of a nursery, ask if you can just sit and watch the children for a while. You will probably want to know how they select their staff, what they consider the most important things about the care they offer, and to learn about any changes that have taken place in the nursery in the last year. Ask to meet other parents who have children of about the same age as yours who are there, as you can learn a lot from their experiences.

Making it as easy as you can
Though it may seem a counsel of perfection, if you take your child to a caregiver outside your own home, prepare as much as you can overnight, and avoid a mad rush in the morning. Lay breakfast, and put out the clothing she will need, so that you can be relaxed and gentle, and take time for a cuddle. If you have a partner, one of you can do the kitchen jobs while the other can give the child total attention, even if that is only for five precious minutes.

Children feel secure when they have a regular pattern of events. Talk about what will happen next. Make a story out of it.

Never leave your baby in someone else's care without an introductory period in which you stay, but try to remain in the background as much as possible. The height of separation anxiety is between 9 months and 2 years. Your child may need you to be there at least for the first couple of days, and sometimes weeks, before he will trust this stranger. You can ease him in by gradually reducing the time you stay with him. You may want to be there all the time at first, then half the time, and following this an hour or two in the next week as the relationship between child and carer becomes a going concern. If your child is being cared for in your own home, try to arrange it so that you are away for only an hour or so at first. As the child adjusts and becomes confident and happy, extend the time.

A transitional object, something which your child associates with you, can help her cope with your absence. It could be a scarf, a handbag, or anything familiar. When a baby is in a strange environment, you could take the mobile that she usually sees when she is in her cot, a loved doll, teddy bear, or blanket. A psychologist who has written a book on childcare says that children get very attached to their car seats, and, if your child is in a strange environment, leaving the seat gives the message that before long she will be going home again with you in your car.[9]

'She started going to the minder at 7 months and was OK until she began to walk. Then she screamed when I left. We had to go through the easing-in programme all over again.'

When you leave, never just slip away and hope your child will not notice. Say goodbye, even though she becomes distressed. You may be able to develop a goodbye ritual—a rhyme, a hug, a song, similar to a goodnight ritual.

But make it short. Do not hang around anxiously, or wait outside the door and then pop back in because the child is crying. This trains her to cry so that you keep on returning.

It will be an ordeal for you at work if your child was distressed as you left. Though you may long to be reassured that all is well, calling up three or four times to check interrupts the carer in building a relationship with your child, is distracting for her, and may wake a sleeping baby.

If you can manage it, arrange a regular time to have a chat with the caregiver. You want to get an idea of what your child has been doing, how tired she gets, what she is eating and drinking, and whether there have been any difficulties.

After you have been out to work, or when you have scooped the child up from a minder's, make a point of giving your undivided attention when you come in if you possibly can, even if it is only for a short time. Enjoy a snack together, share a shower or bath, get on the bed with a favourite picture book, or keep a stock of best loved playthings for this special half hour. When a child is having to adjust to the challenge of a new environment and being cared for by different people, he may get very tired and cross, and protest by being as difficult as he can once back with you.

When a caregiver is introduced at the right time for a particular child, it can expand and develop her social world, and this even when separation has at first been painful for you both. She learns that when you go away from her you come back. This is important in the unfolding of trust between you. The certainty of continuity, the rock on which she depends, and the sure knowledge that your temporary absence is always followed by your return and the reaching out of loving arms to her, build security for a child of a kind that may be stronger than when a mother never leaves her child, and when she is concerned to satisfy every need herself.

All over the world in traditional cultures children are cared for by other women, relatives and neighbours, who share the same value system, and who look after them in much the same way. There are often wide differences in values between mothers and childminders in Western societies. A mother cannot be sure that the carer has the same attitudes and values that she hopes to inculcate in her child. So there is often an element of uncertainty. Yet a child often readily adjusts to different standards and beliefs in a variety of environments. And women from very different backgrounds form strong relationships as they love and care for a child. This community of loving women is a powerful foundation on which any child can become aware of the female bonds of love and reciprocity which are the basis of human society.

Building your support system

Whether or not you are working outside the home, every mother benefits from a support system to help her cope when the going gets tough. This is vital if you are a mother alone, or if you have a partner who does not share in parenting or consider time spent with the baby a personal priority.

Women taking time off from work often use their maternity leave to start building up that network, and to make links with people in the local community. You will meet them at postnatal exercise classes, at parents' discussion groups, at the school gate, in a place of worship. You may want to go out of your way to meet women with babies of the same age, and older women whose children have left home who may be available to help.

There may be a working mothers' association where you can join with other mothers to make proposals for more flexible working conditions, improved childcare, and job-share schemes. It is often more effective when an organization makes constructive suggestions of this kind than when one individual asks for special consideration and arrangements that suit her.

Start up or join a baby-sitting co-operative if you want to get out in the evenings. Explore the possibilities of nanny-sharing, and take turns to have someone else's children with you for a day, then switch round when you want a day out.

No mother can be everything to her child, however hard she tries. Sometimes women feel guilty about actually enjoying going out to work, seeking any separate existence from a baby. They feel that, if they were good mothers, they should be giving 100 per cent care every hour of every day. If a woman is able and willing to commit herself to this, and has joy in doing so, that's fine. But it is not something that should ever be imposed on women. For many mothers it is impractical to give total, undivided attention to a baby day and night, if only because they have other children. A woman and her baby both benefit when other people share loving responsibility.

Theories of attachment and the mystique of bonding, which have done a great deal to improve care of newborns in hospitals, are often stretched and distorted to become rules of an almost religious intensity stating that you should never put a baby down, never let anyone else care for your child—or it may lead to emotional damage. Gurus and mentors who have forgotten, or never known, what it is like to be with a baby for twenty-four hours and to carry the sole burden of responsibility for another life, call for impossible standards of maternal devotion and the total surrender of self. This highly contrived mother–child exclusiveness is an invention of the twentieth century, and has no cultural validity outside wealthy Western countries in which extended families rarely exist, and where mothers and babies are often cut off from other human contact for hours on end.

If a woman is to nurture her child, she needs to be supported and nurtured herself. That includes recognition of the right to realize her potential as a person other than in her role as a mother.

For the child, being loved and cared for by several people can be an enriching experience. When you gradually introduce your baby to a social world in a positive and supportive way, you create the foundations for relationships later in life, for learning the art of giving and getting, and the development of self-confidence.

One woman's support group

My partner. We try to divide the work 50/50.

I went to school with Tina. James is 8 and adores the baby.

Mrs Smith lives next door and cares for Ben occasionally so that we can get out to the theatre or a concert.

Mrs Smith's daughter, Laura, baby-sits after school.

My sister-in-law is generous with hand-me-downs and nursery equipment.

My mother and father have her for a few hours each week. I leave breastmilk in the fridge.

John and Lucy, a couple we met at postnatal discussion group.

Vivien and Ann. Vivien is a nursery-school teacher, Ann a children's librarian, and they are both willing to help when they can.

Anima and Melissa. Jan has Ben when I want a break to do something on my own, and I take Melissa when she wants to go out.

My health visitor—I can discuss any health queries with her.

Our GP.

My breastfeeding counsellor.

Claire is training to be a nursery nurse. She comes in to help one day a week as part of her practical work so I can get on with my studies.

The transition to parenthood is, for men as well as for women, a leap into the dark. Whether you plan carefully ahead or whether you are surprised by pregnancy, you have to take courage in both hands as you start out on an amazing journey that takes you far into the future, way beyond birth and babies, and on to your own death. For being a parent does not stop when your children are no longer children. You continue to be a mother and father through their adulthood, too, and for as long as you live.

It starts with an intimate sexual act between two people which they may consider no one's concern but their own. It may be an expression of commitment to each other, or merely a casual encounter. A child is conceived. A woman tells other people she is pregnant. A baby is born. Relationships change, coalesce, crystallize around this new human being, and bonds of love and caring are formed.

With the birth of a child, lives become connected and bonds that may have been weak are strengthened. Family, friends, even sometimes total strangers reach out and greet the new life as if this child holds out hope for their future, too. Women gather to support each other in love and reciprocity. In traditional cultures whole communities are bound more closely together.

With the birth of a child, the shape of life changes irrevocably. Past connects up with future. Links with the past through parents and grandparents have a significance which may never have been previously acknowledged. The future—not just our own personal future—but the future of the world that this child will have to live in—comes to matter in a way it may never have done before. Fundamental values—our deepest beliefs and the spirit in which we live our lives—are challenged.

A man begins the long and often difficult process of learning how to be a father. A woman starts out on the painful, arduous, and exciting journey to motherhood. She sails in turbulent emotional seas, plunges through states of alternating exhaustion and exhilaration, treks through arid desert thinking that she can never be a good enough mother, and needs to summon all her energy and determination to scale mountains. It is a journey in which she always comes face to face with herself. And, as she grows to be a mother, she discovers, often for the first time, her own power.

GLOSSARY

AIDS Auto-immune deficiency syndrome

agoraphobia fear of open spaces

anaemia deficiency in quality or quantity of red corpuscles in the blood

anal sphincter ring-shaped muscle around the anus

antibodie elements in the blood that resist disease

areola a ring of pigmentation that surrounds the nipple

autolysis breaking-up of living tissues

catheter a fine hollow tube for removing or inserting fluid into a body cavity

cerebral palsy brain damage when something has gone wrong in pregnancy, or sometimes childbirth. Co-ordination of movement is affected

circumcision cutting off of a circular portion of the skin around the top of the penis; **female circumcision** excision of the labia minora and sometimes the clitoris.

clitoris a woman's sexual organ formed of erectile tissue, at the upper end of the vagina

coccyx tail bone of the spine

coeliac disease a condition in which the body cannot metabolize certain carbohydrates and fats, and for which a child needs a gluten-free diet

coitus sexual intercourse

colic pain due to spasmodic contraction of digestive muscles

colostrum first fluid from the mother's breasts after childbirth, containing more protein but less fat and sugar than later milk

colporrhaphy repair of the vagina

congenital conditions existing at or before birth, not necessarily hereditary

convulsions spasmodic or prolonged contraction of muscle

cystitis inflammation of the bladder

cystocele sagging of the front surface of the bladder into the vagina

cytotoxic damaging to cell structure and division

detrusor muscle whose action is to push down

Down's syndrome used to be called 'Mongolism'; a chromosome abnormality that causes mental handicap

dyspareunia painful intercourse

electroconvulsive therapy passage of an electric current through the frontal lobes of the brain, which causes a convulsion

electrolyte compound which when dissolved in a solution will dissociate into ions

endometrium mucous membrane lining the uterus

enterocele sagging of the intestine into the deepest part of the vagina

episiotomy cut through skin and muscles to speed delivery

external os opening to the outside (*os* is literally 'mouth')

faradism electricity with a rapidly alternating current

galactagogue an agent causing increased secretion of milk

gastroenteritis inflammation of the stomach and intestine due to viral or bacterial infection

glottis space between the vocal cords

gluteals buttock muscles

gonorrhoea a sexually transmitted disease

HIV human immuno-deficiency virus

haematoma swelling filled with blood

haemoglobin pigment that makes blood cells red

haemophilia a genetic disease transmitted by women only, to male offspring, characterized by delayed or absence of clotting power of the blood

haemorrhoids piles; varicose veins of the rectum

hara-obi Japanese pregnant woman's comfort sash; also worn post-partum

hysterectomy surgical removal of the uterus

hysteria a psychoneurosis

ilium upper part of the pelvic bone

immunological body's defence mechanism

impotent a man's inability to perform sexual intercourse

involution tightening of the uterus after birth

linea nigra dark line down the centre of the abdomen which may appear during pregnancy

lochia bleeding after birth

lumbar curve muscles in the small of the back

manic depression a mental illness characterized by mania and/or depression

mastitis inflammation of the breast

meningocele a protrusion of the meninges through the skull or spinal column, forming a cyst filled with cerebro-spinal fluid, *see* spina bifida

mucous concerning or secreting mucus

neuroma a tumour consisting of nervous tissue

oestrogen a steroid hormone, controlling female sexual development

opiate any medicine containing opium

ovulation rupture of the mature graafian follicle when the ovum is released from the ovary

oxytocin pituitary hormone which stimulates uterine contractions and ejection of milk

parturition act of giving birth

perineometer a device to measure the strength of pelvic-floor muscles

perineum area between the vagina and the anus

placenta organ which develops with the embryo in the uterus and through which the unborn baby is nourished

polyp a tag of mucous membrane

post-partum haemorrhage more than 500 ml blood loss after birth

primigravida a woman pregnant for the first time

progesterone hormone which plays an important part in the regulation of the menstrual cycle and in pregnancy

prolactin milk-producing hormone which stimulates the mammary gland

prolapse downward displacement of an organ

psychosis mental illness affecting the personality

pubic symphysis at the front of the pubis

pubo-coccygeous muscle slung between the pubic bone and the coccyx

puerperal time after childbirth

puerperium period of about six weeks following childbirth when the reproductive organs are returning to their normal state

recti muscles muscles running down the middle of the abdomen

rectocele sagging of the rectum into the anus

rectovaginal fistula a tear from the vagina into the rectum

REM sleep rapid-eye-movement type of deep sleep

ribozo strip of cloth a mother winds round her body to 'wear' her baby

rubella German measles

sacro-iliac the joints connecting the sacrum to the pelvis

sacro lumbar the area where the sacrum joins the pelvis.

sacrum a triangular bone composed of five united vertebrae, between the lowest lumbar vertebra and the coccyx; it forms the back of the pelvis

secondary post-partum haemorrhage a gush of very heavy bleeding later than twenty-four hours after childbirth

spina bifida a congenital defect of the spine in which the spinal cord protrudes through the back

sternum breast bone

thrombosis clot in a blood vessel

toxic shock severe bacterial infection, with flu-like symptoms, sometimes resulting from a tampon which has been worn too long

uterine prolapse sagging of the uterus into the vagina

uterus womb

vaginismus vaginal muscle spasm

vernix creamy protective covering on skin of baby during the last months of pregnancy.

vertebra one of thirty-three bones forming the spine

NOTES

Chapter 1 The Roller-Coaster Year

1. V. Bergum, *Woman to Mother* (Gramby, Mass.: Bergin & Garvey, 1989); P. Caplan, *The Myth of Women's Masochism* (London: Methuen, 1986); N. Chodorow, *The Reproduction of Mothering* (Berkeley, Calif.: University of California Press, 1978; J. Lazarre, *The Mother Knot* (New York: Dell Publishing, 1976); J. Raphael-Leff, *Psychological Processes of Childbearing* (London: Chapman & Hall, 1991); A. Oakley, *Women Confined* (Oxford: Martin Robertson, 1980; L. G. Peppers and R. J. Knapp, *Motherhood and Mourning* (New York: Praeger, 1980); A. Rossiter, *From Private to Public: A Feminist Exploration of Early Mothering* (Toronto: Women's Press, 1988).
2. S. Kitzinger, *Ourselves as Mothers* (London: Transworld/Doubleday, 1992).
3. Quoted in Chodorow, *Reproduction of Mothering*
4. S. Kitzinger, *The Crying Baby* (Harmondsworth: Penguin, 1990).
5. Reported in J. O'Farrell, 'Childbirth and the Disabled Woman', *New Generation [Digest]* (Mar. 1993).

Chapter 2 How your Body Changes

1. G. M. Stirrat, *Obstetrics* (London: Grant McIntyre, 1981).
2. T. H. Bloomfield and H. Gordon, 'Reaction to Blood Loss at Delivery', *British Journal of Obstetrics and Gynaecology*, 10, suppl. 2 (1990), 5.
3. H. R. Mahomed, 'Iron and Folate Supplementation in Pregnancy', in I. Chalmers, M. Enkin, and M. Keirse (eds.), *Effective Care in Pregnancy and Childbirth*, 2 vols. (Oxford: Oxford University Press, 1989), i. 301–5.
4. M. Tisserand, *Aromatherapy for Women* (London: Thorsons, 1985).
5. C. MacArthur, M. Lewis, and E. G. Knox, *Health after Childbirth* (London: University of Birmingham and HMSO, 1991).
6. Ibid. 236.
7. M. Cassidy, 'Doctor and Patient', *Lancet*, 1 (1938), 175–9.

8. D. Armstrong, 'What do Patients Want?', *British Medical Journal*, 303 (1991), 261.
9. A. Grant and J. Sleep, 'Relief of Perineal Pain and Discomfort after Childbirth', in Chalmers, Enkin, and Keirse, ii. 1347–58.
10. MacArthur, Lewis and Knox, *Health after Childbirth*; R. Russell, P. Groves, N. Taub, J. O'Dowd, R. Reynolds, 'Assessing Long-Term Backache after Childbirth', *British Medical Journal*, 306 (1993), 1299–303.
11. C. MacArthur, M. Lewis, E. G. Knox, and J. S. Crawford, 'Epidural Anaesthesia and Long-Term Backache after Childbirth', *British Medical Journal*, 301 (1990), 9–12.
12. Russell, Groves, Taub, O'Dowd and Reynolds, referring to S. Kitzinger, *Some Women's Experiences of Epidurals: A Descriptive Study* (London: National Childbirth Trust, 1987).
13. MacArthur, Lewis, and Knox, *Health after Childbirth*.
14. Ibid.
15. S. Clement, *The Caesarean Experience* (London: Pandora, 1991).
16. Ibid.

Chapter 3 Enjoying your Body

1. M. Feldenkrais, *Awareness through Movement* (Harmondsworth: Penguin, 1980).
2. E. Noble, *Essential Exercises for the Childbearing Year*, 3rd edn. (Boston: Houghton Mifflin, 1988).
3. P. Simkin, J. Whalley, and A. Keppler, *Pregnancy, Childbirth and the Newborn* (Deephaven, Minn.: Meadowbrook, n.d.), 208.
4. Childbirth Graphics Ltd., PO Box 20540, Rochester, NY 14602-0540.
5. Ibid.
6. S. K. Olkin, *Positive Parenting Fitness* (New York: Avery, 1992).
7. Noble, *Essential Exercises for the Childbearing Year*, 8.

Chapter 4 Your Pelvic Floor, Bladder, and Vagina

1. I. L.C. Fergusson, 'Genital Prolapse', *British Journal of Hospital Medicine* (1981), 67–72.

2. W. Greenshields, 'What Every Woman should Know', *New Generation*, 4/4 (1985), 9–10.

3. E. Montgomery, *Regaining Bladder Control* (Bristol: Wright, 1974).

4. E. Montgomery, 'Pelvic Power', *Community Outlook* (Sept. 1986), 33–4.

5. P. E. Chiarelli with D. Mandelstam, *Women's Waterworks: Curing Incontinence* (Rushcutters Bay, Australia: Gore & Osment, 1991; distributed in the UK by the Incontinence Advisory Service at the Disabled Living Foundation).

6. J. Pusey, C. Hodge, P. Wilkinson, and R. Johanson, 'Maternal Impressions of Forceps or the Silc-Cup', *British Journal of Obstetrics and Gynaecology*, 98/5 (1991), 487–8.

7. K. S. Olah, N. Bridges, J. Denning, and D. Farrar, 'The Conservative Management of Patients with Sumptoms of Stress Incontinence', *American Journal of Obstetrics and Gynaecology*, 162 (1990), 87–92.

8. L. Cardozo, 'Urinary Incontinence in Woman: Have We Anything New to Offer?', *British Medical Journal*, 303 (1991), 1453–7.

9. S. Kitzinger, *Episiotomy:Physical and Emotional Aspects* (London: National Childbirth Trust, 1981); S. Kitzinger and R. Walters, *Some Women's Experiences of Episiotomy* (London: National Childbirth Trust, 1981).

10. R. E. Allen, G. L. Hosker, A. R. B. Smith, and D. W. Warrell, 'Pelvic Floor Damage and Childbirth: A Neurophysiological Study', *British Journal of Obstetrics and Gynaecology*, 97/9 (1990), 770–9; H. Gordon and M. Logue, 'Perineal Muscle Function after Childbirth', *Lancet*, 2 (1985), 123–5.

11. J. Sleep and A. Grant, 'West Berkshire Perineal Management Trail: Three Year Follow Up', *British Medical Journal*, 295 (1987) 749–51.

12. G. Rockner, V. Wahlberg, and A. Olunda, 'Episiotomy and Perineal Trauma during Childbirth', *Journal of Advanced Nursing*, 14 (1989), 264–8; Kitzinger and Walters, *Some Women's Experiences of Episiotomy*.

13. Gordon and Logue, 'Perineal Muscle Function after Childbirth'; S. Kitzinger and P. Simkin, *Episiotomy and the Second Stage of Labour*, 2nd edn. (Seattle: Penny Press Inc., 1990).

14. M. Enkin, personal communication.

15. M. C. Klein *et al.*, 'Does Episiotomy Prevent Perineal Trauma and Pelvic Floor Relaxation?', *The Online Journal of Current Clinical Trial*, 10/1 (Montreal, 1992).

16. Kitzinger and Walters, *Some Women's Experiences of Episiotomy*.

17. Klein *et al.*, 'Does Episiotomy Prevent Perineal Trauma and Pelvic Floor Relaxation?'; Rockner, Wahlberg, and Olunda, 'Episiotomy and Perineal Trauma during Childbirth'.

18. G. White and M. White, 'Breastfeeding and Drugs in Human Milk', *Veterinary and Human Toxicology*, 26, suppl. 1 (1984), 3.

19. S. J. Snooks, 'Faecal Incontinence due to External Anal Sphincter Division in Childbirth is Associated with Damage to the Innervation of the Pelvic Floor Musculature: A Double Pathology', *British Journal of Obstetrics and Gynaecology*, 92 (1985), 824–8.

Chapter 5 Breastfeeding

1. C. M. Jain, *The Baby Challenge* (London: Tavistock/Routledge, 1990).

2. M. Renfrew, C. Fisher, and S. Arms, *Bestfeeding* (Berkeley, Calif.: Celestial Arts, 1990).

3. M. Minchin, 'Positioning for Breastfeeding', *Birth*, 16/2 (1989), 67–74.

4. B. Hall, 'Changing Composition of Milk and Early Development of an Appetite Control', *Lancet*, 1 (1975), 779–81.

5. S. Kitzinger, *Breastfeeding your Baby* (London: Dorling Kindersley, 1989), 12–17.

6. Ibid.

7. A. S. Glasier, A. S. McNeilly, and P. W. Howie, 'The Prolactin Response to Suckling', *Clinical Endocrinology* 21 (1984), 109–16.

8. J. Akre (ed.), 'Infant Feeding: The Physiological Basis', *Bulletin of World Health Organisation*, 67, suppl. (1989), 1–108.

9. J. C. Martines, M. Rea, and I. de Zoysa, 'Breastfeeding in the First Six Months: No Need for Extra Fluids', *British Medical Journal*, 304 (1992), 1068–9.

10. M. W. Woolridge, J. D. Baum, and R. F. Drewett, 'Effect of a Traditional and of a New Nipple Shield on Sucking Patterns and Milk Flow', *Early Human Development* 4 (1980), 357–64.

11. M. Gunther, *Infant Feeding* (London: Methuen, 1980).

12. A. C. Thomsen, T. Espersen, and S. Maigaard, 'Course and Treatment of Milk Stasis, Non-Infectious Inflammation of the Breasts and Infectious Mastitis in Nursing Women', *American Journal of Obstetrics and Gynecology*, 149 (1984), 429–95.

13. A. M. Prentice, R. G. Whitehead, and S. B. Roberts, 'Dietary Supplementation of Lactating Gambian Women, i. Effect on Breastmilk Volume and Quality', *Human Nutrition and Clinical Nutrition*, 37 (c) (1983),53–64.

14. S. Kitzinger, *The Experience of Breastfeeding* (Harmondsworth: Penguin, 1989).

15. J. M. Morse, 'The Cultural Context of Infant Feeding in Fiji', *The Ecology of Food and Nutrition,* 14 (1984), 287–96.

Chapter 6 Eating Well

1. D. B. Jelliffe and P. E. F. Jelliffe, *Human Milk in the Modern World* (Oxford: Oxford University Press, 1978).

2. Anthony Trollope (1847).

3. Jelliffe and Jelliffe, *Human Milk in the Modern World,* 61–3.

4. *Surgeon General's Report on Nutrition and Health,* No. 71 (Washington DC: US Department of Health and Human Services, 1988).

5. *Recommended Daily Amounts of Food Energy Nutrients for Groups of People in the UK,* report by medical committee on medical aspects of food policy (London: HMSO, 1981).

6. Expert Advisory Group, *Folic Acid and the Prevention of Fetal Deformities,* (London: HMSO, 1993).

7. A. S. Triswell, 'ABC of Nutrition: Other Nutritional Deficiences in Affluent Communities', *British Medical Journal,* 291 (1985) 1333–7.

8. Ibid.

9. Jelliffe and Jelife, *Human Milk in the Modern World.*

10. J. C. Dearlove and B. M. Dearlove, 'Prolactin, Fluid Balance and Lactation', *Journal of Obstetrics and Gynecology,* 88/6 (1981), 652–4

Chapter 7 Feelings about Yourself

1. S. M. Tucks, 'The Outcome of Pregnancies in Elderly Primagravidae', paper presented at European Congress of Perinatal Medicine, Dublin, 1984.

2. *South Wales Echo,* 29 Sept. 1981.

3. J. Berryman, 'Perspectives on Later Motherhood', in A.Phoenix, A. Woollett, and E. Lloyd (eds.), *Motherhood: Meanings, Practices and Ideologies* (London: Sage, 1991).

4. J. Raphael-Leff, *Psychological Processes of Childbearing* (London: Chapman and Hall, 1991).

5. S. Kitzinger, *Ourselves as Mothers* (London: Transworld/Doubleday, 1992).

Chapter 8 Unhappiness after Childbirth

1. R. Kumar and K. M. Robson, 'A Prospective Study of Emotional Disorders in Childbearing Women', *British Journal of Psychiatry,* 144 (1984), 35–47.

2. S. Kitzinger, *Homebirth and Other Alternatives to*

Hospital (London: Dorling Kindersley, 1991).

3. L. Kaij and A. Nilsson, 'Emotional Psychotic Illness following Childbirth', in S. J. Howell (ed.), *Modern Perspectives in Psycho-Obstetrics* (London: Oliver & Boyd, 1972); K. Dalton, *Depression after Childbirth* (Oxford: Oxford University Press, 1980); J. L. Cox, *Postnatal Depression: A Guide for Health Professionals* (Edinburgh: Churchill Livingstone, 1986).

4. Ibid. 14.

5. W. A. Brown, 'Psychiatric Problems during the Postpartum Period', in W. A. Brown (ed.), *Psychological Care during Pregnancy* (New York: Raven Press, 1981).

6. C. Dix, *The New Mother Syndrome* (London: Unwin, 1986).

7. H. Deutsch, *The Psychology of Women,* ii. *Motherhood* (New York: Grune & Stratton, 1945); L. Chertok, *Motherhood and Personality* (London: Tavistock, 1969).

8. G. Douglas, 'Puerperal Depression and Excessive Compliance with the Mother', *British Journal of Medical Psychology,* 36 (1963), 271–8.

9. T. Spitzer, *Psychobattery: A Chronicle of Psychotherapeutic Abuse* (Clifton, NJ: Human Press, 1980); M. L. Gross, *The Psychological Society: A Critical Analysis of Psychotherapy, Psychoanalysis and the Psychological Revolution* (New York: Random House, 1978), 41.

10. P. Rutter, *Sex in the Forbidden Zone* (London: Unwin, 1990); A. Burgess and C. Hartmann, *Sexual Exploitation of Health Professionals* (New York: Praeger, 1986).

11. C. Kitzinger and R. Perkins, *Changing our Minds: Lesbian Feminism and Psychology* (London: Onlywomen Press; New York: New York University Press, 1993), 6.

12. P. Romito, 'Unhappiness after Childbirth', in I. Chalmers, M. Enkin, and M. Keirse (eds.), *Effective Care in Pregnancy and Childbirth,* 2 vols. (Oxford: Oxford University Press, 1989).

13. A. Oakley, 'Beyond the Yellow Wallpaper, or Taking Women Seriously', in A. Oakley (ed.), *Telling the Truth about Jerusalem* (Oxford: Blackwell, 1986).

14. B. Brown and T. Harris, *Social Origins of Depression* (London: Tavistock, 1978).

15. A. Rossiter, *From Private to Public: A Feminist Exploration of Early Mothering* (Toronto: Women's Press, 1988).

16. J. Kitzinger, 'Recalling the Pain', *Nursing Times,* 86 (1990), 38–40.

17. J. Kitzinger, 'The Internal Exam', *The Practitioner,* 23 (16 July 1990), 698–700; S. Kitzinger, 'Birth and Violence against Women', in H. Roberts (ed.),

Women's Health Matters (London: Routledge, 1991).

18. R. Kumar, 'Admitting Mentally Ill Mothers with their Babies into Psychiatric Hospitals', *Bulletin of Royal College of Psychiatrists*, 10 (1986), 169–72.

19. J. Raphael-Leff, *Psychological Processes of Childbearing* (London: Chapman & Hall, 1991).

20. D. Austin, 'When a Mother's Place is in the Home', *Independent*, 25 August 1992.

21. Raphael-Leff, *Psychological Processes of Childbearing*, 481.

Chapter 9 Your Baby's Personality

1. M. Brady, *Having a Baby Easily*, 4th edn. (London: Health for All Publishing, 1948), 127–9.

2. G. Bedell, 'The Age of the Little Emperors', *Independent on Sunday*, 28 Feb. 1993.

3. S. Emmerson, *The Times*, 20 February 1993.

4. M. Myles, *Textbook for Midwives*, 9th edn. (London: Churchill Livingstone, 1981); F. Leboyer, *Birth without Violence* (Glasgow: Fontana, 1977).

5. D. Chamberlain, 'Newborn Senses', in B. K. Rothman (ed.), *Encyclopedia of Childbearing* (Phoenix: Oryx, 1993).

6. A. Macfarlane, *The Psychology of Childbirth* (London: Fontana).

7. D. Chamberlain, 'Newborn Intelligence', in Rothman, *Encyclopedia of Childbearing*

8. D. Chamberlain, 'Babies are not what we Thought', *International Journal of Prenatal and Perinatal Studies*, 4/3–4 (1992), 1–17.

9. Ibid.

10. Ibid.

11. S. Montanaro, 'Quattrocchi', *Montessori Today* (May – June 1988), 15–17.

12. M.Kaitz, P. Lapidot, R. Bronner, and A. Eidelman, 'Parturient Women can Recognize their Infants by Touch', *Developmental Psychology*, 28 (1992), 35–9.

13. T. Heinl, *The Baby Massage Book* (London: Coventure/Thorsons, 1982).

14. J. J. McKenna, 'Rethinking "Healthy" Infant Sleep', *Breastfeeding Abstracts*, La Leche League International Quarterly (Feb. 1993).

15. A. Whitelaw and K. Sleath, 'Myth of the Marsupial Mother: Home Care of Very Low Birth Weight Babies in Bogota, Columbia', *Lancet*, 1 (1985), 1206–8.

16. S. B. Saines, 'West African Baby Wearing', *Mothering* (summer 1990), 104–5.

17. Chamberlain, 'Newborn Intelligence'.

18. G. Keeley and B. Keeley, *Simply Lullabies* (Keeley Designs, Freepost, Leighton Buzzard, Beds. LU7 8YZ).

19. V. A. Hunziker and R. G. Barr, 'Increased Carrying Reduces Infant Crying: A Randomised Control Trial', *Pediatrics*, 77 (1986), 641–8.

20. I. St James Roberts and T. Halil, 'Infant Crying Patterns in the First Year: Normative and Clinical Findings', *Journal of Child Psychology and Psychiatry*, 32 (1991), 951–68; L. Lothe and T. Lindberg, 'Cow's Milk Whey Protein Elicits Symptoms of Infantile Colic in Colicky Formula-Fed Infants: A Double Blind Crossover Study', *Pediatrics*, 83 (1989), 262–6.

21. B. Taubmann, 'Clinical Trial of the Treatment of Colic by Modification of Parent – Child Interaction', *Journal of Pediatrics*, 74 (1984), 998–1003; B. Taubmann, 'Parental Counselling Compared with Elimination of Cow's Milk or Soy Milk Protein for the Treatment of Infant Colic Syndrome: A Randomised Trial', *Journal of Pediatrics*, 81 (1988), 756–61.

22. S. McKenzie, 'Troublesome Crying in Infants: The Effect of Advice to Reduce Stimulation', *Archives of Diseases of Childhood*, 66 (1991), 1416–20.

23. D. Chamberlain, *Babies Remember Birth* (Los Angeles, Calif.: Tarcher, 1988).

24. R. G. Barr, 'The Normal Crying Curve: Hoops and Hurdles', in B. Lester, J. Newman, and F. Pederson (eds.), *Biological and Social Aspects of Infant Crying* (New York: Plenum Press, 1992); R. St James Roberts, 'Managing Infants who Cry Persistently', *British Medical Journal*, 304 (1992), 997–8.

25. For a detailed description of one baby's development during the first year, see N. McClure and J. Burton, *A Baby's Story* (London: Michael Joseph, 1989).

Chapter 10 Feelings about Your Baby

1. M. Klaus and J. Kennell, *Maternal Infant Bonding* (St Louis: Mosby, 1976).

2. D. Eyer, *Mother – Infant Bonding: A Scientific Fiction* (Princeton, NJ: Yale University Press, 1993).

3. J. Z. Rubin, F. J. Provenzao, and J. L. Luriaz, 'The Eye of the Beholder: Parent's View on Sex of Newborns', *American Journal of Orthopsychiatry*, 44 (1974), 512–19.

4. C. A. Seavey, P. A. Katz, and S. R. Zalk, 'Baby X: The Effect of Gender Labels on Adult Responses to Infants', *Sex Roles*, 1 (1975), 103–9.

5. C. Smith and B. Lloyd, 'Maternal Behaviour and Perceived Sex of Infants: Revisited', *Child Development*, 49 (1978), 1263–6.

6. R. Rosenthal and L. Jacobson, *Pygmalion in the Classroom: Teacher Expectations and Pupils' Intellectual Development* (New York: Holt, Reinhart, & Winston, 1968).

7. M. D. Ainsworth, S. M. Bell, and D. J. Stayton, 'Individual Differences in the Development of Some Attachment Behaviors', *Merrill-Palmer Quarterly*, 18/2 (1972), 123–43.

8. R. Rubin, *Maternal Identity and the Maternal Experience* (New York: Springer, 1984), 128–45.

9. N. Black, 'Cerebral Palsy Rarely Caused by Birth Trauma', *British Medical Journal*, 301 (1990), 781.

10. T. Cubitt, 'Crying out for Succour', *British Medical Journal*, 306 (1993), 800.

11. C. S. Bradbeer, 'Mothers with HIV', *British Medical Journal*, 209 (1989), 806–7; European Collaborative Study, 'Children Born to Women with HIV 1 Infection: Natural History and Risk of Transmission', *Lancet*, 337 (1991), 252–60.

12. S. Kitzinger, 'Death of a Baby', in *Woman's Experience of Sex* (Harmondsworth: Penguin, 1986), 292–7.

13. T. O'Dowd, 'The Needs of Fathers', *British Medical Journal*, 306 (1993), 1484–5.

14. E. Delight and J. Goodall, 'Babies with Spina Bifida Treated without Surgery: Parents' Views on Home versus Hospital Care', *British Medical Journal*, 297 (1988), 1230–3.

15. S. Kitzinger and C. Kitzinger, *Talking with Children about Things that Matter* (London: Pandora Press, 1989 182–205.

Chapter 11 Becoming a Father

1. C. Turnbull, *Wayward Servants* (London: Eyre and Spottiswoode, 1966).

2. M. Mead, *Male and Female: A Study of the Sexes* (New York: Morrow, 1949).

3. S. Kitzinger, *The Experience of Breastfeeding* Harmondsworth: Penguin, 1987).

4. R. Israeloff, *Coming to Terms* (New York: Knopf, 1984, 127–8.

5. C. Lewis, *Becoming a Father* (Milton Keynes: Open University Press, 1986).

6. S. Kitzinger, *Ourselves as Mothers* (London: Transworld/Doubleday, 1992).

7. *The Times*, 4 Sept. 1971

8. M. Greenberg, *The Birth of a Father* (New York: Continuum, 1985).

9. M. Greenberg, 'Fathers: Falling in Love with your Newborn', in E. Shiff (ed.), *Experts Advise Parents* (New York: Delacorte Press, 1987).

10. C. Lewis, *Becoming a Father*, 150.

11. R. Scragg *et al.*, 'Bed sharing, smoking, and alcohol in the sudden infant death syndrome', *British Medical Journal*, 307 (1993) 1312–1318.

Chapter 12 Changing Relationships

1. G. Bourne, *Pregnancy* (London: Pan, 1979).

2. J. Newson and E. Newson, *Four Years Old in an Urban Community* (Harmondsworth: Penguin, 1968).

3. J. Newson and E. Newson, *Seven Years Old in the Home Environment* (Harmondsworth: Penguin, 1976).

4. S. Kitzinger and C. Kitzinger, *Talking with Children about Things that Matter* (London: Pandora Press, 1989).

5. J. Raphael-Leff, *Psychological Processes of Childbearing* (London: Chapman & Hall, 1991), 484.

6. J. Hendry, *Marriage in China and Japan* (London: Croom Helm, 1981).

7. P. Munn, 'Mothering more than One Child', in A. Phoenix, A. Woollett, and E. Lloyd (eds.), *Motherhood: Meanings, Practices and Ideologies* (London: Sage, 1991).

8. J. Moyes, 'Will her World still Revolve around me?' *Independent*, 28 Apr. 1993.

9. Munn, 'Mothering more than One Child'.

10. General Household survey 22 (London: HMSO, 1991).

11. B. Brown and T. Harris, *Social Origins of Depression* (London: Tavistock, 1978).

12. Ibid.

Chapter 13 Sex

1. E. Adler and J. Bancroft, 'Sexual Behaviour of Lactating Women', *Journal of Reproductive and Infant Psychology*, 1 (1983), 47–53.

2. E. Adler and J. Bancroft, 'The Relationship between Breast Feeding Persistence, Sexuality and Mood in Postpartum Women', *Psychological Medicine*, 18 (1988), 389–96.

3. D. Lipp, 'Mothering after Incest', *Mothering* (spring 1992), 115–20.

4. S. Kitzinger, *Homebirth and Other Alternatives to Hospital* (London: Dorling Kindersley, 1991).

5. Anon., 'A Father's View of Sexuality in Childbirth', *New Generation*, 11/2 (June 1992), 36.

6. S. Kitzinger, *Ourselves as Mothers* (London: Bantam, 1993).

7. M. A. Kay, 'The Mexican American', in A. L. Clarke (ed.), *Culture, Childbearing, Health Professionals* (Philadelphia: F. A. Davis, 1978), 88–108.

8. K. H. Singer, *The New Sex Therapy* (London: Bailliere Tindall, 1974).

9. W. H. Masters and V. E. Johnson, *Human Sexual Inadequacy* (London: J. & A. Churchill Ltd., 1970).

10. S. Kitzinger, *The Experience of Childbirth* (Harmondsworth: Penguin, 1984); S. Kitzinger,

The New Pregnancy and Childbirth
(Harmondsworth: Penguin, 1989).

11. S. Kitzinger, *Some Women's Experiences of Episiotomy* (London: National Childbirth Trust, 1981).

12. S. Kitzinger, *Woman's Experience of Sex* (Harmondsworth: Penguin, 1986).

13. K. M. Robson, H. A. Brant, and R. Kumar, 'Maternal Sexuality during First Pregnancy and after Childbirth', *British Journal of Ovbstetrics and Gynaecology*, 88 (1991), 882–9.

14. W. B. Shute, 'Episiotomy: A Physiologic Appraisal and a New Painless Technic', *Obstetrics and Gynecology* 14 (1959), 467.

15. *Health Policy and Planning*, 8 (1993), 33–42, quoted by Minerva, *British Medical Journal*, 306 (1993), 1280.

16. Masters and Johnson, *Human Sexual Inadequacy*, 263.

17. Family Health International, 'Breastfeeding as a Family Planning Method', *Lancet*, 11 (1988), 1204–5.

18. Anon., 'Widening the Choice', *Family Planning Today*, 1 (1991), 1.

19. M. Monier and M. Laird, 'Contraceptives: A Look at the Future', *American Journal of Nursing*, 89/4 (1989), 249–51.

20. A. Szarewski, *Contraception* (Oxford: Oxford University Press, 1994).

21. Ibid.

22. *IPPF Medical Bulletin*, 24/6 (1990), 3–4.

Chapter 14 Coming Up for Air

1. S. Kitzinger, *Ourselves as Mothers* (London: Bantam, 1993).

2. C. Wood, 'Mood Change and Perceptions of Vitality: A Comparison of the Effects of Relaxation, Visualization and Yoga', *Journal of Royal Society of Medicine*, 86 (May 1993), 254–8.

3. S. Zain, 'One Woman's Week . . . with Three Children (Two Full-time Jobs and No Pay)', *La Leche League GB News* (Nov. – Dec. 1992), 10–11.

4. S. J. Ryburn, 'Labor after Birth', *Childbirth Instructor*, 1/1 (1991), 27–8.

5. E. Reifsnider and S. T. Myers, 'Employed Mothers can Breastfeed too!', *American Journal of Maternal/Child Nursing*, 10 (July – Aug. 1985), 256–9.

6. Incomes Data Services Report, 1993.

7. P. Hewitt, in the Mischcon Lecture, University College, London, 10 May 1993.

8. K. Vora, 'Who Cares for Children when their Mothers Go back to Work?', *European*, 5–7 Oct. 1990.

9. B. Siegel-Gorelick, *The Working Parent's Guide to Child Care* (Boston: Little, Brown, 1983)

NOTE ON SOURCES FOR SCHEMATIC DRAWINGS

The bladder diagram on p. 63 is based on illustrations in Pauline E. Chiarelli, *Women's Waterworks: Curing Incontinence* (Rushcutters Bay: Gore & Osment Publishing Pty Ltd, 1991).

Helpful Organizations

BRITAIN

General

Caesarean Support Group
  81 Elizabeth Way, Cambridge CB4 1BQ
  ✆ 0223 314211

Cicely Northcote Trust
  Northcote House, 37a Royal Street, London
  SE1 7LL ✆ 071 261 1959
  *Runs pioneering social projects, concerned with, for
  example, isolated mothers with children under three,
  liaison between health service, and ethnic minority
  groups.*

Exploring Parenthood
  39–41 North Road, London N7 9DP
  ✆ 071-607-9647

Home-Start Consultancy
  Mrs Margaret Harrison, 2 Salisbury Road,
  Leicester LE1 7QR
  ✆ 0533 554988; Fax 0533 549232
  *Support, friendship, and practical help to families in
  their own homes, who have at least one child under
  five and who are experiencing difficulties.*

In Touch
  10 Norman Road, Sale, Cheshire M33 3DF
  ✆ 061 905 2440
  Information agency for parents.

Meet-a-Mum-Association (MAMA)
  58 Malden Avenue, South Norwood, London
  SE25 4HF ✆ 081 656 7318/665 0357

National Childminding Association
  8 Masons Hill, Bromley, Kent BR2 9EY
  ✆ 081 464 6164

National Childbirth Trust (NCT)
  Alexandra House, Oldham Terrace, London
  W3 6NH ✆ 081 992 8637
  Postnatal groups.

New Ways to Work
  309 Upper Street, London N1 2TY
  ✆ 071 266 4026
  *Promotes job-sharing and other flexible ways of
  working.*

Parent Network
  44–46 Caversham Road, London NW5 2DS
  ✆ 071 485 8535

Working Mothers' Association
  77 Holloway Road, London N7 8JZ
  ✆ 071 700 5771

Abuse

Child Abuse Survivors Network
  PO Box 1, London N1 7SN

Incest Survivors Network
  ✆ 071 385 2617

Lifeline – Help for Victims of Violence in the Home
  PO Box 251, Marlborough, Wilts SN8 1EA

Parents Anonymous
  6–9 Manor Gardens, London N7 6LA
  ✆ 071 263 8918
  *Advice for parents who feel they may abuse their
  children.*

Rape Crisis Centre
  PO Box 69, London WC1X 9NJ
  ✆ 071 278 3956 (office hours)
  ✆ 071 837 1600 (24-hour service)
  *Counselling and medical and legal advice for women
  and girls who have been raped or sexually abused.*

Alternative healing

British Acupuncture Association and Register
  34 Alderney Street, London SW1V 4EU
  ✆ 071 834 1012/834 3353

British Chiropractic Association
  Premier House, 10 Greycoat Place, London
  SW1P 1SB ✆ 071 222 8866

British College of Naturopathy and Osteopathy
Frazer House, 6 Netherall Gardens, London
NW3 5RR ✆ 071 435 8728

British Homoeopathic Association
27a Devonshire Street, London, W1N 1RJ
✆ 071 935 2163

Institute for Complementary Medicine
21 Portland Place, London WC1N 3AF

The Society of Homoeopaths
2 Artizan Road, Northampton, NN1 4HU
✆ 0604 21400

Breastfeeding

Association for Breastfeeding Mothers,
Sydenham Green, Health Centre, Homshaw
Close, London SE26 4TH ✆ 081 778 4769

Breast Pumps, Special Care Products,
PO Box 288, West Byfleet, Weybridge, Surrey
KT14 6HG

La Leche League of Great Britain
PO Box BM 3424, London WC1 6XX
✆ 071 242 1278
Help, advice, and support for breastfeeding mothers.

National Childbirth Trust (NCT)
Alexandra House, Oldham Terrace, London
W3 6NH ✆ 081 992 8637
Breastfeeding and postnatal support.

Crying baby

CRY-SIS
BM Cry-sis, London WC1N 3XX
✆ 071 404 5011
*Support, help, and advice to parents of excessively
crying babies or children who do not sleep.*

Death of a baby

Compassionate Friends
6 Denmark Street, Bristol BS1 5DQ
✆ 0272 292778
*Support and help for parents who have lost a child of
any age.*

Cruse – Bereavement Care,
Cruse House, 126 Sheen Road, Richmond,
Surrey TW9 1UR ✆ 081 940 4818

Foundation for the Study of Infant Deaths (Cot
Death Research and Support)
15 Belgrave Square, London SW1X 8PS
✆ 071 235 1721/235 0965

Parents Lifeline
Station House, 73d Stapleton Hall Road, London
N4 3QF ✆ 071 263 2265
*Support for parents whose children are critically ill in
hospital; bereavement counselling.*

Stillbirth and Neonatal Death Society
28 Portland Place, London W1N 4DE
✆ 071 436 5881

Disabilities and illnesses

Action on Aids
1st Floor, Milton Court Centre, Moor Lane,
London EC2 ✆ 071 601 7357

Action for Victims of Medical Accidents
Bank Chambers, 1 London Road, Forest Hill,
London SE23 3TP ✆ 081 291 2793

ALLERGY
Christine Bunyan, 27 Holcot Lane, Anchorage
Park, Portsmouth, Hampshire ✆ 0705 673744
*Information on milk-free diets, weaning, and soya
products.*

Association for Brain-Damaged Children,
Clifton House, 3 St. Paul's Road, Foleshill,
Coventry CV6 5DE ✆ 0203 313817

Association for Children with Heart Disorders
35 Upper Bank End Road, Holmfirth, West Yorks
HD7 1EP ✆ 0484 685431

Association for Spina Bifida and Hydrocephalus,
22 Upper Woburn Place, London WC1H 0EP
✆ 071 388 1382

BLISS-LINK/NIPPERS
17–21 Emerald St, London WC1N 3QL
✆ 071 831 8996
*Network support service for parents of babies in
intensive and special care.*

Children's Aid Team (CATS)
75–77 Granville Road, London N22 5LP
✆ 081 888 4189
*Help for mentally-handicapped people. 24-hour
service.*

Cleft Lip and Palate Association
1 Eastwood Gardens, Kenton, Newcastle-upon-Tyne NE3 3DQ ✆ 091 285 9396

Contact a Family
16 Strutton Ground, London SW1P 2HP
✆ 071 222 2695
Advice service for families who have handicapped children.

Cystic Fibrosis Research Trust
Alexandra House, 5 Blyth Road, Bromley, Kent BR1 3RS ✆ 081 464 7211/2

Dial UK (Disablement Information and Advice Lines)
Victoria Buildings, 117 High Street, Clay Cross, Nr. Chesterfield, Derbyshire S45 9DZ
✆ 0246 250055

Downs' Syndrome Association
12–13 Clapham Common South Side, London SW4 7AA ✆ 071 720 0008

Equipment for Disabled People
Mary Marlborough Lodge, Nuffield Orthopaedic Centre, Headington, Oxford OX3 7LD
✆ 0865 750103

Hypercalcaemia (William Syndrome) Infantile Hypercalcaemia Foundation,
37 Mulberry Green, Harlow, Essex CN17 0EY
✆ 02792 7214

Incontinence Foundation
✆ 091 213 0050
Information and confidential help.

Kith and Kids
Chesnut Cottage, Stanstead Road, Hunsdon, Cheshire SG12 8PZ ✆ 0920 870741
Support for physically and mentally handicapped children and their families.

MENCAP (Royal Society for Mentally Handicapped Children and Adults)
123 Golden Lane, London EC1Y 0RT
✆ 071 253 9433

National Association for the Welfare of Children in Hospital (NAWCH)
Argyle House, 29–31 Euston Road, London NW1 2SD ✆ 071 833 2041

National Eczema Society
Tavistock House, North Tavistock Square, London WC1H 9SR ✆ 071 388 4097

Network for the Handicapped
16 Princeton Street, London WC1R 4BB
✆ 071 831 8031/831 7740

Parents with Disabilities Group
National Childbirth Trust,
Alexandra House, Oldham Terrace,
London W3 6NH
✆ 081 992 8637

Research Trust for Metabolic Diseases in Children
53 Beam Street, Nantwich, Cheshire CW5 5NF
✆ 0270 629782/626834 (24 hours)

RNIB Parents Telephone Service
60 St John's Road, Sevenoaks, Kent TN13 3NA
✆ 0732 452176
Support by phone for parents with visually handicapped child and parents who themselves are visually handicapped. Evenings and weekends only.

SENSE, National Deaf–Blind and Rubella Association
311 Gray's Inn Road, London WC1X 8PT
✆ 071 278 1005
Provides educational needs of deaf–blind children, parent/baby courses, counselling and information and home visiting.

Sickle Cell Information Centre
St Leonard's Hospital, Nuttall Street, London N1 5LZ ✆ 071 601 7762/739 8484

Sickle Cell Society
Green Lodge, Barretts Green Road, Harlesden, London NW10 7AP ✆ 081 961 7795

Spastics Society
12 Park Crescent, London W1N 4EQ
✆ 071 636 5020

STEPS, National Association for Children with Congenital Abnormalities of Lower Limbs, including dislocated hips
15 Statham Close, Lymm, Cheshire WA13 9NN
✆ 0925 757525

Technical Equipment for Disabled People (REMAP)
25 Mortimer Street, London W1N 8AB
✆ 071 637 5400

Voluntary Council for Handicapped Children
8 Wakley Street, London EC1V 7QE
✆ 071 278 9441

Marriage guidance

Relate
   Herbert Gray College, Little Church Street,
   Rugby, Warwicks CV21 3AP © 0788 73241

United Kingdom Marital Research Fund
   Marriage Research Centre, Central Middlesex
   Hospital, Acton Lane, London NW10 7NS
   © 081 965 2367
   For couples with relationship and/or sexual problems.

Multiple births

Multiple Births Foundation
   Queen Charlotte's and Chelsea Hospital
   Goldhawk Road, London W6 OXG
   © 081 740 3519

Twins and Multiple Births Association (TAMBA)
   41 Fortuna Way, Aylesbury Park, Grimsby,
   S. Humberside DN37 9SJ © 051 348 0020

Single parents

Gingerbread
   35 Wellington Street, London WC2E 7BN
   © 071 240 0953
   Runs self-help groups for one-parent families.

National Council for One-Parent Families
   255 Kentish Town Road, London NW5 2LX
   © 071 267 1361

Unhappiness after childbirth

Agoraphobia Information Service,
   4 Manorbrook, London SE3 9AW
   © 081 318 5026

Association for Postnatal Illness,
   7 Gowan Avenue, London SW6 6RH
   © 071 731 4867

Birth Crisis Network (Ann Dally)
   10 Portnish Close, Woodley, Reading, Berks,
   RG4 3AR © 0734 698275
   *Support after birth in which you have been
   disempowered. Available 9am–4pm*

British Association for Counselling
   37a Sheep Street, Rugby, Warwickshire
   CV21 3BX © 0788 78328/9

British Association of Psychotherapists
   c/o 121 Hendon Lane, London N3 3PR
   © 081 346 1747

Brook Advisory Centres
   153a East Street, London SE17 2SD
   © 071 708 1390
   *Offers free contraceptive advice, pregnancy testing,
   counselling for sexual and emotional problems.*

Depressives Anonymous (Fellowship of)
   36 Chestnut Avenue, Beverley, North Humberside
   HU17 9QU © 0482 860619

Depressives Associated
   PO Box 5, Castletown, Portland, Dorset
   DT5 1BQ

Institute of Family Therapy
   43 New Cavendish Street, London W1M 7RG
   © 071 935 1651

NCH Careline
   85 Highbury Park, London N5 1UD
   London © 081 514 1177; Luton
   © 0582 422751; Maidstone © 0662 56677;
   Birmingham © 021 440 5970;
   Leeds © 0532 456456;
   Manchester © 061 236 9873;
   Norwich © 0603 660679; Preston
   © 0772 24006; Taunton © 0823 333191;
   Cardiff © 0222 29461;
   Glasgow © 041 221 6722;
   Glenrothes © 0592 759651.
   *Telephone counselling for children and families under
   stress.*

Parentline–OPUS
   106 Godstone Road, Whyteleaf, Surrey CR3 0EB
   © 081 645 0469
   *Umbrella organization of self-help groups for parents
   under stress. Provides a 24-hour telephone service.*

Phobic Action
   Greater London House
   547–551 High Road, London E11 4PR
   © 081 558 6012 (helpline);
   © 081 553 3463 (office)
   *Support and information to phobia/anxiety/neurosis
   sufferers.*

Psychotherapy Centre
1 Wythburn Place, London W1H 5WL
℗ 071 723 6713
Refers enquirers to nearest practitioner, quickly arranges appointments.

Samaritans
17 Uxbridge Road, Slough, Berks SL1 1SN
℗ 0753 32713/4
Telephone number of local office in telephone directory.

Westminster Pastoral Foundation
23 Kensington Square, London, W8 5HN
℗ 071 937 6956

Women's Therapy Centre
6 Manor Gardens, London N7 6LA
℗ 071 263 6200
Counselling and psychotherapy for women by women. Monday to Friday, 1.30–4pm.

Women from different backgrounds

American Women's Health Center
94 Harley Street, London W1N 1AF
℗ 071 935 4853

Asian Women's Resource Centre
27 Santley Street, London SW4
℗ 071 274 8854

Catholic Marriage Advisory Council
Clitherow House, 1 Blythe Mews, Blythe Road, London W14 0NW
℗ 071 371 1341

Chinese Health Information Centre
34 Princess Street, Manchester M1 4JP
℗ 061 228 0138

Chinese Information and Advice Centre
68 Shaftesbury Avenue, London W1V 7DF
℗ 071 836 8291/494 3273

Cypriot Women's League
376 St. Anne's Road, London N15 3JL
℗ 081 800 8398

Federation of Spanish Organisations
116 Ladbroke Grove, London W10 5NE
℗ 071 221 2007

Inochi No Denwa
Samaritans Japanese Line
℗ 071 287 5493
Available Tuesdays and Wednesdays from 2pm to 9pm

The Japanese Women's Association in Great Britain
36 Adam and Eve Mews, London W8

Jewish Marriage Education Council
23 Ravenshurst Avenue, London NW4 4EL
℗ 081 203 6311/203 6211 (24-hour crisis line)

Latin American Women's Rights Service
Albany Centre, Douglas Way, Deptford, London SE8 6NA ℗ 081 694 8176

Nakayoshi Kai – The Japanese Friendship Group
PO Box 2185, Barnet, Herts. EN5 5RB

AUSTRALIA

Most of the organizations are listed in the sections for each state or territory, but there are also some central helplines and national organizations that you can contact wherever you live. These are listed first.

Parents' Helplines

Breastfeeding ℗ 00555 1271 *(advice for beginners)*

Crying ℗ 00555 1272

Sleep problems ℗ 00555 1273

When to call the doctor ℗ 00555 1274

General problems

Health commissions and hospitals in each state run baby health or infant welfare centres. Check phone book under: Early Childhood Health Centres (NSW); Child Health Centres (Qld Government Health Dept.); Infant Welfare Centres: (Vic Government Local); Child Health Services (WA); Child, Adolescent and Family Health Services (SA Government).

VISA (Vomiting Infants Support Association), PO Box 139, Broadway Qld 4006 or phone 07 229 1090; VISA, PO Box 105, East Gosford NSW 2250.

To make a complaint about care

Contact the Complaints unit or Health Services Commission in your state or territory found by contacting the State/Territory Department of Health in your capital city. You could also contact the Royal Australian College of Obstetricians and Gynaecologists, 254 Albert St., East Melbourne Vic 3002, ☏ 03 416 3314. If the problem is connected with a neonatologist/paediatrician, contact the Australian College of Paediatrics, PO Box 38, Parkville Vic 3052.

Young parents

Mothers under 18 will find support and information from the Young Parents Program in Queensland: 07 357 9381. If you live outside Brisbane or in another state, call anyway. YYP will be able to advise you on starting your own group, or tell you about any existing groups.

Disabled children

For support and information about the following disabilities, check your phone book for the office in your state, or ring the national headquarters listed here.

The Spastic Centre, Australian Cystic Fibrosis Association
  ☏ 02 564 3089

Cleft Pals, Diabetes Australia ☏ 06 247 5211

Australian Down's Syndrome Association
  ☏ 08 232 0688/008 088 882

National Epilepsy Association of Australia
  ☏ 02 891 6118

Muscular Dystrophy Association, Spina Bifida Association, Osteogenesis Imperfecta Society
  ☏ 02 869 1486

Association for Genetic Support of Australia
  ☏ 02 416 0647

Parent to Parent Association, NSW Society for Children and Young Adults with Physical Disabilities ☏ 02 890 0100

New South Wales

Associates in Childbirth Education
  PO Box 366, Camperdown NSW 2050

Transition to parenthood.

Child Abuse Prevention Service
  ☏ 02 344 7646 (24 hours)

Child Protection Unit ☏ 02 818 5555

Contact: Children's Services ☏ 02 212 4144

Cot Death/SIDS ☏ 02 639 5343;

Newcastle ☏ 049 46 9392

Domestic Violence ☏ 02 637 3741

Hearing Impaired ☏ 02 560 6433

Intellectual Disabilities ☏ 02 809 7134

Karitane Mothercraft Society ☏ 02 399 7111

Maternity Alliance, ☏ 047 82 2008

Multiple Births ☏ 02 621 2424

Nursing Mothers ☏ 02 639 8686

Outreach Domiciliary Service
  ☏ 02 958 3076/02 568 3633

Single Parents ☏ 02 682 6677

Still Birth and Neonatal Death Support
  ☏ 02 450 1565

Tresillian Family Care Centres (24-hour counselling line) ☏ 02 569 5400, Petersham ☏ 02 568 3633; Willoughby ☏ 02 958 8931

Visually Impaired ☏ 02 327 5698

Welfare of Children in Hospital
  ☏ 02 633 ll80/633 1988

Women's Health Centre
  ☏ 02 689 8203/789 3499/601 3555

Victoria

Child Protection Services ☏ 03 882 8193

Cot Death/SIDS ☏ 03 882 7022/822 9611

Domestic Violence and Incest ☏ 03 387 9155

Hearing Impaired ✆ 03 650 1164

Intellectual Disabilities ✆ 03 419 9277

Multiple Births ✆ 03 726 5579

Nursing Mothers ✆ 03 878 3304

O'Connell Family Centre Canterbury
✆ 03 882 2326; Tweddle Baby Hospital
Footscray ✆ 03 689 1577

Queen Elizabeth Centre ✆ 03 347 2777

Single Parents ✆ 03 836 3211

Still Birth and Neonatal Death Support
✆ 03 882 8336

Visually Impaired ✆ 03 529 3544

Welfare of Children in Hospital ✆ 03 650 2864

Women's Health Centre
✆ 03 654 6844/008 136 570

Queensland

Child Abuse ✆ 07 227 7111/224 7588/227 5999

Cot Death/SIDS ✆ 07 341 1176/832 4500

Department of Family Services ✆ 07 224 2111

Domestic Violence ✆ 07 857 6299

Hearing Impaired ✆ 07 356 8255

Intellectual Disabilities ✆ 07 224 8031/391 6912

Mothercraft Home, Fortitude Valley
✆ 07 252 8555; at Clayfield ✆ 07 262 4863

Multiple Births ✆ 07 205 3816

Nursing Mothers ✆ 07 266 3119

Still Birth and Neonatal Death Support
✆ 07 207 1397

Visually Impaired ✆ 07 371 7488

Welfare of Children in Hospital ✆ 07 253 8111

Women's Health Centre
✆ 07 253 8111/844 1944/229 1580

South Australia

Child Abuse ✆ 08 267 7000/272 1222

Child, Adolescent and Family Health Services
(24-hour telephone counselling) ✆ 08 236 0400

Children's Interests Bureau ✆ 08 226 7052

Cot Death/SIDS ✆ 08 363 1963

Domestic Violence ✆ 08 232 0040/232 3300

Hearing Impaired ✆ 08 223 3335

Intellectual Disabilities ✆ 08 239 0179/223 7522

Multiple Births ✆ 08 373 1292

Nursing Mothers ✆ 08 339 6783

Single Parents ✆ 08 2321 6514/223
6155/347 1109

Still Birth and Neonatal Death Support
✆ 08 277 0304

Torrens House Mothercraft Service Adelaide
✆ 08 223 2477; 24-hour telephone counselling
✆ 008 18 8082

Visually Impaired ✆ 08 261 4611

Welfare of Children in Hospital ✆ 08 267 7347

Women's Health Centre
✆ 08 223 1244/008 188 158

Western Australia

Child Abuse
✆ (09)272 1466/321 1111/008 188 158

Childcare Service Board ✆ 09 222 2894

Cot Death/SIDS ✆ 09 220 0620

Domestic Violence
✆ 09 336 2144/325 1111/008 199 008

Hearing Impaired ✆ 09 443 2677

Intellectual Disabilities ✆ 09 220 0649/322 3377

Multiple Births ✆ 09 447 7491

Ngala Mothercraft Home ✆ 09 367 7855

Nursing Mothers ✆ 09 309 5393

Single Parents ✆ 09 325 4575

Still Birth and Neonatal Death Support
✆ 09 370 2687

Visually Impaired ✆ 09 362 8202

Welfare of Children in Hospital ✆ 09 321 4821

Women's Health Centre ✆ 09 222 0444/321 2383

Tasmania

Child Abuse ✆ 002 30 2529/30 2921

Cot Death/SIDS ✆ 004 31 8540

Domestic Violence ✆ 002 30 2529/35 2111

Family Day Care ✆ 002 23 3238

Hearing Impaired ✆ 002 34 9877

Intellectual Disabilities ✆ 002 73 1149

Mothercraft Home ✆ 002 30 2700
  Alternatively, contact your Early Childhood Centre

Multiple Births ✆ 002 49 4393

Nursing Mothers ✆ 002 23 2609

Parenting Centre ✆ 008 80 8178

Single Parents ✆ 002 34 7172

Still Birth and Neonatal Death Support
✆ 002 43 5464

Visually Impaired ✆ 002 34 4666

Welfare of Children in Hospital ✆ 002 23 7263

Women's Health Centre ✆ 002 34 2166

Australian Capital Territory

Child Abuse ✆ 06 275 8213/247 0519

Cot Death/SIDS ✆ 06 258 6174

Health (child care) ✆ 06 205 5111

Hearing Impaired ✆ 06 282 3671

Intellectual Disabilities ✆ 06 246 3093

Multiple Births ✆ 06 247 9661

Nursing Mothers ✆ 06 258 8928

Queen Elizabeth II Home Canberra
✆ 06 248 0813

Single Parents ✆ 06 239 6878/248 6333

Visually Impaired ✆ 06 295 3333

Welfare of Children in Hospital ✆ 06 258 7162

Women's Health Centre ✆ 06 245 4650

Northern Territory

Child Abuse ✆ 089 81 4733/41 1644

Community Welfare ✆ 089 89 2400

Cot Death/SIDS ✆ 089 322 448

Domestic Violence ✆ 089 27 4581

Hearing Impaired ✆ 089 45 2016

Nursing Mothers ✆ 089 32 2838

Single Parents ✆ 089 85 3394

Visually Impaired ✆ 089 27 1235

Women's Health Centre ✆ 089 27 7166

NEW ZEALAND

Contact the Plunket Karitane Family Support Units in Auckland, Mt Eden, Newtown, or Christchurch.

Help is available at Alice Springs Hospital or the Royal Darwin Hospital.

Birthplace Support Group Inc, PO Box 1070
  Fremantle 6160 *(support group aspects of birthing and parenting).*

Nursing Mothers Association of Australia

PO Box 231, Nunawading, Vic 3131
  ✆ 03877 5011 *or Parents Centres Australia in New South Wales or the La Leche League in NSW offer advice and support, check your telephone directory.*

Index